• ANABAPTIST PORTRAITS •

• ANABAPTIST PORTRAITS •

John Allen Moore

Foreword by Leonard Gross

HERALD PRESS
Scottdale, Pennsylvania
Kitchener, Ontario
1984

Library of Congress Cataloging in Publication Data

Moore, John Allen.
  Anabaptist portraits.

  Bibliography: p.
  1. Anabaptists—Biography. 2. Anabaptists—History.
I. Title.
BX4940.M66 1984   284'.3 [B]   84-12769
ISBN: 0-8361-3361-7 (pbk.)

The reproductions of the paintings on pages 15, 45, 67, 95, and 123 (also on the cover) are from the picture files of Jan Gleysteen (Conrad Grebel, Felix Mantz, and George Blaurock painted by Oliver Wendell Schenk; Michael Sattler and Hans Denck painted by Ivan Moon). The likeness on page 163, from an old etching, is the only known portrait of Balthasar Hubmaier.

Dedicated
to
My Wife
Pauline Willingham Moore

• CONTENTS •

• FOREWORD •

In our twentieth-century Western world we take for granted the idea of religious liberty, where the church is voluntary, and separate from the state. It is hard for us to imagine a time, 450 years ago, when those who proclaimed these very ideas were persecuted and killed for their faith.

Yet we continue today in the faith of such martyrs who dared to think new thoughts, dared to believe new dreams, dared to enter into a new vision. Those Anabaptists of Reformation days and their spiritual children, the Mennonites, Baptists, Brethren, Quakers, Methodists, and many other groups which have entered this free church tradition, have helped bring about change within Western society, from the idea that church must be part of established society for unity to prevail, to the idea that church and state must be separate for the good of both entities.

Anabaptist Portraits takes us back to that time within the Reformation context when men and women who dared to think "free church" thoughts, and express and live out these thoughts and convictions, also suffered for conscience' sake, even unto death.

The author, John Allen Moore, tells us this story, broadly enough for all those within the believers' church tradition to see themselves reflected, historically and prototypically. For here are Conrad Grebel, Felix Mantz, and George Blaurock, the radical Swiss Brethren leaders who dared to enact their thoughts and forge ahead in the light of conscience. Michael Sattler follows, who helps give concrete spirit, substance, and structure to the fledgling movement, setting the peaceable community of faith in a manner that would influence the Mennonite movement for the next four and more centuries. Hans Denck is also there, the great proponent and interpreter of conscience, discipleship, and tolerance, who learned that love as a means is essential to peace as an end. Yet the story would not be complete without the great theological reflecting of Balthasar Hubmaier, who gave verbal expression to so many tenets of faith from the free church perspective, such as the Lord's Supper, congregational discipline, and the idea of freedom of the will.

It is the breadth and depth of this unwieldy mixture of components, some compatible, some less than compatible, that launched the modern free church movement. Pilgram Marpeck and Menno Simons would take up some of these same ideas and spread them more broadly within Upper German and Low Country areas, respectively, during the decades which followed the turbulent 1520s when the six Anabaptists portrayed in this volume were active. Other groups would emerge as well—the later Mennonites, the Baptists, the Society of Friends (Quakers), the Methodists. These and other parallel movements were nourished indirectly if not directly by the Reformation-era Anabaptists.

The author, wisely, allows the Anabaptist story to be told in its own words, through the chronicling of human interaction. Moore permits his Anabaptist types to speak for themselves. Yet in his choice, Moore shows his own broadminded understanding of radical Anabaptism. To include a Denck, for example, is Moore's way of saying that the Anabaptist movement was variegated, and at points contradictory. There was, to be sure, a center which was common to all Anabaptists. This was believer's baptism, the "port of entry" into the gathered church, where allegiance to its Lord God is taken to be higher than allegiance accorded the magistracy.

We need to come to terms with our most recent past—the hopes and disappointments of the twentieth century, including those of the Vietnam interlude. Yet we would be the poorer, and less than faithful, if we at the same time would allow the excitement of our early free church history to pale, where the waters ran fresh, and if not absolutely pure, at least with conviction! John Allen Moore reminds us of these exciting times, and with artistic creativity, paints his words, combining idea and event, persons and the dreams that inspire and motivate them.

The six Anabaptist portraits in this book are of course not the whole of the Anabaptist story. They are rather a selection of those early Anabaptists of the 1520s who most directly molded the Anabaptist movement and whose ideas—directly and indirectly— became part of the broad free church or believers' church legacy. Their concerns are our concerns, their questions, our questions— their attempted answers taking an upward turn which we had better look into and understand, before consciously choosing other alternatives.

The author has not included a conclusion, nor is it indicated. The six portraits themselves tell the whole, interpretive story. Moore, as a Baptist scholar, complements Mennonite interpretation. He is sympathetic, undergirding, accurate, and writes from a posture of faith. The reader can also sense in Moore the depth of a cultural and geographical awareness of the European scene that he is describing on every page. Moore spent much of his adult life in Europe, walking the very streets where Grebel, Mantz, and Blaurock, as well as Sattler, Denck, and Hubmaier, themselves walked.

We too may walk where these Anabaptists walked, learning to know them and their faith—six significant spiritual forebears, and forerunners of essential elements of modern society as we know it.

—Leonard Gross
Mennonite Historical Committee
Goshen, Indiana

• AUTHOR'S PREFACE •

Even moderate, peaceful, New Testament-based Anabaptists—as contrasted with those of Münster, Germany, in 1534-35—were of various types and emphases. The differences, as well as the much more important similarities, are evident in the subjects of this collection of biographical sketches.

The first three—Grebel, Mantz, and Blaurock—represent the very first chapter in the history of Anabaptism. Sattler fits nobly within the Swiss Brethren fellowship, although his origins and much of his work were in South Germany. Denck, a cooperating Anabaptist leader in South Germany for a period of time, was essentially an undogmatic spiritualist in approach—uncomfortable in any rigid mold of precept or practice. Hubmaier differed from the others in holding that a good Christian might participate in government—the magistracy, the judiciary, and law enforcement, even to the extent of capital punishment for heinous crime—when officially and rightly called on to do so.

The six biographies have been written as separate stories, each complete in itself. Some repetition, especially in the first three accounts, is therefore by design. All six of the men here presented were pioneers in the Anabaptist movement, which ranks as a worthy part of the sixteenth-century Reformation in Europe.

—John Allen Moore
Brownwood, Texas

• CONRAD GREBEL •

1
• CONRAD GREBEL •
Founder of the Swiss
Brethren

The little city of Zurich, snuggled about the banks of the Limmat River where it flows from the Lake of Zurich, nestled a population of five or six thousand within its walls at the end of the fifteenth century when Conrad Grebel was born. The canton of Zurich, then under the administration of the city, had belonged to the Swiss Confederation since 1351; it occupied a position of strength in federal affairs.

Jacob Grebel, father of Conrad, enjoyed prominence as a leading member of the city and cantonal government, being first a part of the Council of Two Hundred, then later also of the inner council which largely directed local affairs. He represented Zurich from time to time at meetings of the confederation, which then consisted of fourteen cantons. Descended from several generations of influential and well-to-do Grebels, he had inherited a large iron business from his father.

Conrad came third in a family of six children. In 1499, about a year after Conrad's birth, the Zurich council appointed Jacob Grebel as *Vogt*, or chief magistrate, of the Grüningen district, southeast of Zurich. Until 1512 the family lived in the "castle" there, where years later Conrad would be imprisoned.

The elder Grebel sent Conrad, when the latter reached the age of seven or eight, to the Latin school in Zurich, which legend says Charlemagne had founded. It was called Latin school because most of the instruction was in that language, which bore no resemblance whatever to the Swiss German dialect the boy had grown up with at home. The school had a reputation for unruliness and frequent fights among the boys, but Conrad advanced as a student in Latin literature, logic, debating, and liturgical music. At about the age of sixteen Conrad proceeded to Basel, fifty-five miles northwest of Zurich, and enrolled in the university there.

Lively Student Days

A new humanism flourished in Basel, with emphasis on the study of Greek and Latin classics and more open inquiry than had been allowed scholastics during the Middle Ages. The wandering scholar, Erasmus of Rotterdam, mentor of Christian humanists (there were other kinds), himself had settled in Basel for a time and so left his imprint there. Young Heinrich Loriti—called Glarean because he came from Glarus, Switzerland—already in 1514 ranked as perhaps the most prominent Swiss humanist in Basel. Ten years older than Conrad, he had settled in Basel just a few months before Conrad entered the city.

As a student in the philosophical faculty or college, Conrad was obliged to live in one of the *bursae* or private dormitories. Each of these was supervised by a graduate scholar who held a master's degree; he directed his charges in their studies, drilling them according to need and giving some lectures to them. Conrad, along with twenty-five or thirty others, chose to live in the *bursa* of Glarean, who was an outstanding scholar in Latin language and literature as well as in Greek, geography, and mathematics. Glarean enforced strict discipline and was loved by many of the students, especially Conrad Grebel. The latter studied in Basel from October 1514 to May of the following year.

Jacob Grebel, always avaricious (it would help to bring him to his death), transferred his son to the University of Vienna when he was able to secure a "pension" or scholarship for him, from Emperor Maximilian, providing funds to over four years of study there.

Another attraction at Vienna, for Swiss students, was the presence on the faculty of Joachim von Watt of St. Gall, called Vadian. He was a physician as well as a specialist in classical geography and other studies. Conrad developed a close relationship with Vadian as his mentor, and the latter praised young Grebel later as the most outstanding of all Swiss students in Vienna. Conrad wrote in one of his letters that Vadian was "loved and cherished and respected by me as a most devoted father."

Vadian chose Conrad, along with two others, to accompany him on a hike up Mt. Pilatus in Switzerland. This ascent is credited as one of the first of any mountain for scientific purposes. To Conrad Grebel Vadian dedicated the first edition (1518) of his *Commentary on Pomponious Mela*, a commentary on the Roman geographer of the first century. Vadian chose young Grebel to write the introduction to the second edition, of 1522.

Conrad studied in Vienna three years. The city was enjoying its golden age—the last years of Emperor Maximilian's reign—a wealthy, pleasure-loving, international business and imperial center. It had the reputation, evidently deserved, of barbaric morals. Students frequently engaged in ganglike street brawls, and Conrad joined in. In one altercation, his hand was "half cut off." About this time he also began to suffer from painful swelling in his joints and especially in his feet. This tormented him intermittently to the end of his life, and even walking sometimes caused difficulty. He bore infirmity with considerable patience, conscience convicting him that it resulted from a sinful life, including his having "consorted with females carnally," to mention but one of Conrad's personal confessions.

Decline and Fall of Serious Studies

In June 1518 Conrad and Vadian left Vienna suddenly, probably because of the outbreak of the dreaded plague there, and they traveled together to Switzerland. Conrad had apparently heard that his favorite teacher Glarean was now at the University of Paris and desired to study with him there. Jacob Grebel had discovered a way of obtaining a royal French scholarship for Conrad, larger than the imperial one in Vienna, and he profited from such "pensions" more than his son did. Receiving such a grant was now illegal for a citizen of Zurich. It implied support in the enlisting of Swiss mercenaries, in this case for France; and the French king was unpopular in Switzerland.

In order to justify receiving the scholarship, Conrad gave up his Zurich citizenship during this period, but his father, of course, did not. Jacob Grebel, opposed by church reformer Ulrich Zwingli and many in the council, was eventually beheaded on October 30, 1526, convicted of receiving illegal stipends from foreign rulers.

Conrad arrived in Paris on October 20, 1518, and remained there four semesters; it was almost without exception an unhappy and fruitless time. He enrolled immediately in Glarean's *bursa*, but within two months was grumbling about housing conditions; and the dispute climaxed in a drunken bout which ended the friendly relationship of the two young men. With two other students Conrad rented quarters and employed a house servant, but he gave little attention to his studies.

To make matters worse, Conrad was embroiled on May 1, 1519, in what others referred to as a student brawl; two Frenchmen were killed. For reasons of personal safety, he and other students who were involved left the city. Soon, however, they returned and gave a complete account of the affair to the police. Apparently a band of French brigands attacked the students, and in the fight that ensued they killed two of their assailants. Conrad later spoke of it as "our war against the bandits."

This further worsened Conrad's relationship with Glarean, who banned him from even occasional attendance at instruction classes at the *bursa*. When reports of the affair reached Zurich, they caused a disastrous deterioration in Conrad's relationship with his father. Parisian officials obviously did not consider that the students had committed any crime. They were not punished in any way, or even brought to trial.

Another interruption in studies resulted when the plague

broke out in Paris in the summer of 1519. Over thirty thousand Parisians died. The epidemic raged in other areas at the same time. Vadian was in Switzerland for his marriage to Dorothea Grebel, sister of Conrad's, and he remained six months in a Swiss village to escape the plague's ravages in St. Gall. Conrad, with some other students, fled Paris and resided five months in a nearby village. When they moved back to the city, letters awaited him from his father and from Vadian, both extremely critical of his participation in the "student brawl" and otherwise. Jacob Grebel accused his son of profligacy and culpable violence, ordering him to return home—although without sending funds for the trip.

From this time Conrad and his father were never really reconciled. Of necessity they would reside for long periods of time under the same roof; but because of the father's continued use of funds for himself that were intended for Conrad's study, because of the violent incident in Paris and for other reasons that developed later, Conrad would never really be welcome in the home of his parents.

Of necessity also he had returned to Glarean's *bursa* in Paris, although Glarean would not allow Conrad to attend classes there. Since the elder Grebel would not send sufficient funds for living expenses, continuing meanwhile to accuse Conrad of wastefulness, the latter was obliged to live at the *bursa*, thus reducing current outlay while building up indebtedness. Several months elapsed before Conrad was able to get enough money together for the journey home.

Struggle for a Foothold in Life

By early July we find Conrad back in Zurich. He hoped to continue his studies and to this end secured a two-year papal stipend for work at the University of Pisa in Italy. He evidently changed his mind and decided to study again in Basel. He went to Basel but remained only ten weeks. He then returned home, resumed Zurich citizenship, and determined to give up the idea of any further study abroad. He hoped to contribute to the cultural life of his homeland as a humanist scholar, but no opportunities emerged. Swelling and pain in the joints of his feet and hands continued to bother him.

He worked occasionally in his father's ironware shop. Sometimes he was able to find a few students to tutor in the classical languages. This provided some income, but not enough. He joined a few others, local pastors and other young scholars, reading literary and Christian classical writings under the leadership of the leading pastor in Zurich, Ulrich Zwingli. In general it was for Conrad an unhappy period, and he wallowed in despair with no clear goals for life.

The young humanist admired Zwingli, then thirty-six, for his scholarship and his leading of church reform in the Zurich area. Zwingli had been the "people's priest" at the Grossmünster, Zurich's principal church, for a year and a half when Conrad returned from Paris. Rather than follow the stated liturgical plan for services, Zwingli began from the first to preach through the New Testament in an expository way. Besides Sunday services there were others, one almost every day of the week.

Zwingli, originally a humanist of the Erasmian type, gradually made a clean break with medieval church authority—which Erasmus never did. Zwingli studied the Scriptures in the original languages (he studied Hebrew later), along with other ancient Christian writings. He taught and preached that the church and an individual's Christian life should be reformed according to the example of Christ and the apostles. His reforms, although gradual, were more radical than those of Martin Luther, involving simple biblical worship and a symbolic interpretation of the two recognized sacraments or ordinances, baptism and the Lord's Supper.

Zwingli had great respect and appreciation for the young scholar Grebel and included a poem by him as an appendix to a book Zwingli published in 1522. Grebel's poem, sixteen lines in Latin, celebrated God's overthrow of Catholic hierarchy by the "olden light of truth." It pictured the enslavement of people and promotion of superstition through the proclamations of bishops, then the victory of the gospel in church reform, based on the "Gospel Word" alone. Zwingli's preaching and Conrad's more personal contacts with the reformer, along with his own Bible study, gradually won him to active Christian discipleship. This decisive change in his life came apparently in the spring of 1522.

Problems Also in Romance

Before the process toward Christian commitment reached its climax, there was another change in Conrad's situation. He fell in love. The girl may have been from a Zurich family, but she apparently resided in Basel at this time. We hear of her only by the name of Barbara, and Conrad called her his *Holokosme*—his "whole world." He wanted very much to marry immediately, but Barbara's family apparently ranked much lower on the social scale, and the elder Grebels opposed this relationship vociferously. Conrad, financially unable to set up a home of his own, felt himself at an impasse—unwilling to disobey his parents but incapable, he thought, of living without his beloved *Holokosme*. He spent two months with her in Basel.

"My beloved is with me," he wrote Vadian, now settled in St. Gall. "We get along fine together, except that now and then we have little quarrels as is the manner of lovers. The quarrel is usually short and peace comes quickly. She says that she is mine, and I am hers so absolutely that I could not be hers more completely.... At last the heart of your poor Grebel is enraptured, hence rejoice with me if you love me."

Conrad worked for Cratander, a printer of humanistic works, during his two months in Basel; he edited and proofread materials with which he was familiar from previous studies. Cratander intended this as a lasting relationship, but on sudden impulse Grebel returned to Zurich, continuing his efforts to find a solution in his personal predicament.

His father left on a week-long business trip and Conrad took advantage of the opportunity to bring Barbara to Zurich and have the wedding. It took place on February 6, 1522, in the Fraumünster, Zurich's second largest church, with a few young relatives and friends attending. Conrad's mother, "enraged beyond measure," remained at home, weeping incessantly. Conrad commissioned two or three of his friends to intercede with his father upon his return. The young couple expected to be expelled from the Grebel home and compelled to leave Zurich. Although they were not forced out, they lived unhappily with the elder Grebels for about two years, with parental opposition to the marriage continuing unabated. Conrad had no money and no regular work. Concerning his mother, he wrote to Vadian at the end of 1522, "Against me she is ungodly and against my wife she rages."

At about that time the younger Grebels' first child was born, a son named Theophil, and nine months later the second, Josua. Conrad complained in letters to Vadian that his father had completely abandoned him, refusing to pay funds that were due from the "pension," making him completely dependent on strangers and forcing him to borrow heavily; the debts oppressed him, and he remained in poor health.

Fellow Worker in Zwinglian Reform

Despite everything, Conrad began manifesting a positive attitude. Beginning in June 1523, after a nine-month period from which we have no record of his activities, his letters to Vadian reflect a new spirit. The problems remained, but young Grebel met them patiently, as a believing Christian. No longer did he write in classical humanist fashion about the deities of ancient Rome and the philosophers of Athens. In every letter there were references to the Bible and its teachings. His children received biblical names, although Conrad's parents disapproved.

He wrote about church reformers of his day, about religion and ethical questions. He offered to pray for his friends and requested their prayers. He affirmed his readiness for Christian service, fighting for the gospel against the enemies of evangelical doctrine, however much "the world" might oppose. Included among those enemies was the "superstitious church of the bishops." Converted under the ministry of Zwingli and through study of the Bible, Conrad said he had been "born again by the spirit of God," had "become a new creature," had "put on Christ." He asked fellow believers to pray for him that he might be called to "the office of minister."

For almost a year and a half after his conversion, Conrad, as a lay leader, supported Zwinglian reform with enthusiasm, and the Zurich church leader regarded his younger colleague as "a man of the highest integrity." Zwingli preached more and more against ecclesiastical abuses, veneration of images, the mass as sacrifice, moral laxity among priests and nuns, obligatory tithes and fasts. Conrad took the lead in one of the many public manifestations against abuses—in this case, the conduct of monks. The council called him and others to answer for the disturbance, July 7, 1522. The hearing resulted in no judicial action. After harsh recriminations between accused and accusers, the council dismissed the men without punishment.

The council of Zurich arranged, under Zwingli's lead, a public disputation for January 29, 1523. As a large body of interested persons gathered at the *rathus*, or council hall, the burgomaster called the meeting to order and gave the opening address. Zurich still nominally belonged to the diocese of the bishop of Constance. He sent a representative as an observer to the public disputation, but his protests against change in ecclesiastical usage were rejected.

Zwingli declared that the Bible was the church's judge, in teaching and practice—none other was needed. Proposed reform did not constitute departure from valid ancient custom, he declared, but a return to the most ancient of all, New Testament Christianity. For the occasion Zwingli had prepared sixty-seven theses asserting Scripture as sole authority, the church as associations of believers with Christ as immediate head and only mediator, and salvation by faith. The theses urged clerical marriage, rejected fasts, purgatory, and works for sanctification. They affirmed the divine authority of civil rulers "insofar as they command nothing contrary to God."

After extensive discussion the council declared that Zwingli had prevailed, and ordered that he and the other clergymen continue to preach the gospel. In such a way the

Reformation was formally instituted in Zurich, under the aegis of the Zurich government council.

Breach in the Groundwork of Unity

By the summer of 1523 there was widespread demand in the Zurich area for doing away with "abominations of the papal church." Zwingli personally seems to have favored some radical reforms. For years he had preached against obligatory tithes and usury, the mass, and the use of images; but he made no real changes in forms of worship. A gradualist at heart, he felt uneasiness at unruly developments.

Not only were theologically untrained laymen conducting Bible study groups, but bands of radicals tore down public crucifixes and images. Wilhelm Reublin, pastor in Wytikon, near Zurich, broke fasts openly, and urged the common people to resist obligatory tithes. Then in April 1523 he married publicly—the first priest in Switzerland to do so. Among those interested in reform, varying ideas competed as to what constituted the "pure gospel" which had been authorized for preaching and practice in Zurich.

Unsure how far reforms should or could go at the time, Zwingli arranged with the council to call another public disputation for October 26-29, 1523. It would deal specifically with images and the mass, which seemed to be the most urgent questions. Vadian of St. Gall was asked to serve as one of the moderators of this assembly.

On the first day Zwingli, Grebel, and a number of others spoke against the veneration of images. Some participants urged patience with the weak in faith who were not ready for radical change. On the second day the mass, as traditionally observed, was repeatedly denounced as an abomination before God. Grebel and a few others then desired of Zwingli some indication as to procedures for abolishing the mass, and the latter replied, "My lords [members of the council] will decide what regulations are to be adopted in the future in regard to the mass."

Zwingli had countered as strongly as anyone the two "abominations," but encouraged by the council's support for the Reformation in Zurich following the January disputation, he believed it would order reforms as fast as the people were ready for them. This procedure, he felt, would give the strongest possible undergirding for his work. His brusque statement at the October disputation shocked Grebel, pastor Simon Stumpf of the nearby parish of Höngg, and a few other persons—although its full and fateful significance surely did not come home to anyone, including Zwingli, at the time. The latter, who had taught dependence on Bible teachings alone for the church, even against state authority if necessary, now submitted the church to that authority.

"Master Ulrich," Stumpf declared, "you do not have the right to place the decision on this matter in the hands of my lords, for the decision has already been made; the Spirit of God decides."

Zwingli then tried to explain that he was turning over to the council, not what the truth is for the church, but only the implementation of that truth—in this case, procedures for discontinuing the mass (which would not be approved by the council until Easter 1525). Stumpf asserted that for him, in a matter so clear in the New Testament, it was simply not a decision for the council to make. "If my lords adopt and decide on some other course that would be against the decision of God," he asserted, "I will ask Christ for his Spirit, and I will preach and act against it."

This called forth a ringing testimony from Zwingli: "That is right. I will also preach and act against it if they decide otherwise. I am not putting the decision in their hands. They are not over the Word of God, and this goes not only for them but for the whole world." He then reiterated his distinction between the ascertaining of truth and its implementation, the latter being applied in this case.

Search for the Truth

There now began a period of increasing estrangement between Zwingli and the council on one hand, and Conrad Grebel and the radicals on the other. For a time the latter still hoped to win Zwingli to their point of view, even as Zwingli hoped to retain Grebel and others as faithful supporters.

Conrad drew up a plan of church reform based on his new understandings of New Testament teachings. These indicated a voluntary and regenerate church membership. Zwingli would later testify that the proposals, upon presentation, did not seem so bad. He and Leo Jud, pastor in the St. Peter's Church, had received Grebel and his associates in a friendly spirit. It seemed that except for the idea of voluntary church membership, the radicals were still at one with the reform leader on every major point of faith and practice. After repeated talks on the matter in dispute, however, there was no agreement but only a strengthening of positions taken.

Simon Stumpf and Felix Mantz—another young humanist scholar who advocated radical obedience to the Scriptures—had separate discussions with Zwingli, also without success. Another person who felt the same way was Andreas Castelberger, bookseller from the Graubünden area, called "Andreas on the Crutches" because of lameness. For more than a year he, a layman, had conducted Bible study meetings attended by large numbers of people. Stumpf was expelled from Zurich as a dissident in December 1523, and the same fate later befell Castelberger.

"The gospel is in a very poor way with us here (if you will believe a suspected character [Grebel], rather than a liar [Zwingli])," Conrad wrote Vadian December 18, 1523, "and this evil condition began at the time when you, by the wise decision of the council, served as president of the disputation. At that time (God sees and hears) the Word was overthrown, trodden under foot, and enslaved by its most learned heralds.... Here is an axiom: who thinks, believes, or says that Zwingli is performing his duties as a shepherd, he thinks, believes, and says ungodly things."

Conrad's outward circumstances and problems continued much the same—only his attitude toward them had changed to that of patient acceptance. His debts had risen to sixty guilders, which would be more than a year's income for many a respected citizen.

The decision of Zwingli to leave to civil authorities the determination of the church's course constituted for much of

Reformed Christendom the watershed between those units that would become "state churches" and those that would be "free churches." In modern times most of the latter developed at least in a spiritual sense from these forerunners who took a radical biblical view in the Zurich controversy 1523-25. They insisted that ecclesiastical doctrine be practiced consistently and not remain theory only until such a time when state authorities should be moved to act on it. This does not mean the radicals wanted a separatist church—the thought probably never entered their minds at this time. They wanted only that which they considered a New Testament kind of church.

Finally, Grebel decided to counter Zwingli and his colleagues boldly and openly in the area of church reform. Writing to Vadian on September 3, 1524, he quoted Job 32:16: "I have waited and they have not spoken, they stand there and do not reply." Grebel, Mantz, Stumpf, and perhaps others had laid a proposed program before Zwingli, yet he had opposed or ignored them on the issues. Conrad, constantly now in study of the Scriptures, applied various passages to what he considered the Zwinglian dictatorship.

He saw a parallel in Israel's leaders turning from trust in God to trust in themselves and in the enemies of God: " 'Woe to the rebellious children,' says the Lord, 'who carry out a plan, but not mine, and who make a league, but not of my spirit, that they add sin to sin' " (Isaiah 30:1) and "Is it not enough for you to feed on the good pasture, that you must tread down with your feet the rest of your pasture; and to drink of clear water, that you must foul the rest with your feet? And must my sheep eat what you have trodden with your feet, and drink what you have fouled with your feet?" (Ezekiel 34:17-19).

Additional Issues Raised

Wilhelm Reublin of Wytikon was the first priest in the canton of Zurich to preach against infant baptism. Early in 1524 he announced, "If I had a child, I would not have it baptized before it came to maturity and could choose its own godparents." Some parents followed his advice, withholding their children from baptism. The council imprisoned Reublin a short time for his part in this.

In Zollikon, another village adjoining Zurich, fathers were withholding their infant children from baptism. Encouragement for this came from Johannes Brötli, who had served as priest in the town of Quarten before he settled in Zollikon. Brötli had converted to Zwinglian evangelical reform, and later to the views of Grebel. Infant baptism was not yet a major concern to Conrad Grebel, but soon it would be.

Despairing of valid reform leadership in Zurich, Grebel and the new group of "brethren" who gathered about him turned elsewhere. Conrad wrote to Martin Luther urging him to voluntarism and greater spiritual reform in the church, the abandonment of "false forbearance" (holding back from radical change and from church discipline) and the simple following of biblical teaching. Luther did not reply directly but indicated to friends a rather cordial reaction. Meanwhile, as surely as with Zwingli, he was turning toward the state-church concept and the suppression of "enthusiasts."

Grebel thought he saw some hope in the work of Carlstadt (Andreas Rudolf Bodenstein), former professor at the University of Wittenberg, who had been forced out of this position by his colleague Luther and banished because of Carlstadt's strong advocacy of the priesthood of believers, and his opposition to the mass and to infant baptism. At different times Grebel and Andreas Castelberg both wrote to Carlstadt on behalf of the brethren in Zurich.

On September 5, 1524, Grebel wrote, in some haste and without keeping a copy of the letter, to Thomas Müntzer, later called "the most controversial figure of the period of the German Reformation." He had served as priest, then as provost of a monastery, and still later as father-confessor in a nunnery. Converted to evangelical views, he wanted to establish a church of the "spirit of the fear of God," but his plan seemed visionary and confused. During the previous year, he had been priest or evangelical pastor in Allstedt, near Wittenberg. There he attempted to substitute German for Latin in the mass, and he discouraged infant baptism.

Müntzer had written several tracts concerning basic Christian faith, baptism, and the mass. Grebel and his brethren in Zurich knew Müntzer, who would soon become a fiery social revolutionary, solely from five of these tracts that were printed in Switzerland; they were written in a time when Müntzer was still expressing himself generally in a moderate way. A few days before Grebel wrote Müntzer, however, the latter had fled from Allstedt into hiding due to controversies already stirred up there. So the letter never reached its addressee and was returned to Switzerland.

This letter—about four thousand words, including a postscript—reveals, more than any other source, the ideas of Conrad Grebel and his friends in Zurich at the time. They were obviously a not-yet-organized group of between fifteen and twenty persons who met with some regularity for Bible study, prayer, and discussion.

The Undelivered Letter

"Every man wants to be saved by superficial faith," Grebel wrote to Müntzer, "without fruits of faith, without the baptism of testing and trial, without love and hope, without right Christian practices; one wants to persist in all the old ways of one's own vices and in the common ritualistic antichristian observance of baptism and the Lord's Supper, in contempt for the divine Word, esteeming the word of the pope and anti-papal preachers, which is not the same as the divine Word nor in conformity with it."

Grebel admits, "We were in the same error also as long as we heard and read only the evangelical preachers who are to blame for all this, in the wages of our sins. But after we also took the Scripture in hand and consulted it on all kinds of matters, we have become somewhat informed and have discovered the great and hurtful shortcomings of the pastors, of ours also [pastors in Zurich]. . . . The cause of all this is the false caution, the concealing of the divine Word and mixing the human with it. Yes, we say it brings harm to all and hinders entirely the cause of God. . . ."

Along with his commendation of Müntzer's tracts on the Lord's Supper, baptism, and personal faith, Grebel does not hesitate to warn Müntzer, "We beg and admonish you as a brother ... preach the divine Word only, set up and defend only divine usages, esteem as good and right only what can be found in unmistakably clear Scripture; reject, hate, and curse all devices, words, usages, and opinions of all men including your own."

Specifically in connection with a discussion of the Lord's Supper but applying it more broadly, Grebel continues, "If we are not in the right, teach us better.... You should drop [the clergy's liturgical] singing and the mass; act in all things according to the Word.... If that cannot be done, it would be better if all things remained in Latin, without changing and accommodating. If the right cannot be established, then neither should you minister according to your own or priestly antichristian usage.... It is much more desirable that a few be rightly taught through the Word of God, believing and walking aright ... than that many out of a mixed teaching believe falsely and hypocritically."

Grebel chides those living from tithe taxes: "You must really cut yourselves loose and be completely clear of priestly benefices.... If your benefices, as with us, are from interest and tithes, which are both true usury, and if you do not get your support from an entire church, would you give up your benefices? You know well how a pastor should be supported.... Serve with the Word and establish a Christian congregation with the help of Christ and his rule, as we find it instituted in Matthew 18 and applied in the epistles...."

"Moreover," the letter continues, "the gospel and its adherents are not to be protected by the sword, nor are they thus to protect themselves, which as we learn from our brother Hans Huiuf is your opinion and practice. True Christian believers are sheep among wolves, sheep for the slaughter; they must be baptized in trepidation and distress, tribulation, persecution, suffering and death; they must be tried with fire and reach the fatherland of eternal rest not by the snuffing out of their bodily but their spiritual enemies. Also, they use neither the world's sword nor war, since all killing has been done away with by them. . . .

"Infant baptism," Grebel goes on, "is a senseless, blasphemous abomination, contrary to all Scripture. . . ." Perhaps he had some inkling that despite Müntzer's criticism of it, the latter had not abandoned the practice consistently; for Grebel wrote, "We hope that you are not acting against the eternal Word, wisdom, and commandment of God, according to which only believers are to be baptized, and that you are not baptizing children." As a matter of fact, Müntzer had continued to baptize infants when requested by parents to do so.

Grebel advises also against other abuses: "We ask you not to use nor to receive the old antichristian customs such as the sacrament, mass, signs, etc., but to hold and act according to the Word alone."

Conrad Grebel signed the letter, along with Castelberger, Mantz, and several others. At this point they heard from a member of their group (Hans Huiuf), who had received a message from his brother in the Wittenberg area, that Müntzer was advocating the use of force by godly people against persecuting worldly powers; Grebel consequently wrote a postscript of about 850 words to accompany the original letter to Müntzer.

"If it is true that you are willing to defend war" or other things "which you do not find clearly in the Word," he writes, "then I admonish you by the common salvation of us all that you will cease therefrom and from all notions of your own. . . . Be strong. You have the Bible . . . for defense against the idolatrous caution of Luther, [and] . . . against deceitful, weakened faith . . . in which they do not teach Christ as they should. . . . And if you must suffer for it, you well know that it cannot be otherwise. Christ must suffer still more in his members. But he will strengthen and keep them steadfast to the end. . . . We too shall in time see persecution. Therefore, pray to God for us."

First Baptism Disputation

The Zurich council, because the question of infant baptism had come to the fore, announced a public disputation on the matter for January 17, 1525. More and more, small children were being withheld from the rite, especially in Wytikon and Zollikon. On the fourteenth of that month, Conrad Grebel wrote Vadian regarding his daughter, then eight days old, that she "has not yet been baptized and watered in the Romish water bath." It was intended that this disputation would be the last word as far as any questioning of infant baptism was concerned, but it proved to be really just the beginning.

Heinrich Bullinger, Zwingli's successor and a hostile witness so far as the Brethren were concerned, recalled the event years later, summarizing how Grebel, Mantz, Reublin, and others defended their position that "children could not have faith, and so do not understand what baptism is. Baptism should be administered to believers, to whom the gospel has been previously preached, who understand it and then themselves request it, putting to death the old Adam, desiring to live a new life. Of all that, children know nothing whatsoever; therefore, baptism does not belong to them."

Bullinger then reports how the opponents of infant baptism read passages from the Gospels and Acts to show "that the apostles had not baptized children but only adults with understanding—therefore it should still be done in such a way. And since [children] are not to be baptized, therefore infant baptism is not valid." Bullinger no doubt faithfully reports the radicals' argument; but in the continuing words of his last sentence, "therefore one should have himself baptized again," Bullinger surely either adds his own conclusion or confuses what was said at the disputation with developments soon to come.

Zwingli and other pastors argued that the New Testament used the word "baptism" with varied meanings, e.g., the inner baptism of faith or the outer baptism with water. They declared infant baptism, corresponding to circumcision in the old covenant, to be a valid symbol of the child's being externally reckoned as belonging to the people of God.

On the day following the disputation the council issued a mandate ordering parents to bring unbaptized children to the priests within a week for baptism; anyone who continued to withhold infants from this rite would be banished from the canton. Three days later the council published another edict. It forbade further meetings of the groups which had been gathering for prayer and Bible study. It ordered Grebel and Mantz, Zurich citizens, to cease speaking about the issues in question.

The council banished several non-citizens who had taken part in the argument against infant baptism. Those affected by this order were Reublin, Brötli, Castelberger, and Ludwig Haetzer, a native of Bischofszell, Switzerland, who had participated in and written the official report of the disputation in October 1523. He had previously served as a priest and later opposed infant baptism but never did espouse believer's baptism.

Birthday of the Movement

Faced with the order to cease their meetings and all reform activity, the Brethren had to decide what course they would follow. They gathered secretly on a Saturday, almost certainly the evening of January 21, in the Mantz home. A difficult decision confronted the harried group of about fifteen bold believers. They could not continue as in the past with their fellowship, Bible study, and witness. They must submit to the official church with its obligatory infant baptism and obnoxious state supervision, or go their own way in defiance of established authority in church and state.

Fearful but determined, they resolved, after prayer and Bible reading, to obey God rather than men. They fell again to their knees in prayer, begging guidance and strength from the Lord. After some time in agonizing supplication, George Blaurock stood and asked Conrad Grebel, as recognized leader of the group, to baptize him on confession of his faith in Christ. He knelt down, once again, to receive baptism. Grebel reached for one of Frau Mantz's small kitchen dippers, partially filled it with water, and poured it on Blaurock's head, probably while quoting appropriate words from Scripture. Blaurock then baptized the others who were present, each on his or her own profession of faith.

"And so in this way with one another, in profound fear of

God and surrendered to him," concludes the ancient account of this event, "they confirmed one another in the service of the gospel; thus they began to teach and stand by the faith. In this way they began breaking away from the world and its evil works."

This was the birth date not only of the Anabaptists but of almost the entire evangelical free church movement, as it is known. The small group of believers never called themselves Anabaptists, or rebaptizers, for they regarded infant baptism as no baptism at all, and that of believers as alone worthy of the name. Simply "brethren" or earnest fellow Christians among themselves, they were sometimes referred to by others as the Swiss Brethren. *Wiedertäufer* (Anabaptists or rebaptizers) was long the disparaging epithet of those who desired to defame them. Later, users of German who wished to be more objective called them *Täufer* (baptizers or baptists). In English, the term "Anabaptist" has lost its pejorative connotation.

The Brethren insisted—as Zwingli had of his own work earlier—that they were not starting anything new, only trying to return the church, at least that part of it they could be a part of, as closely as possible to its original New Testament character.

In the days following, Grebel and Mantz spent their time in meetings, often with just one family and perhaps a few visitors, in the homes of those who had been baptized by Blaurock, or others who seemed interested, especially in Zollikon. Ordinarily the service consisted of the reading of a passage from the Bible and its exposition, a period of prayer, the baptism of those who desired it, and a simple celebration of the Lord's Supper. This latter ordinance was observed with ordinary bread and wine from the pantry of whatever home they were meeting in. The leaders admonished converts regarding the new kind of life they were to live.

Missionary Labors Near and Far

Grebel decided to leave Mantz and Blaurock in charge of the flourishing movement in Zollikon while he proceeded on a mission of his own in Schaffhausen, thirty miles north of

Zurich. The first of the Brethren to take the new ideas into other regions, Grebel hoped to influence the leaders of church reform in the northern Swiss town. He went directly to the pastors, Dr. Sebastian Hofmeister (who had been a chairman of the 1523 Zurich disputation on images and the mass) and his associate Dr. Sebastian Meyer. Johannes Brötli and Wilhelm Reublin, having been expelled from Zurich, joined Grebel in Schaffhausen for a brief time. All three were dinner guests of Dr. Hofmeister. "Dr. Sebastian agrees with us in the matter of baptism," Brötli wrote following this meeting. Neither of the Schaffhausen pastors joined the Brethren, however; Hofmeister wavered for a time, but he later denounced Anabaptism in Zurich and Bern.

Grebel continued hopeful and tried to win others as well during his two months in Schaffhausen. We hear in particular of his contacts with a young Frenchman, Anemund de Coct, who resided there and manifested interest in church reform, even in its more radical aspects; but de Coct died suddenly while Grebel was still in Schaffhausen.

The Brethren as a rule seem to have manifested no special interest in the form of baptism. They were concerned, however, to follow Scripture to the letter. A few began to notice the implications for immersion in the wording of New Testament passages. In addition, immersion seemed to suggest completeness of surrender to, and identification with, Jesus Christ in his death, burial, and resurrection, as well as the candidate's death to sin, arising to walk in newness of life. For practically all Anabaptists symbolizing these teachings did not mandate immersion.

But for one convert at least, it did. Wolfgang Ulimann belonged to an old upper-class family of St. Gall and had been a monk. As he walked with Conrad Grebel along the bank of the Rhine River in the vicinity of Schaffhausen, speaking with his mentor about the significance of the rite, he suddenly asked for baptism. The contemporary chronicler Johannes Kessler of St. Gall (who supported Zwinglian reform) said that Ulimann "was so filled with the knowledge of rebaptism that he did not wish only to be poured over with water from a dish, but to be taken altogether naked into the Rhine by Grebel and pressed under and covered over."

By the end of March Grebel was back in Zurich and active in work with the Brethren, but soon he proceeded to St. Gall. He worked with Ulimann in the burgeoning Anabaptist movement there, preaching and conducting Bible study meetings. Grebel stayed two weeks, and hundreds of people thronged the hall of the weavers' guild to hear him. (Ulimann's father was or had been the guildmaster.) Many converts requested baptism, and on Palm Sunday, following a procession through the city by a large company of friends, as well as the curious, Grebel seems to have baptized several hundred persons in the Sitter River just outside St. Gall. The new movement spread rapidly in and around the town, and authorities seemed rather tolerant; they sponsored several disputations.

As the Anabaptists were not overcome by arguments, however, measures of suppression followed and foreign leaders were expelled. Among the latter was Eberli Bolt, soon to be burned at the stake in his hometown of Lachen as the first Anabaptist martyr. Vadian led in establishing Zwinglian reform and destroying the Anabaptist movement in St. Gall. In June, two months after Grebel's large baptismal service at the Sitter River, authorities forbade the radicals to hold any more meetings and banished Ulimann. After serving the Brethren's cause in several areas, Ulimann was leading a group of Anabaptist refugees to Moravia in 1528 when authorities seized them in Swabia. He and ten other men were beheaded; the women were drowned for their faith.

Finding a Field of Work

During a period of about six weeks after his return to Zurich from St. Gall, Conrad Grebel, still suffering from his old foot ailment, remained in his father's home with his own little family. He seldom left the house but kept in contact with Brethren of Zurich and Zollikon. "I believe it is known that I receive the brethren here," he wrote Andreas Castelberger. "However, I do not go out, in order to protect my asylum here against a possible imprisonment by Zwingli." Because he was entirely without funds, he sold his books. He wrote Castelberger that he wanted to leave Zurich but feared capture. He had attempted to leave secretly by night along with Felix Mantz, but Conrad's wife threatened to betray Mantz, and Conrad gave up the idea for the moment.

About the first week in June he did get out. Along with Zollikon Brethren leader Jacob Hottinger, he made his way to Waldshut, just across the border in Hapsburg territory, where pastor-theologian Balthasar Hubmaier had recently been baptized into the Brethren movement by Wilhelm Reublin. Hubmaier's views on the Christian's right to take part in government and even in the government's use of force did not please Grebel; we hear nothing further of any relationship between these two strong Anabaptist leaders.

On his return to the Zurich area, Grebel turned his attention to Brethren beginnings in the district of Grüningen, where his father had served twelve years as chief magistrate and where Conrad had spent much of his childhood. Grüningen was well prepared for the Anabaptist movement. The peasants and other citizens of the district, who had previously enjoyed more autonomy, chafed under payment of tithes and other taxes to Zurich; a group of them, in their rage, plundered a monastery. Influenced by evangelical teachings of Zwingli and his colleagues, they demanded the right to call their own pastors instead of having them appointed by authorities in Zurich. These demands and others were rejected; Grüningen seethed in resentment. Anabaptists came with an apolitical message but one that offered spiritual freedom in a congregation of believers, and people flocked to hear them.

Grebel, preaching to the people and holding conferences with the established pastors, labored in this field for over three months. He stood largely alone in leadership of the work; Blaurock and Mantz labored in other parts of Switzerland. It was the longest, as well as the most successful and satisfying, period of ministry during his brief time of service as a Brethren leader, despite his having to move quickly from place to place to avoid capture. The period of work in Grüningen might have lasted considerably longer if it had not been brought to an abrupt end by his arrest.

Early in July Grebel had received a summons, as did his Brethren associate Marx Bosshart of Zollikon, for trial in Zurich on a charge of slander against Zwingli. The allegation maintained that they said of the latter's recently published book on baptism, "Zwingli has written plain lies." The accused Brethren were willing to appear if assured safe conduct, but this the Zurich council denied; it simply repeated the order that they appear. Grebel, under these ominous circumstances, refused. Bosshart and two other Zollikon Brethren did appear in Zurich, where they were immediately thrown into prison. After four weeks Bosshart was released on payment of a fine, the posting of a large bond and promising to desist from preaching and baptizing.

The Authorities Tighten the Noose

Moving from place to place, Grebel worked hard, preaching, speaking with pastors, strengthening Brethren groups; and so the movement grew steadily. Meanwhile, Zurich authorities tried to apprehend the Anabaptist leaders. Chief magistrate Jörg Berger, in the same position earlier occupied by Jacob Grebel, made it his particular objective to achieve this purpose of his superiors in Zurich.

Two Anabaptist refugees from Waldshut held services and baptized thirty persons before Berger succeeded in arresting them. When Berger heard that Blaurock was in the town of Hinwil, he went there and eventually was able to arrest him. As he took Blaurock away, an unruly crowd, sympathetic with the Anabaptists, followed. As they reached an open field near the village of Betzholz, they found Grebel and Mantz beginning a service. Berger listened, as the preachers held forth. Having secured assistance from a nearby village, he succeeded in arresting Grebel (Mantz escaped for the time being). He took Grebel and Blaurock to the Grüningen castle and threw them into the prison pit, later transferring them to Zurich. Soon Mantz also was captured and imprisoned.

Hoping to solve the Anabaptist problem and that of the restless peasants of Grüningen, Berger suggested a disputation to which twelve impartial men from his district should be invited. They would later report to the Grüningen people, who should believe them—although the people were skeptical about official pronouncements from Zurich. Others also had been urging a public discussion of the issues. The Zurich council agreed and set the date of November 6 for the disputation to begin. Authorities planned for this to be in the council hall, where others had taken place, but it proved to be too small. Hundreds came (one estimate of nine hundred may be an exaggeration), and it was moved to the Grossmünster. Four presiding officers were named—including Dr. Sebastian Hofmeister, now of Zurich, and Vadian of St. Gall—to see that debate proceeded in an orderly manner.

Chief participants were Zwingli and the other two leading pastors of Zurich on one side, Grebel, Mantz, and Blaurock on the other. Brethren leader Michael Sattler of Stauffen in South Germany also took part. The discussion, which continued for three days, centered around questions regarding baptism. Zwingli and his colleagues said children of Christians were no less children of God than their parents, so why should baptism be denied them? Baptism had taken the place of circumcision, they argued, and the New Testament had nothing to say about rebaptism, which meant that those who rebaptize crucify Christ anew. The Brethren reiterated the necessity for faith to precede valid baptism.

After the disputation things were no better but rather worse for the Brethren. The twelve representatives from Grüningen reported at home that the Anabaptists had received a fair hearing. The Zurich council gave the victory, of course, to Zwingli and his colleagues. Grebel, Mantz, and Blaurock were returned to prison. Following trial, these three received sentence on November 18, "because of their Anabaptism and their unbecoming conduct, to lie in the tower on a diet of bread and water" and no one was to visit them except the prison guard. They were to lie there "as long as God should please and as seems good to my lords." Sattler and other non-Zurichers were banished. Throughout the coming winter more Anabaptists were arrested and thrown into the tower prison. Grebel and others conducted Bible reading periods regularly for fellow prisoners, admonishing and encouraging them.

The council, determined to rid its area of the Anabaptist challenge, gave a new trial to the prisoners March 5 and 6, 1526, then on the next day condemned them to life imprisonment. It issued another mandate sternly forbidding the rebaptism of anyone and set death by drowning as the penalty for all who performed it. This, councilors felt, should end the heresy once and for all. One of them, Jacob Grebel, strongly opposed the death penalty for Anabaptists.

Grebel's Final Labors

The "lifelong" imprisonment of incarcerated Brethren lasted only two weeks from the time it was proclaimed. Someone left a prison window open and the drawbridge down—perhaps intentionally to aid the imprisoned Anabaptists—and the entire group escaped. Grebel, Mantz, and Blaurock at first opposed the idea of taking advantage of the opportunity but finally agreed. There was a rope conveniently at hand to enable them to climb out of the high window and they scrambled over the bridge to freedom. As they discussed where they might go, one of the group jested, since they were so unwanted in their own part of the world, "Let us go to the red Indians across the ocean." They scattered far and wide, except for two men who chose to remain in Zurich, and these were promptly arrested; they gave the account of the escape which has come down to us.

In the final trials Grebel requested permission to have a statement of his views printed, as he had sought since the summer of 1524; he felt he expressed himself better in writing. He always insisted that he and his Brethren were never given, in the hearings before Zwingli and other pastors and in trials held by the council, sufficient opportunity to answer the accusations that were being made.

Finally, not in Zurich but perhaps in Basel, he apparently succeeded in getting a pamphlet of maybe 1,500 words published. It circulated widely among the Brethren and was much used by them; they felt its arguments against infant baptism unanswerable. No copy survives, but in a book answering these arguments of Grebel, Zwingli quoted most of the Anabaptist's writing verbatim. The Grebel volume was itself a rebuttal to a previous book by Zwingli threatening these enemies of his. Entitled *Those Who Incite to Rebellion*, it repeated the old argument for infant baptism— that the apostles baptized entire families (those of Stephanus, Lydia, and an unnamed person) which must have included children. There is no justification for presuming small children in these families, Grebel countered; one must follow the positive instruction of the Word of God, and none was to be found for infant baptism.

For a period of several months after the prison escape, Grebel carried out an "underground" itinerant ministry, secretly visiting persecuted groups and individual believers in the area north of Zurich and in the cantons of Appenzell and Graubünden. Worn down by the rigors of long imprisonment, the months of difficult travel and the strain of evading arrest, Grebel arrived in 1526 in the village of Maienfeld, southeast of Zurich. A little group of harassed Anabaptists existed in the area, but he probably went there seeking rest and recuperation in the home of his oldest sister, who married and settled in Maienfeld around this time.

Conrad Grebel, aged about twenty-eight, died there of the plague not long after arrival, in the summer of 1526.

• FELIX MANTZ •

2
• FELIX MANTZ •
Anabaptist Martyr

A small circle of colleagues and scholars gathered regularly around Ulrich Zwingli, church reformer in Zurich, during the year 1522 to read Latin and Greek classics, but especially the Bible—so far as possible in its original languages. Already proficient in Latin and Greek, Zwingli and a few others of the group engaged a famous Hebrew scholar, Andreas Böschenstein, to instruct them in the language of his specialty while he was in Zurich during this period.

The person within the group who apparently profited most from Böschenstein's instruction, and from Old Testament readings with Zwingli, was Felix Mantz. The illegitimate son of a clergyman serving at the Grossmünster, collegiate church in Zurich, Felix was in his early twenties at the time. He had studied and done well in Latin, Greek, and other subjects offered to students of his day, probably for about two years of the time at the University of Paris.

Zwingli, people's priest at the Grossmünster since the beginning of 1519, had humanistic and theological training at the universities of Basel and Vienna. Attracted to the Christian humanism of Erasmus during an earlier ministry, even before coming to Zurich, Zwingli espoused the principle of scriptural authority for the church and soon went far beyond Erasmus in reform principles.

Along with biblical authority, other principles began to

fall into place in the foundations of Zwinglian reform, notably that of salvation only through the work of Christ in atonement and the believer receiving it through faith. Sacraments were reduced to two, baptism and the Lord's Supper. In making these symbolic only, Zwingli differed from Martin Luther. The Zurich reformer remained a humanist in his faith, believing that reason would prevail and that he could in time convince the great majority of the people and the city council to go along with his reforms. He would wait patiently for this reform, even if it could not proceed as fast as one would like. He arranged a public disputation of the issues in January 1523 and won the council's support for reformation in principle on the basis of biblical, rather than Catholic hierarchical, authority. He anticipated the gradual elimination of abuses such as the observance of the mass as a sacrifice.

He ran into serious opposition, not only from a few who desired to stay with the old ways of medieval Catholicism, but also with those who would not compromise what they regarded as basic Bible teachings in order to hold everybody in the church whether there were any personal faith or not. These evangelical dissidents, feeling that the church was a fellowship of believers and not an institution of the state, opposed Zwingli's decision to await the council's approval for outward changes in ecclesiastical activities and worship.

Formation of Parties

Felix Mantz, who sympathized with the dissident views, held informal discussions with Zwingli late in 1523 or early in the following year, arguing for a freer church, more straightforward preaching and consistent reforms, including church discipline for blatant sinners. Others also were speaking with Zwingli, and with Leo Jud after the latter came to Zurich in February 1523 as priest of St. Peter's Church.

As the priestly members of the college of canons in the Grossmünster died, Zwingli planned to designate for other purposes the ecclesiastical annuity income which had been used for their support. His favorite plan was to employ at the Grossmünster teachers of Latin, Greek, Hebrew, biblical theology, and other subjects. Grebel was apparently in line to receive the appointment as tutor in Greek, and Mantz in Hebrew. Zwingli considered both men well qualified. But their defection from the course he was setting in church reform disqualified them, in his view, and nothing came of it. Only in mid-1525 could the proposed institution be set up. It was called simply *Prophezei*—"School of the Prophets," one might say; and it met at the outset in the choir area of the Grossmünster. Here were the very first makings of the University of Zurich.

At a public disputation on images and the mass in October 1523, Zwingli had made clear his decision to go only so far in reform as should be approved by the Zurich council. Those who insisted on a consistent biblical course, as they understood it, began to look to one another for fellowship, then to other reformers who seemed to share some of their views.

Felix Mantz, in September 1524, joined with Grebel and others in a letter to Thomas Müntzer in Germany. Representatives of the little group—gathering regularly now for Bible study and prayer—wrote also to Martin Luther and Andreas Carlstadt. Mantz played a particular part in the relationship with Carlstadt.

The latter had written a number of tracts opposing, among other things, infant baptism and sacramentalism in the Lord's Supper. In October 1524 Carlstadt's son-in-law and supporter, Dr. Gerhard Westerburg, brought eight of these tract manuscripts to Switzerland for printing. Mantz accompanied Westerberg from Zurich to Basel and assisted in arrangements for having the tracts printed there. Just at this time Carlstadt himself, who had been banished from the Wittenberg area of Germany because of his reform work, came to Zurich on a hasty visit and proceeded to Basel; then he and Westerberg just as suddenly departed for Germany.

Printing arrangements were left to young Mantz, who insisted the tracts be published. The printers, fearful of offending the authorities, printed some of the tracts but not all. Mantz brought some of those that were printed back with him to Zurich. The brethren used these extensively, and later secured more copies from the printers in Basel.

Mantz and other leaders of the radical reform group met more or less formally for talks with Zwingli and his colleagues in December 1524. These have been referred to as the "Tuesday discussions." After two meetings plans to continue came to nought because of strong feelings on both sides and sheer incompatibility.

Mantz's Letter of Defense

One gets a good idea of how the Tuesday and earlier discussions went from a writing of Mantz's to the Zurich council at about this time. Some eighteen hundred words in length, it has often been called the "Protest and Defense." In the opening section Mantz denies that there is the least bit of truth in recent accusations against him and others as being seditious troublemakers. Mantz knew about a book Zwingli was writing against him and his friends at this time entitled, *Those Who Incite to Rebellion.*

Mantz in his writing shows that the points of difference between him and his fellow-believers on one hand, and their official attackers on the other, were purely religious, such as on the question of infant baptism. Those opposed to this medieval practice had been repeatedly faced by the established pastors in uneven controversy; the latter had brought forth their views, Mantz says in his writing, but failed to support them with Scripture.

"We were not permitted to have our say, and even Scripture could not be heard," Mantz complained. "When we wanted to declare something concerning the truth, they stifled the words in our throats. . . . " They demanded Scripture proofs, "but they should themselves provide them for their position and stand by the truth. . . . Christ did not teach and the apostles did not practice child-baptism, but only this which baptism signifies, that those should be baptized who mend their ways, take on the new life, die to old vices, are buried with Christ and through baptism arise with him in newness of life."

After describing events in connection with Cornelius (Acts 10) and Paul (Acts 22), Mantz comments: "From these words we see very clearly what baptism is and when baptism should be administered, namely when one is converted through the Word of God and his heart is changed. Afterwards he desires to walk in newness of life, as Paul clearly shows in Romans 6 [:4], dead to the old life, circumcised in heart, dead to vices, buried with him in newness of life, etc. To attribute these experiences, just described, to children is itself unscriptural and even contrary to all Scripture." The Bible is full of such evidences, Mantz declares, and "baptism is nothing else than the dying of the old man and the putting on of the new."

Toward the end of his writing Mantz pleads with the council to impress upon Zwingli and others who would defend infant baptism to do so in writing, then he (Mantz) would reply in like manner. "Speaking does not come easy for me; I just can't do it," he confesses. "So often earlier he [Zwingli] has attacked me with so much speaking that I could not reply or, due to his long speeches, I could not get to answer.... If there is anyone at all, whoever he be, who holds from divine Scripture that young newborn little children should be baptized, he can show all this to you, my lords, scripturally and in writing and I will give an answer to each one; I can't do much in disputation and don't desire to, but want to deal only with holy Scripture."

The home of the Mantzes, mother and son, was a favorite place in Zurich for meetings of the radicals. These meetings were attended by perhaps a dozen or so persons as a rule. Their house was on Neustadt Street, which extended southward from the Grossmünster church. A considerable number of the concubines of Grossmünster priests had their houses in this area. They were an accepted part of late medieval society, and children of such unions often bore the surnames of their illegitimate fathers, as Felix did. His mother apparently shared her son's aspirations for thoroughgoing reform in the church.

Brethren Beginnings and Early Development

"Since certain persons are speaking of the erroneous idea that young children should not be baptized until they are older," read the council's mandate calling a public disputation on the subject, "all those, cleric or lay, who want to maintain such a view should appear next Tuesday morning before the council in the city hall and present reasons from true divine Scripture for their position.... Afterward our lords [the council] will take further action, as seems best to them."

This disputation did take place as announced, January 17, 1525, in the city hall council chamber. In the only actual description of the event that has come down to us Mantz is mentioned first among the radicals who participated, then Grebel and Wilhelm Reublin, pastor in the village of Wytikon just outside Zurich. Others who surely took part on the side of the radicals were: Johannes Brötli of Zollikon, near Zurich, who had been a priest; Andreas Castelberger, who had led Bible study groups; and George Blaurock, who had recently arrived. Arguments were the same as in private discussions earlier.

Authorities regarded this as the final opportunity for the radicals to express their views. The council's decisions afterward might have been anticipated, but they turned out to be even harsher than expected. Zwingli and his colleagues were declared victorious in their arguments in favor of infant baptism, and parents with unbaptized children were ordered to have them baptized within a week or the families would be banished. Further meetings of the radical group were forbidden. Mantz and Grebel were ordered to cease speaking about the matters in dispute. Four non-Zurichers received an order to leave the area "within eight days": Reublin, Brötli, Castelberger, and Ludwig Haetzer, a former priest.

What were the radicals to do? They met, evidently on the evening of January 21 in the home of the Mantzes. After prayer, the record in the almost-contemporary *Old Hutterian Chronicle* states that Blaurock requested and received believer's baptism from Grebel, then Blaurock baptized the rest—probably Grebel first, then Felix Mantz, and maybe a dozen or so others.

The act of receiving for those radicals was not a subjective experience only. It symbolized a deep commitment to Christian mission. Doubtless that *Old Hutterian Chronicle* seized on its essence in pointing out not only their devotion to the Lord and to the fellowship of faith but also their covenant with one another "in the service of the gospel." The newly baptized started their witnessing early on the next day, a Sunday. Mantz and Grebel systematically visited homes where interest in the new ideas had been expressed, especially in Zollikon.

Jörg Schad, one of those visited, later testified in court that he had "all his days gone about in vice and sin; this troubled him and caused him to pray God for grace, mercy, and acceptation; God showed mercy to him as he confessed his sin. God then promised him, if he would forsake sin, he would also forgive him. This caused him to request the sign of brotherly love [baptism], that he should do good to his neighbor even as unto himself. And so he requested baptism ... Felix Mantz was the baptizer."

This rite was observed in an ordinary farmer's home, as was the case with another simple ceremony which the Brethren (as they called themselves) observed. Rudolf Breitinger of Zollikon gave testimony of how the Lord's Supper was administered by Felix Mantz. Concerning himself Breitinger said that "no one forced him to take part, except his Creator and Savior. A loaf of bread was cut up and the Word of God appropriately spoken. After that Felix Mantz distributed it to us and whoever so desired ate of it."

At an evening meeting in the home of Rüdi Thomann in Zollikon, Mantz baptized a man from the nearby community of Zumikon, Hans Bruggbach. Responding to the call to repentance in a Bible passage being studied, Hans "stood up, wept, and wailed what a great sinner he was and asked those present to pray to God for him." Blaurock questioned him about his faith and his desire for baptism. When Blaurock received a positive response, Mantz stood and asked, "Who will say that I should not baptize this man?" Blaurock answered, "No one!" Mantz took a household dipper, filled it partially with water, and "baptized him in the name of God the Father, God the Son, and God the Holy Spirit. Then

Jacob Hottinger stood and requested baptism ... [whom] also Felix Mantz baptized." After the service, others departed for their homes, but Mantz and Blaurock remained to spend the night in Rüdi Thomann's home.

Standing Firm While Many Weaken

The Anabaptist movement grew fast in Zollikon during an amazing week before some of its non-Zurich leaders would have to depart. The Brethren had, during this time, at least one baptism from each of about a third of the homes in the village. Any knowledgeable observer could know that the time of relative freedom for their activity would be cut short. It was almost certainly on Monday, January 30, that the blow fell. Police, mainly from Zurich, rounded up as many of the new converts as they could and locked them in the old Augustine cloister in Zurich. Mantz and Blaurock were imprisoned separately.

Zurich pastors and members of the council had conversations with the incarcerated group seeking to prove that Scripture contained nothing on rebaptism, which was therefore wrong.

Almost all were able to maintain their position for a time, but the learned pastors finally overcame their arguments and the radicals promised to give up Anabaptism. They were required to take an oath to this effect, pay the costs of their confinement, and bail of a thousand gulden for the group. Having satisfied these conditions, they were released on February 8, 1525.

Felix Mantz and George Blaurock remained in prison. They were subjected to a series of hearings. Mantz prepared a statement of his views on baptism and the Lord's Supper, addressing it to the Zurich council. First mentioning the incarnation of Christ and how salvation occurs through trust in him, Mantz then called attention to the commissioning of disciples and their consistent Christian living. He referred to the giving of the external sign of baptism.

"Among those also whom I have instructed, certain ones have come to me in tears asking that I baptize them," the writer continued. "These I could not turn away but did unto them as they requested and spoke the name of Christ over them; that they might learn love and unity and the sharing of all things; ... that they might always be mindful of the death of Christ, and not forget his shed blood, the ordinance of Christ which he observed in the Supper, breaking bread with one another and drinking the wine; that we keep in mind that we are redeemed by the body of Christ and washed by his blood; that we therefore be one, each the other's brother or sister in Christ our Lord."

The council sentenced Mantz on February 18: he could be released upon posting a hundred-gulden bond and paying the costs of his incarceration. Beforehand, however, he would need to appear before the small and large councils and be summarily warned against administering baptism and the Lord's Supper—otherwise, the authorities would deal with him again.

Blaurock, who was released at this time, was soon to be back in prison again—along with others from Zollikon. Mantz, however, refused to accept his own sentence. He did not recognize the authority of the state to regulate in matters of faith. One week after the sentence, the council reaffirmed it, adding that Mantz should remain in the tower prison on a diet of "mush, water, and bread until he had enough and would take the oath no longer to disturb the peace." Mantz was placed repeatedly before Zwingli for further efforts on the part of the latter to dissuade him from his dissident course, but in vain. Mantz again requested that Zwingli put his arguments in writing; then he, Mantz, would reply, also in writing. Mantz remained in prison.

Johannes Brötli, one of those who had been banished, wrote from the town of Hallau in northern Switzerland of his disappointment at the recantation and surrender by most of the Zollikon brethren but of his joy in the loyalty of Mantz: "O, how strong, as I hear, is my brother Felix Mantz and Jörg [Blaurock]—but especially Felix Mantz. God be praised!"

Continuing Persecution—and Mission Work

Despite their promise to give up Anabaptist activity, the Zollikon Brethren were at it again soon after returning home. The layman Jörg Schad baptized forty persons in one day—probably a Sunday afternoon—in the Zollikon state church! Another brother baptized thirty. On March 16 the council struck again and arrested everyone they could find who seemed involved in the new movement. There were trials in the following week. Further discussion took place also on the question of baptism. Mantz and Blaurock were brought in one at a time to defend their side with powerful leaders of church, school, and state maintaining the other. This is often referred to as the second public disputation on baptism.

In the March trials most of the imprisoned Anabaptists surrendered again, took an oath to keep the peace, paid their incarceration costs and fines of a silver mark each. They were then released.

A few, including Mantz and Blaurock, stood their ground when others wavered. The civil record reads, for the hearing of March 25, "Felix Mantz holds to his old views, will not give in; but when Master Ulrich [Zwingli] writes on baptism, he [Mantz] will also."

Blaurock was sent back to his native area. Mantz remained in prison, but sometime in the coming weeks he found an opportunity to escape. He at first did not intend to take advantage of it until prisoners in other cells asked him to bring some tools which would enable them to get out as well. Mantz then let himself down with a rope, went to his mother's home, and brought tools back to the others to facilitate their escape.

Mantz hid out in Zurich for a time, then planned to leave the city with his friend Conrad Grebel; but the latter's wife thwarted the scheme. What was Grebel to do next? He had mentioned to Mantz the interest of Dr. Sebastian Hofmeister of Schaffhausen in the idea of believer's baptism, so Mantz decided to visit him; Mantz, in any case, could not safely remain in Zurich.

Hofmeister received Mantz and spoke with him at length. Their conversations dealt chiefly with questions about the nature of the church and its relationship to the state. Mantz recognized the need for government but held that a true

Christian should not hold office because this would inevitably involve the use of force and the sword which did not belong to the life in Christ. He urged the building up of churches free of state control and composed of believers who were baptized on their confession of faith and of seeking to live consistent Christian lives. Hofmeister was having trouble getting the Schaffhausen council to accept a moderate Zwinglian-type reformation and he was soon to be expelled. Understandably, the talks between him and the more radical Mantz remained fruitless.

Mantz joined Blaurock in the latter's native Graubünden and their efforts were crowned with some success. This joint activity came to a close with Mantz's arrest in mid-July. Authorities sent him under guard to Zurich, just as Blaurock may have been returned by Zurich, a few months before, to Chur. "He has caused much annoyance and discord among our people in the matter of rebaptizing adults and in quackish preaching," Chur wrote to Zurich. "We regard him a headstrong and obstinate person; we have sent him to you, as a native from there, with the friendly request that you will accept your own citizen and keep him with you so that we are rid of him, and our people can then remain calmer, so that we should not be obliged, the next time he returns, to deal with him more harshly."

Out of Prison and Back in Again

Mantz was again thrown into prison upon arrival in Zurich. Brought to trial he was asked to give an account of his escape the preceding spring. He also referred to Zwingli's recently published book, *Concerning Baptism, Rebaptism, and Infant Baptism,* and offered to write a reply. Mantz testified that "he wished to stand by the truth that infant baptism originated not with God but with men; true baptism takes place in confession to God, in the believer's commitment to a new and better life and to being a disciple of Christ. And whoever desires of him [Mantz] that water be applied [in baptism] in the name of God, he would not be able to deny it to him."

Mantz evidently expressed himself in a manner difficult

for the court clerk to record. For this or some other reason, Mantz himself wrote several lines of the official record of the trial. Mantz had asked a question of his judges and when he came to write it down he took the opportunity to present a short theological prologue: "Christ acknowledged his Father, even unto death, and whoever acknowledges him before men will be his disciple and will be acknowledged by him before his heavenly Father. Now I ask whether it is not right for me so to confess Christ the crucified one." This, he had been doing, the record of Mantz's testimony continues, "which was commanded by the one who sent him." Another section in Mantz's handwriting states, "Christ Jesus sits at the right hand of God ... he will come again to judge each one according to his work, etc."

After three months in prison Mantz was released, upon taking an oath no longer to disturb the peace, and being warned to cease baptizing or inciting to adult baptism.

In choosing his next field of labor Mantz decided to join Grebel and Blaurock in Grüningen. Felix Mantz seems to have been a person not at all ambitious for prominence and high leadership. His movements, as in Schaffhausen and Chur, reflect a preference for work where others had prepared the way. He served happily as helper and supporter. He had a quiet and studious nature, and did not find it easy to evangelize among the common people, or to argue for his point of view. He seems never to have urged seekers to be baptized but always emphasized that it was their free decision. Although his natural inclinations lay elsewhere, he went out among the people, working as a radical reformer, out of deep convictions and commitment to the cause.

Already on the day after his release Mantz was with Grebel at the hamlet of Betholz in Grüningen preparing to conduct a service in an open field. Zurich's magistrate for Grüningen, Jörg Berger—who had arrested Blaurock in nearby Hinwil and was taking him to the Grüningen castle—advised the assembled radicals to give up their separatist activity. They replied that they must first be convinced, from holy Scripture, of a better way. Berger then espied Grebel and Mantz and succeeded in arresting the former. Mantz escaped, but he remained in the Grüningen area.

Mantz continued his work among the people and they, being sympathetic toward his views and opposed to Zurich authority, hid him successfully. Berger, protesting to Zurich his inability to capture Mantz, wrote on October 31, "Now he has really in these three weeks caused much disturbance in the district." Berger claimed he had found out where Mantz was at the time, but it was apparently several days before he was able to arrest Mantz and add him to the number of those Anabaptists already imprisoned in Zurich.

More Disputation, Less Tolerance

Mantz and others, including non-Anabaptist sympathizers in Grüningen, continued to protest that Zwingli and the council gave no real opportunity to the Brethren to express their views; "my lords" in Zurich therefore called another public disputation, which convened November 6-8. In contrast to the so-called second Anabaptist disputation the preceding March, where Mantz and Blaurock stood as defendants before fourteen harsh judges, Brethren came from afar to take part in this one—St. Gall, Chur, and Zofingen are mentioned. Some of these out-of-town visitors gathered at "Sister Mantz's house."

The Anabaptist leaders Grebel, Mantz, and Blaurock, placed on one side of the Grossmünster church, were opposed—along with others—by the three leading state church pastors of Zurich: Ulrich Zwingli, Leo Jud, and Kaspar Grossman. Discussions lasted from Monday until Wednesday. Arguments were the same as always, and of course the council declared Zwingli and his associates winners.

Grebel, Mantz, and Blaurock were returned to prison. Taken before the council and warned against further activity, they held to their principles. On November 18 the council decreed that the three Anabaptist leaders "be placed together in the New Tower, be given mush and bread to eat and water to drink. And no one shall go to them or from them except the designated guard. So long as it pleases God and my lords think it good."

The movement continued to grow in Grüningen. Chief magistrate Berger wrote repeatedly to the Zurich council. "The baptizers are making me entirely gray-headed," he said. In the course of the winter more and more were imprisoned, including the outstanding Anabaptist theologian from Waldshut, Balthasar Hubmaier. The three Brethren leaders of the Zurich area, in prison also during the time he was in Zurich, probably had no contact with him. Some of those newly arrested were thrown into the New Tower, others into the Wellenberg.

Frustrated in its hope of suppressing the faith-rebels by pastoral talks, disputations, fines, and imprisonment, the council determined, in the spring of 1526, to enforce the most stringent measures. There was a series of hearings and trials in March; the first of these was for Felix Mantz, and it was held on the fifth of the month. Some of the Brethren gave in, were fined and released; others stood firm. In his trial Mantz once again was allowed space in the official record book—this time, to record his entire testimony! It evidently had been discovered that in his case this was a more satisfactory way, for everyone concerned, to get the matter down exactly. Perhaps it helped to satisfy his repeated request to explain his views in writing rather than orally.

"That infant baptism is not right and not the baptism of Christ you must and will come to know," Mantz wrote. "You have not permitted me to write . . . as I have always desired of you. I have not disputed but rather testified to my faith. I am baptized with the new baptism of Christ—that, I will acknowledge to the end, in the power of him who will strengthen me by his truth. Regarding other matters and charges under your law I shall give true justification, as is only right."

After the various Anabaptists had been heard, the council mandated death for any further rebaptizing. The three leaders and fifteen others, including six women, stood firm and received the sentence: "They are to be put in the New Tower together, with straw to lie on and nothing given to them except water, and bread to eat. And the warder who looks after them shall on his sworn oath allow no one to come to or leave them. So let them die and rot." (The last two words were later struck through.) The door was to be left open, however, for any who might still decide to "take a stand against what he had done and from his errors and choose to be obedient." It was specifically stated that the Anabaptist women—young or old—in prison should be treated in the exact same harsh fashion as the men.

The situation changed suddenly, however, when on March 21 the entire group of incarcerated Anabaptists escaped from prison through a window that had been left open.

Widespread Evangelism and Church Growth

For the next period we need imagination to get a picture of Mantz's activity. This was all "underground" work and therefore unrecorded. The fugitive preacher changed his field of work frequently to elude police. He visited in the homes of believers and friends of the gospel where he taught and preached, held secret services in homes and in the forests, counseled and encouraged the people. Although still in his middle twenties, Mantz was respected as a veteran Anabaptist leader who had held faithfully to his convictions and who survived three imprisonments. The Brethren received him gladly.

Prayer and exposition of Scripture constituted important parts of services he conducted. If the text were from the Old Testament Mantz seems as a rule to have translated the passage directly from the Hebrew, which was followed by its exposition and application. He did this in no vain display of knowledge, which would have been contrary to his nature, but to help people understand the Word of God. When specifically requested to do so, he baptized. One such case during this period was a woman of the village of Embrach, north of Zurich; this baptism would constitute fateful evidence against him in his last trial. At most of the services, it seems, the Lord's Supper was observed.

After a couple of months Mantz went, with Blaurock, back to the Grüningen area, southeast of Zurich. The strengthening of Anabaptist activity in the district troubled chief magistrate Berger exceedingly; he announced that anyone harboring Anabaptists would be punished in the same manner as they.

Still in the early summer of 1526 we find Mantz in the Basel area of Switzerland, far to the west and a bit to the north of Zurich. A hostile contemporary witness of this period (J. Gastius) declared that "wherever he went ordinary men and women always accompanied him as if he were a visible divinity, and they hung, transfixed and bewitched, on his every word. He loved the fields and the forests, the sure hiding places of heresy. Whatever he said or ordered was held to be a word of God." The same observer described one service in an open field near Basel: Mantz began by reading from something he had written down. This was probably a poem of faith which he had composed.

Mantz's work in the Basel area seems to have been quite successful. Believers were strengthened, converts won and new groups established. One of the many Brethren later arrested and brought before the Basel council ingenuously asked his accusers: "Why do you, gentlemen of the council, not permit us our own church in which we can make known the true teachings of Christ, baptize the repentant, observe the Lord's Supper, and practice church discipline?"

During the summer we find Mantz in northeastern Switzerland. On the way there, he stopped over in the town of Wil, where he met with his brother evangelist, George Blaurock. Opponents later accused them of having claimed that they had escaped miraculously through closed doors the preceding March, but both men vociferously denied having made any such claim. It is likely that local Anabaptists had embellished the plain account of Mantz and his colleague in this way.

In any case such extreme and fantastic ideas seem to have prevailed among Brethren groups in that part of Switzerland and further eastward. Mantz joined his friend Conrad Grebel in the area about midsummer and they worked hard to quell extremism. When the moderates from Zurich observed, according to a contemporary witness (J. Kessler), "such crass error and fantasies in these people they were very greatly displeased; they explained that such things were not the intention in the beginnings of the movement.... But many would not listen to them ... [and] even regarded them as false prophets and scribes and turned them away." This seems to have been Grebel's last area of work.

Mantz proceeded to the nearby cantonal capital, St. Gall. His activity there resulted in his arrest, along with a brother from Grüningen; their incarceration was brief, however. They took an oath to preserve the peace and then were released, and banished from St. Gall territory.

Last Labors and Trial

Mantz made bold to return to Zurich's Grüningen district, where the Brethren enjoyed greatest success and where Blaurock was working. It was not a choice for ease or safety. Zurich authorities, supported by magistrate Berger in Grüningen, had redoubled efforts to wipe out the Anabaptist movement. On November 19 the council issued a mandate confirming the penalty of death for those who rebaptized and made the same punishment applicable for anyone who held an Anabaptist preaching service—making clear that the new measures were taken with Grüningen particularly in mind. Magistrate Berger hunted the radical leaders diligently, enlisting the help of assistants and informers. He finally succeeded in arresting a group of Anabaptists gathered in the woods, December 3, 1526. Among them were Mantz and Blaurock. A week and a half later they were all taken to prison in Zurich.

Zurich authorities, determined to crush the radical movement through extreme measures, prepared the way with a series of hearings, with testimony from Zwingli and other hostile witnesses. The officials also gathered pertinent documents from earlier trials. Principal charges against Mantz were that he had tried to set up a separate church whose members must be sinless; that he taught, a Christian ought not to hold state office or bear the sword; true Christians should hold all things in common; and that, despite his earlier oath to desist, he had baptized at least one person.

Mantz, with Blaurock, was brought before the council for hearings, point by point, on the charges. He did not deny trying to set up a separatist church; its members were not sinless but such as were determined to hear the Word of God and follow Christ. He acknowledged being against a Christian's holding office or bearing the sword, adding that the opposing view had no scriptural support. He denied having taught communism, affirming, however, love's duty that each one must help his neighbor when the latter suffered want. As for having baptized in the canton of Zurich since the March 7 edict, he admitted that about two weeks thereafter he had baptized the above-mentioned woman in Embrach. Furthermore, he added, he would administer baptism to anyone who requested him to, assuming that the candidate would receive previous instruction in the faith. Knowing full well the fateful weight of his words, the brave young Brethren leader held back not a whit in his honest and open testimony.

Mantz, having twice escaped from prison, was placed this time in the secure Wellenberg tower. He penned a letter, most likely during these final days, which was his testament to the Brethren. It warns against false prophets who claim to be pastors and teachers but in reality hate and persecute true believers; they are actually "thieves and murderers" (of the truth) who "under false pretenses, pour out innocent blood." True "sheep of Christ" are known by their love. At the end of the letter Mantz affirmed that despite all hostility and persecution he would "remain steadfastly by Christ."

This farewell writing of Mantz has come down to us also in poetic form—eighteen stanzas, each of seven lines; it was later set to music and used as a hymn. It is not clear whether the poetic version comes from Mantz, but the guess here is that it does. The hymn begins "With all my heart I'll sing, my heart rejoices in God" and continues through eighteen stanzas of seven lines each, praising the love of God, warning against false prophets, anticipating the early return of the Lord, declaring that the true believer will stand by Christ, who knows his need and will not fail.

The trial concluded and the sentence was pronounced on

Mantz and Blaurock, January 5, 1527. It was not proved that the latter had administered baptism in the canton of Zurich after the March edict, and he was not a citizen of Zurich; so Blaurock was flogged, and then banished forever from the canton of Zurich. In stark contrast to their treatment of Blaurock, the council decided to make a frightful example of Mantz, which they thought would surely suffice to destroy the Anabaptist movement. For him the judgment was death.

Martyred for the Cause

The sentencing began with a review of the radicals' baptizing activity, against tradition and the public order, and against the explanations of the Zurich pastors that only infant baptism—certainly not rebaptism—was biblical. By providing disputations, warnings, treatment good and bad of the accused, the council said it had tried to divert them from their erroneous views and practice all in vain. It declared that Mantz had been "one of the real beginners and chief promoters" of the Anabaptist movement.

He had been treated mildly heretofore, the council affirmed (here at the close of his fourth harsh imprisonment); it had warned him and he had taken an oath to desist. Despite all this he admitted now to having instructed and baptized a woman in Embrach and on his own initiative declared he would do the same kind of thing in the future. He was declared guilty of trying to set up a separatist church, of objecting to a Christian's taking state office or bearing the sword. All this, according to the sentence, made for disorder and insurrection.

The verdict therefore was execution by drowning and "if anyone, whoever he may be, should hereafter presume in word or deed to censure or revenge his death, privately or publicly, this one is likewise guilty and liable to the same punishment as he." His possessions would "fall to my lords to be disposed of as they choose." Zwingli, eager to be free of the Anabaptist challenge, agreed fully with the council's action.

The sentence described in some detail the procedure for execution which was carried out on the same day, a Saturday, at about three o'clock in the afternoon. Mantz was taken from his cell in the Wellenberg, rowed in a small boat to the fishmarket area by the city hall. The sentence was likely read to him there in the presence of many onlookers. He called out in praise to God who was giving him the privilege of dying for divine truth. He was taken along the street for a short distance on the east side of the Limmat to the slaughterhouse building. Some state church pastors were in the crowd and they argued with him about baptism. Also among the people observing the tragic drama were Felix Mantz's mother and brother (the latter mentioned nowhere else); they encouraged him to stand firm in the faith.

At this point he was put again into the boat and brought to a little fisherman's hut in the middle of the river. The official executioner, who had already bound his hands together, here "slipped them over the knees and pushed a short stick through under the knees above the arms" and, immobilized in such a way, he was "thrown into the water. . . . "

Just before being pushed over the side of the fisherman's platform into the water, Mantz cried out loudly in Latin, "Into your hands, Lord, I commend my spirit." Although the sentence had read that he was to remain "in the water to die and rot," his body was in fact removed shortly afterward and buried in the cemetery of St. Jacob's Church.

• GEORGE BLAUROCK •

3

• BLAUROCK •
He Was
Called Strong George

Early in the year 1525 an ex-priest by the name of Georg Cajacob—or Jorg vom Haus Jacob—made his way to Zurich. With him was his wife, Els. He had formerly (1516-1518) served as vicar in Trins, a village of his native Graubünden. This mountainous territory, also called Grisons, was then an autonomous commonwealth united by treaty with the confederation of Swiss cantons.

Cajacob had left the Catholic Church but remained dissatisfied. He was looking for Ulrich Zwingli, leader of reform in Zurich, and soon was talking with him. The reformer was then forty-one years of age, of medium height and slight build; he wore, day in and day out, his scholar's robe. He was trying, in line with his humanist training, to enlighten people through his preaching and entice them gradually from superstitions and ecclesiastical abuses. He had found the Bible to be the sole and sufficient authority in matters of faith.

George Cajacob, born about 1491, came of humble origin as the son of a Graubünden peasant. A man of striking appearance, he had black hair with a bald spot in the middle. Fiery eyes betrayed an impulsive disposition. He had attended a university or two—Leipzig, in any case—but not for very long; higher education had not molded him. He was a man of the people, indifferent to theological niceties that intrigued scholars; but he seemed to desire one thing very earnestly, to know and do the will of God.

Choosing Sides for Reform

Cajacob's talks with Zwingli left him still dissatisfied. It amazed this man of simple and straightforward thinking that the learned reformer had been preaching for years against church abuses, such as baptism and the mass, but still administered these rites in medieval forms as before. The city council had approved reform in general in January 1523, ignoring papal authority, leaving it to Zwingli and other recognized pastors to preach the gospel, yet implicitly reserving to itself veto rights on external changes. Zwingli was willing to wait until council and people were ready; George Cajacob was not one to wait.

He heard from someone that there was a little group of men in town "more zealous than Zwingli"; Conrad Grebel and Felix Mantz, young laymen and citizens of the town, were the best known of this group. There were gatherings for Bible study and prayer. These people desired changes in the forms of worship which would bring them in conformity with New Testament teachings. They also opposed the baptism of infants but had not yet drawn the logical conclusion of rebaptizing believers. The church, it was already clear to them, should be a fellowship of committed Christians with the Bible as sole authority for faith and life.

Cajacob liked what he heard about these people; he went to visit Grebel and Mantz. He had talked with these younger men but for a short time, when he felt himself at one with them. At least they had the courage of their convictions and were not prepared to compromise as they felt Zwingli was doing. They well knew that their way would be costly and declared themselves willing to pay the price.

Zwingli still hoped, as did the council, to win over those opposing infant baptism. A public disputation on the question was called for January 17, 1525. Grebel, Mantz, and the Wytikon pastor, Wilhelm Reublin, were the main speakers for antipedobaptists at the disputation, but newcomer Cajacob apparently also raised a question or made a brief comment at some point during the discussions. Someone asked who it was that had spoken and another replied, "That fellow wearing the blue coat." Others heard this and thereafter he was called "Bluecoat"—Blaurock.

Following the disputation the council ordered all parents who were withholding their children from baptism to have them baptized within a week or be banished. Further meetings of the radicals were forbidden and four of them, not from Zurich, were banished. The little group of earnest believers, as yet quite unorganized, found itself ordered to cease even informal gatherings for Bible study and prayer or face prosecution for illegal activity.

Starting the New Movement

The radicals met secretly the evening of that Saturday, January 21, on which the final decrees had been issued by the council. Surely it was a solemn group, a crucial moment. They could not continue as before; they must conform to orders of the council or go forward conscientiously into a perilous future. Following a period of soul-searching prayer, George Blaurock arose and asked Conrad Grebel for God's sake to baptize him on confession of his faith. The ex-priest knelt down to receive the rite. Grebel took some water in a dipper and poured it on Blaurock's head, probably while quoting appropriate Scripture. Others who were present likewise requested baptism and Blaurock administered the ordinance to each of them on profession of his or her faith.

From the time of his baptism George Blaurock was a zealot for the cause. To the Brethren, as they called themselves, baptism meant death to the old life of sin and rebirth to walk in newness of life. It was a sign of brotherly love also and a pledge of loyalty to Jesus Christ their captain and Lord. Blaurock and other leaders visited enthusiastically among those who were friendly to the new movement.

The Brethren gathered, usually in the evenings, in various homes, for prayer and praise services. After the reading of some portion of the Bible and discussion of it, those who accepted the gospel as presented were baptized. Usually also there was a simple observance of the Lord's Supper. In contrast to the elaborate service of the mass, still being observed in the Zurich churches, these believers developed from relevant New Testament passages a simple and solemn rite. Ordinary bread and wine, from the pantry of their host, were used. The Supper was explained as a memorial of the "rose-colored blood" shed by the Savior, also as "a sign of brotherly love and peace."

Effective Witness in a Zollikon Home

Most aggressive among the Brethren, both in evangelism and in administering the ordinances, was Blaurock. On Wednesday, January 25, he learned that Rüdi Thomann in the nearby village of Zollikon had invited some of the Brethren for a meal and conversation about spiritual matters. Thomann was a good friend of Reublin and Brötli, the latter being a former priest who had turned Anabaptist in Zollikon; they were among the four who had been ordered to leave the canton in a week's time. Thomann had not yet identified himself with the Brethren, but he was concerned about the matter and wished to give a farewell supper for his friends.

Before the supper was completed, Blaurock and Mantz arrived; two or three others came in later. When the dishes had been cleared away, all sat around the table and had a simple service of worship. They read and discussed passages from the New Testament concerning the grace of God and the need for repentance and rebirth. Suddenly Hans Bruggbach, one of the farmers present, stood with tears running down his face. "I am a great sinner," he cried out, and he asked the others to pray for him. Blaurock inquired whether he wished to receive the grace of God. Hans replied that he did. Mantz stood and asked if anyone would forbid that he baptize Bruggbach. "No one," said Blaurock; and it was done. Likewise with another of the men at the table. Blaurock concluded the service by leading in the observance of the Lord's Supper.

Other visitors then left, but Blaurock and Mantz remained for the night. Very early the next morning these two were awakened by their host, Rüdi Thomann. With him was his son-in-law, Marx Bosshart, who lived in the same house and had been present in the service the evening before. He had been deeply moved at that time but felt unable to make the complete surrender. After going to his room and to bed he had rolled and tossed in sleeplessness. Under deep conviction he prayed God to show him the right way. Toward morning his prayer was answered and peace came, he now related, and the way was clear to him. He must be baptized and become a real Christian. "I was moved so powerfully in my spirit," he testified about the experience in court later, "that I could do nothing else."

Blaurock questioned Marx, at that early-morning encounter, to be sure he understood the step he was taking. "You have been up to now a frivolous young man," said the evangelist, "but you must become a new man. You must put away the old Adam and take on the new. And you must live the better life." Bosshart answered that he would do his best. Then Blaurock asked whether he desired the grace of baptism and he declared that he did. "Come then," said Blaurock, "and I will baptize you." The young man stepped forward and Blaurock poured a bit of water on his head, the rite being accompanied by appropriate remarks.

Turning to Rüdi Thomann the eager evangelist said, "You are an old man, drawing near to the time of death. You also must go the better way." He offered to baptize Thomann also if he were ready for it. He was, and Blaurock administered the ordinance. Others of the household were called in, given the same kind of exhortation and, in the end, baptized. Of those who had been present at the meeting on the evening before only old Heinrich Thomann, a brother of Rüdi's would not be baptized. He had been so shocked to see holy sacraments treated in such an informal way that he "broke out in a sweat," according to his later testimony, and wanted to flee from the place.

The Putsch That Failed

Blaurock was pleased with the response to his preaching and that of the other Brethren, especially in Zollikon where the movement was strongest. There were about ninety independent farmers in the village at the time and approximately a third of them were baptized in that first week, along with at least four hired workers and one woman. Almost all were "small farmers"; names of most leading families were conspicious by their absence from the list of those who received the new teaching and were baptized.

Blaurock was still not satisfied. Convinced that Brethren teaching fairly represented the eternal truth of God, he wanted to reach everyone with it. He felt Zollikon was ripe for coming over to the new movement. He determined on a bold stroke. On Sunday morning, January 29, he appeared in the Zollikon church. As the pastor, Nicolas Billeter, came in to mount the pulpit, Blaurock, who had seated himself in the congregation, arose and asked in a loud voice what the pastor intended to do.

"I am going to preach the Word of God," the latter replied.

"Not you but I have been sent to preach!" the Anabaptist called out.

Billeter tried to explain that he had been designated by his superiors in Zurich to preach there; he referred to the canons of the Grossmünster church, who with the consent of the Zurich council appointed clergymen for Zollikon and many other churches of the area. This was worse than no answer at all for the fiery independent. He continued to talk after the pastor had mounted the pulpit and was trying to begin his sermon. Rather than continue in this way, Billeter came down from the pulpit and started toward the outside door. Some members of the congregation interpreted this as giving in to the disturber and called out to the pastor to come back. He did so, mounting the pulpit once more. He spoke to the people in a reasonable way, warning against disorder. "If anyone wishes to point out error to me," he said, "would this one please come to my home and discuss matters privately. A public service is not the place for such disputing, for it may cause disorder."

The determined Blaurock was not to be hushed by reason. "It is written," he cried, "my house is a house of prayer, but you have made it a den of thieves." To emphasize his words he struck a bench three or four times with a branch-stick he was carrying. This would suggest the cleansing of the temple by Jesus, for Blaurock felt the churches were in need of such a cleansing. This time the radical preacher had gone too far. Deputy magistrate Hans Wüest, who was present in the congregation, came forward and threatened Blaurock with arrest if he did not cease such disturbance immediately. The Anabaptist enthusiast then became quiet. He had failed. The Zollikon congregation was not ready to come over en masse to the new faith.

Hopes Are Dashed Once Again

Far from achieving its purpose, this outburst by Blaurock convinced the Zurich council that further measures must be taken against the radicals. Police appeared in Zollikon on the next day and arrested almost everyone known to have any connection with the movement; twenty-five men were incarcerated in the old Augustine cloister in Zurich—Blaurock and Mantz were imprisoned separately. The twenty-five were questioned one at a time by an investigating board of council representatives and pastors. They gave testimony as to events of the great first week of the Anabaptists, freely confessing their part in baptisms and other activities. One said he had not yet been baptized but would be as soon as he was free again.

Zwingli and his supporters argued that the Bible says nothing of anyone being baptized twice. These simple lay people from Zollikon knew better than to recognize christening as any real kind of baptism, but they were well able to contradict Zwingli on his own ground. They referred to the account in Acts 19 of those who had been baptized into John the Baptist's baptism "of repentance," then after instruction by Paul were "baptized in the name of the Lord Jesus" (Acts 19:4-5).

In reply Zwingli could do no better than to argue that these people had not been baptized into John's baptism but only instructed, then baptized with water for the first time by Paul. Zwingli must have betrayed his own lack of confidence in this weak argument. He tried to make his position more palatable to the Anabaptists by sharing with them his plans to do away with the Catholic mass and substitute in its place a simple Lord's Supper service. (This was indeed to be approved by the council April 11 and instituted in churches the next day.)

The Brethren seem to have interpreted all this as an admission of the rightness of their position, at least in part. A sympathetic friend of the Anabaptists managed to visit them where they were being held and took a message to the Brethren remaining in Zollikon (about ten of those who had been baptized were not arrested) that their incarcerated fellow believers were victorious over Zwingli in the discussions; they were refusing therefore to recant.

Even if it were true that they might be judged by an impartial observer to be winning some of the arguments, that would not change the situation. These Anabaptists were prisoners of those who were their judges and had the power. Soon the Anabaptists realized this and came to terms with harsh reality. On February 7 the council sentenced the twenty-five men to pay costs for their incarceration, post bond of a thousand guilders (which represented the income of the entire group for several months), take an oath regarding rebaptism and all related activities "that they wouldn't do it anymore."

This meant acknowledging infant baptism and not taking part in any kind of separatist church life. The Brethren saw no way out except to conform, at least outwardly, to these requirements. They did so and were released the next day. In a small gesture of generosity the council gave them permission to gather in groups of no more than three or four persons for Bible reading and discussion but not for preaching—and certainly not for baptizing.

Tireless Evangelism in Zurich and Zollikon

Blaurock, Mantz, and one other who had administered baptism were held in prison for further questioning. This came on February 18, when Blaurock testified that so far as he knew he had been the first among them to receive baptism and partake of the Lord's Supper in the manner of the Lord's example. Concerning Zwingli he boldly declared, "He does violence to the Scriptures and falsifies them more than the old pope himself." The fiery Anabaptist offered to defend this position before the council or anywhere else.

Despite this, the council released the non-citizen zealot after a solemn warning, declaring at the same time that he would be required to confront Zwingli with his accusations and produce, in the presence of the reformer and the council, scriptural proof for his assertion. Blaurock surely anticipated this meeting with relish, but things happened so fast afterward that it apparently did not take place in the intended way.

Upon being released Blaurock went to the home of a friend of the Anabaptists a few blocks away on the winding street called Rennweg. The friend was Heinrich Aberli, a baker, who invited three others to join them for supper. They all spoke until late evening of spiritual things, read Scripture, had prayer, observed the Lord's Supper. One of the friends who had come, the furrier Anton Roggenacher, invited Blaurock to his home for the next day, and the Anabaptist leader spent the night there. Early the next morning, Sunday, Roggenacher requested baptism and Blaurock baptized him. The latter then proceeded, with Aberli and two other Brethren, to Zollikon.

In Hans Murer's house, on the bank of the Lake of Zurich, Blaurock led an evangelistic service, while Pastor Billeter conducted the regular service of worship for the village in the church up on the hill. The unauthorized meeting was attended by a large crowd that apparently spilled out into the yard. Blaurock preached there again in the afternoon, perhaps to an even larger group, and baptized eight women. Among those baptized during this period in Zollikon were the wife of the village "mayor," her daughter, and the wife of the deputy magistrate, Hans Wüest.

At an informal meeting in Jacob Hottinger's house in Zollikon the Zurich baker, Heinrich Aberli, who had already been active in the movement, was baptized by Blaurock. The latter said to him, "Brother Heinrich, we all believe in Christ Jesus ... and in this we shall remain steadfast.... Brother Heinrich, do you confess that the Lord Jesus Christ suffered for us, and that what is written of him is true?"

"Yes," answered Aberli.

"Then I baptize you in the name of the Father, the Son, and the Holy Spirit," Blaurock intoned. He took a handful of water and released it on the convert's head, probably quoting at the same time other words from Scripture.

This seems to have been Blaurock's last day, ever, in Zollikon. Grebel remained in Schaffhausen and Mantz was in prison. But the laymen in Zollikon carried on nobly. One of them, Jörg Schad, baptized forty people on one day in the village church!

Struggle of the Brethren for Survival

On the day before Schad's rash act the Zurich council decreed, "Anyone who has submitted to baptism since the affair in the Augustine cloister, whether man or woman, is to be fined one silver mark ... " and "whoever in the future submits to baptism is to be expelled immediately with wife and children."

When the Zurich authorities heard about renewed activity in the Anabaptist movement of Zollikon, they were incensed. Of the twenty-five men who had been released from incarceration on February 8, under oath "that they would not [baptize] anymore," all but three had resumed Anabaptist activity in some fashion. Probably on the testimony of Blaurock they had interpreted their promise as a commitment "not to do it" until called upon by God again to do it. This call some felt quite soon. Rütch Hottinger testified before the council in the latter part of March that in his opinion "what they had promised during the time in the Augustine cloister"—that they would refrain from their activity—they had done. They "desisted" as promised "until God had reproached them for it." His conclusion coincided with that of the other Brethren: "One must obey God rather than men."

This approach did not commend itself in the least to the Zurich authorities. On March 16 they pounced once again on those they reckoned to have taken part in the forbidden baptisms in Zollikon; they arrested and incarcerated nineteen men. Blaurock also was arrested again and imprisoned. For a period of nine days the Anabaptists were questioned by representatives of the council, harangued by Zwingli and other pastors, and threatened with severe punishment.

With the exception of two Hottingers, Schad and Gabriel Giger, this Zollikon group submitted to the browbeating of Zwingli and the authorities, agreeing to conform to Zwinglian rather than Anabaptist reform. The fifteen were fined a silver mark each (approximately the price of a hog), promised they would "refrain from such rebaptism and not speak or act against infant baptism." They were released on March 25 with the warning that if they failed to keep this promise they would be banished with their families from the canton of Zurich.

It had been arranged, meanwhile, for Blaurock and Mantz to be brought from prison and appear before the burgomaster, the three state church pastors of Zurich, other clergymen, two schoolmasters and several councilmen. Zwingli later wrote that as the two were led under guard to or from the city hall, one (doubtless Blaurock) called out with "terrible threats against the city," the other with "words of pity." The hearing began on March 20 and lasted three days. If this were indeed a public disputation on baptism, as claimed, it certainly was a one-sided one, with Blaurock and Mantz standing one at a time before the phalanx of august opponents.

Blaurock, however, was not intimidated and as usual spoke without restraint. Zwingli was much offended at the leading part taken by this man whom he characterized as a "senseless visionary," so ignorant he could not read from the German New Testament as he stood before the council, even though he had been a Catholic priest for some years. One wonders whether Blaurock, zealously wanting to get on with his arguments, might have stumbled a time or two in taking scriptural ammunition for his charges against Zwingli. He had called the Zurich reformer a heretic, a thief, and a murderer, referring to John 10: "He who does not enter the sheepfold by the door but climbs in by another way, that man is a thief and a murderer" (from the German translation). Zwingli would never forgive Blaurock for that.

Blaurock's Labors Far and Wide

Zwingli claimed victory in the debate, as usual, boasting that Anabaptism had been decisively defeated and that the movement was declining rapidly in and around Zurich. The authorities agreed, warning imprisoned Anabaptists that separatist activity would be tolerated no longer. Some of them were frightened into a denial of the new faith—these were fined and released. Blaurock stood steadfast, declaring, "So long as my heavenly Father calls me to baptize, I shall do so; otherwise I shall not." As a result of such stubbornness the council banished Blaurock and four others who were not citizens of Zurich.

"Regarding Blaurock," the council record states, "it is further ordered that he and his wife be put aboard a ship and dispatched toward Chur. And a letter will be sent to the council of Chur that they take care of him and keep him. And to him let it be said that if he comes back again he will get what is coming to him in such a way that he will keep quiet from that time on." Whether this order of the council was carried out at that time is impossible to say, but Blaurock does seem to have worked for a short period in Graubünden during this time. The Anabaptist movement spread rather rapidly there.

"We must now use all our strength against the Catabaptists," Chur reformer Johannes Commander complained. "They gather here, and there are many of our citizens who openly or secretly favor them. That causes us much trouble. The citizens are attracted to them and now I have to work among the people and bear the tribulation."

The council of Chur forbade attendance at Anabaptist meetings, threatening "the loss of body, honor, and goods" to any who took part in them. Blaurock and Mantz—who was also working in the area—were arrested and imprisoned in mid-July. As Mantz was not a citizen there, he was sent back to Zurich. With the intervention of friends, apparently, Blaurock was released after a short time. He then went to

Appenzell, easternmost canton of Switzerland. There as elsewhere the Anabaptist cause flourished under his ministry, and Brethren were encouraged by his bold witness. Later he joined Mantz in the Grüningen highlands southeast of Zurich.

Zwingli's claim to have defeated the Anabaptist movement in and around Zurich was not an empty boast, although the reasons are to be found in official persecution and not in his arguments for infant baptism. Never again were the Brethren to be numerous or influential in Zurich, St. Gall, or any of the larger cities. In many country districts, however, they flourished at this time thanks primarily to the work of George Blaurock. Born a peasant, a peasant at heart he remained, beloved by country people. They might have had difficulty understanding the young scholars Grebel and Mantz, but not Blaurock. He spoke their kind of language. He knew their needs and their way of thinking. He was their interpreter of the gospel. They referred to him affectionately as "Strong George" *(der starke Jörg)* or a "Second Paul."

Another Putsch Fails

After weeks of successful evangelization among the small-farmers of the Grüningen district in the summer and fall of 1525 Blaurock felt that the time had come for making another try at winning an entire community. He appeared in the state church at Hinwil before the pastor arrived on Sunday morning, October 8. Mounting the pulpit he began to address the people who had already assembled. "Whose is this pulpit?" he began, in defense of his irregular act. "If it is God's place, where the Word of God should be proclaimed, then I am here as one sent by the heavenly Father to preach the Word of God." He proceeded then to do it.

After the intruder had been holding forth for a time, Pastor Johannes Brennwald came in. A mild-mannered and cautious man, he waited quietly and allowed Blaurock to continue. However, when the latter began to attack infant baptism, Brennwald felt it his duty to speak out and he did so.

"Do you defend infant baptism and propose to keep it?" asked Blaurock.

"Yes," replied the pastor.

"Then you are antichristian and mislead the people," cried Blaurock in the manner of a prophet. As the two men argued, the people became noisy, most of them supporting the Anabaptist.

A deputy magistrate was present and desired to arrest Blaurock. There were about two hundred people present, and the deputy called on the men to assist him in performing his duty. "Isn't that your business?" one of the men called out; others murmured approval and no one offered to help him.

This could be a dangerous situation. Peasants had been revolting in various parts of Europe. The people of Grüningen had long opposed the rule of Zurich. Both pastor and deputy realized their helplessness and became frightened. They hastened to Grüningen castle, four miles away, and reported the disorder to chief magistrate Jörg Berger. They asked him to bring help and arrest the Anabaptist preacher who had usurped the Hinwil pulpit and was arousing the people.

Berger, with his deputy and the pastor, hurried to the Hinwil church, where about two hundred people remained. There he called on them to cooperate, as had the deputy earlier, but they refused again. He had his men, they said; let them help him. Berger finally succeeded in arresting Blaurock as everyone was leaving the church. He put him on his deputy's horse and they started out for Grüningen castle. Riding along under close guard, Blaurock began to sing. "It was really remarkable," Berger reported to his superiors in Zurich, "how the people young and old ran after him."

As the procession neared the village of Betzholtz, it came upon a large gathering of Anabaptists preparing for a service in the open field. Berger called out, asking them not to baptize any more people and to give up their radical views.

"We do not force anyone," someone in the group replied, "but whenever a person requests it we baptize him; and we will continue to do so until we are taught better from God's holy Scriptures."

Berger recognized two of the leaders, Grebel and Mantz.

They were preparing to speak, despite his warning, and the sullen crowd made it quite evident that they were on the side of the Anabaptists. Berger realized that this might be an even more dangerous situation than that at the Hinwil church. He withdrew to a quieter place and consulted with his deputy and another helper. He decided to send them back to the crowd to keep order as best they could while he rode over to the neighboring village of Ottikon to get help, taking Blaurock with him. From Ottikon he sent back several men to assist the two he had left at Betzholtz. They succeeded in arresting Grebel but Mantz, who had been released from prison in Zurich only the day before, escaped. He would soon be apprehended.

"It was remarkable day," wrote the exhausted chief magistrate that evening in his report to the Zurich council.

Authorities Talk, Then Threaten the Worst

Jörg Berger sent frequent reports to Zurich about the activity of Anabaptists in the Grüningen district. He was a loyal supporter of the council and of Zwinglian reform. He sensed also the seething unrest in his district. In order to convince the people that they were being treated fairly, he recommended (as the Anabaptists of Zollikon had) that another public disputation be held on the question of baptism. He also suggested to the councilors "that from our district you choose twelve nonpartisan and unrelated men to listen carefully" during the disputation, "then they can report back home." Although none of these Grüningen representatives were to be Anabaptist sympathizers, of course, Berger felt that their report would be more credible to restive people of his district than official pronouncements from Zurich. His recommendation was approved and carried out.

Interest in the disputation was so great that, according to one report, nine hundred persons assembled on the appointed day, November 6. It soon became evident that the council chamber in the city hall was too small and the assembly was moved to the Grossmünster church. Arguments on both sides followed the usual course. At the close of discussions, on the eighth, Zwingli and his associates naturally were declared victorious. The twelve representatives from Grüningen reported unanimously that the Anabaptists were sufficiently heard and allowed verily to speak their minds, "and whoever accuses my lords and Zwingli does them an injustice, for no one stifled them in their speaking."

Grebel, Mantz, and Blaurock, brought from their cells to lead the Anabaptist defense, were sent back later to the New Tower prison. They remained there all winter and were given a new hearing March 5, 1526. Blaurock declared he would stand by the baptism of Christ which he had received. He repeated his accusation, based on John 10, that those who baptized infants were thieves and murderers of God's truth. Blaurock then referred his audience to a letter which he had written from prison to the pastors of Zurich. In this communication he had gone into greater detail about his baptismal views. He had attacked infant baptism along with those who administered it, and he requested another public disputation. About his testimony, he said, "I will stand by it until death."

After further hearings an additional twelve men and six women who had refused to deny their faith were locked up together in the New Tower prison. "No one shall have authority to remove them from prison without the knowledge of my lords," the latter ordered, "be they well or ill." "A public notice shall be sent out," the record concludes, "describing the harsh imprisonment of the baptizers. And from this time on whoever baptizes is hereby warned that he will be drowned without mercy and thus be brought from life to death."

So it had come at last! At the end of their resources to deal with the radicals, and determined to silence them, the Zurich council, with the full and enthusiastic support of Zwingli, decreed the ultimate penalty. They chose the form of execution considered the most degrading. Usually it was reserved for condemned women and was deemed particularly humiliating when imposed upon men. Drowning, however, was considered a fitting punishment for those who insisted so much on baptism.

Escape, Manifold Labors, and Recapture

The edict of drowning did not apply to what had happened in the past. Anabaptists in the New Tower had been sentenced to life imprisonment. Instead of being for life, however, it lasted only two weeks. Late on the night of March 21 the guard brought drinking water to the prisoners. They took it, and ate some bread. Suddenly someone noticed that the window had been left unlocked. There was great excitement as the prisoners discussed the situation. A rope was at hand with which they could reach the window and escape. Fortunately, the drawbridge was down so that they were able to slip away.

Following escape, the Brethren leaders worked secretly, and mainly in the country districts, moving quickly from one place to another. However, Grebel died during the summer. For Blaurock and Mantz the most fruitful field of labor was in the Grüningen district. They held services, sometimes in the woods, and crowds assembled to hear them. Not only were the peasants there still interested in the new teaching; they continued to feel sympathy for anyone who was persecuted by the hated Zurich authorities.

Chief magistrate Berger was zealous in his efforts to discourage the spread of Anabaptism, but he did not like the idea of a death penalty for rebaptizers. Early in December 1526 he discovered a group of them during a meeting in the woods and arrested four of the leaders. Among these were Blaurock and Mantz, who were sent to Zurich under heavy guard and imprisoned in the Wellenberg, the old tower in the middle of the Limmat River.

In the trial which followed, both men held firmly to their beliefs. They were accused of teaching communism but denied this except in the sense that a good Christian would share with a brother in need. They were charged with inciting riots and causing general disorder; in denying this they asserted their loyalty to the authorities except in matters against the Word of God.

Attacked in connection with their teachings about the church and its discipline, Blaurock said, "All those who live entirely in open vice and sin, such as drunkards, prostitutes, adulterers, gamblers, revelers, usurers, and the like should be excluded and not at all considered as Christians." He did not insist on discipline for secret sins, probably because no one would know the facts except the persons involved and because it would open the door to abuses. Asked whether he had baptized in the Zurich territory since the warning of the authorities was given, following his previous imprisonment, Blaurock said he did not know that he had. Unwilling to leave the impression that he was submitting under threats, he added, "But if anyone should come to me and request to be taught and baptized, I would not refuse him but would instruct him and baptize him."

"In this regard," he continued, "I would not look upon man, for one is more obligated to God than to man." The astounded clerk added in the official record: "Further, he said and declared openly that my lords the pastors mislead my lords [the council], have done so in the past and will continue in the future, do violence to the Scripture and falsify it and are, together with their followers, thieves, and murders of Christ!" Thus Blaurock repeats his old charge yet once again.

Final Work in Switzerland

Sentence was pronounced against Mantz and Blaurock on the same day, January 5, 1527. Mantz was condemned to death because, it was alleged, he spread Anabaptist errors and baptized in the Zurich canton despite repeated warnings—because he had separated from the Christian church and, leading others to do likewise, had formed a sect; because he taught that a true Christian could not be a magistrate and wield the sword, and because he opposed capital punishment. For these "crimes" he was drowned in the Limmat. Thus died Blaurock's dear friend and intimate co-worker Felix Mantz.

George Blaurock, because he was "a real instigator and leader of anabaptism," was counted as worthy as Mantz of the death sentence. Several times he had been imprisoned and then "mercifully" released in the hope he would give up his errors, but he obstinately refused. In his favor was the fact that it could not be proved that he had baptized anyone in Zurich territory since the last warning. Also, he was not a citizen of Zurich. The authorities hoped the example made of Mantz would be sufficient to defeat the new movement. "By grace," therefore, the council gave Blaurock a milder sentence:

"That he be turned over to the executioner, who should strip him to the waist, bind his hands and, along the way from the Fishmarket to the Lower Gate, beat him with a rod so that the blood flows." There he should be required to take an oath not to return to Zurich territory. "Then if he should afterwards return, be it for a short time or long, he would receive the now well-known sentence of drowning without mercy as had Felix Mantz."

This sentence was carried out that same fateful January 5, 1527. When the bloodied victim reached the Lower Gate, he refused to take the oath. Christ had commanded his followers, "Swear not," and the Brethren took it literally. Ordered to be thrown back again into the Wellenberg prison, Blaurock managed somehow to satisfy his persecutors with an oath of some kind or a promise and was released. As he left the city he shook off the dust of the evil city from his shoes, as Jesus had instructed his disciples, and from his old blue coat if this had been returned to him on that cold January day.

Blaurock did not return to Zurich, not openly at least. He attended a public disputation on Anabaptism in Bern, May 21, that year. He returned there in the January following for a disputation conducted by church and state authorities which lasted almost three weeks. At this disputation it was decided officially that Bern would be Protestant. Eight Anabaptists attended these meetings, as everybody was invited to come and take part. Instead of being given a chance to speak, however, Blaurock and the other Anabaptists were thrown into prison. Zwingli was present at the disputation and a special day was set aside so that he and his supporters could denounce the Anabaptists at length.

The eight men were released from prison with the warning that if any of them returned to Bern territory he would be drowned without mercy. It was not an idle threat; two of the eight were among those Anabaptists drowned in Bernese territory within the next two years.

George Blaurock made his way secretly from place to place in various parts of German-speaking Switzerland. He apparently worked for some time with success in Biel (Bienne). Later he was in Chur and other areas of Graubünden. Wherever he went, the Anabaptist movement flourished. Many converts joined, and the Brethren were encouraged by Blaurock's words as well as by his bold example. He never stayed long in one location, so that for a considerable time authorities were unable to lay hands on him.

Finally they did, in Appenzell, easternmost canton of northern Switzerland. After a brief imprisonment there he was let out with a warning that if he returned to the territory it would cost him dearly in life and limb. In April 1529 he was arrested for a second time in Appenzell and authorities wrote to Zurich for information about him. Sentence was passed a few days later, and it apparently ordered banishment from the territory with threat of execution if he returned.

The New Field in Tyrol

Now regarded as an outlaw in practically every part of German-speaking Switzerland, Blaurock realized that his further presence among the Swiss Brethren could only endanger them more. Still, he had no intention of compromising his call to preach the Word of God to the people. Although often cautious for the sake of the work, personal safety never loomed as a chief concern of George Blaurock. This is evident in his next choice of a field of labor. He left Protestant Switzerland for Catholic Austria, where persecution raged.

The Austrian province of Tyrol bordered districts of northeastern Switzerland and Graubünden, where Blaurock had led a vigorous Anabaptist movement. It was natural that the new teachings should reach into Tyrol, along the valleys of the Etsch and the Inn rivers. There were converts in these areas by 1527 if not the year before. Since the heavily wooded mountain districts afforded some hope of security, persecuted Anabaptists fled to Tyrol from Bavaria and the Salzburg area. The struggle for survival was so difficult in Tyrol, however, that many left for Moravia, almost the only place in Europe where there was a semblance of religious toleration at the time. When persecution broke out there in 1528 some of these harried Brethren returned to Tyrol.

Anabaptist meetings there, frequently attended by seventy or more people, were held, often by night, in the woods, old quarries, deep ravines, abandoned huts, or wherever some secrecy could be assured. This became more and more difficult as their numbers grew. Archduke Ferdinand (now a king, of Hungary-Bohemia) ruled the area. He hated all Protestants and was determined to root out the despised Anabaptists. He promulgated a mandate in 1527 threatening them all with death. Special mounted militiamen were assigned to the heretic hunt and rewarded for ruthlessness. Leonard Schiemer, Anabaptist leader in Tyrol, was seized and executed in January 1528; Hans Schlaffer, a few months later. Schlaffer was followed by Michael Kirschner, who was a successful evangelist for several months and baptized more than a hundred converts.

While still at work in eastern Switzerland Blaurock had come in touch with refugees fleeing from persecution in Tyrol. They told him that Michael Kirschner had been arrested, leaving the Brethren there without a leader. Blaurock saw this as a call from God. Taking with him Hans Langegger, a native of Tyrol, he set out for the Hapsburg country.

The Brethren there welcomed him warmly. He became one of the most popular preachers of the movement in Tyrol, and hundreds were baptized. Blaurock chose Klausen (now Chiusa, Italy) as his center and itinerated down the Eisack Valley as far as Neumarkt (Egna), a distance of thirty-two miles. New congregations sprang up and old ones were revitalized all along the valley. The high mountains on either side were cut from time to time with a smaller valley of some mountain stream which flowed into the Eisack. Every valley meant more villages, and Blaurock could hardly resist the challenge of any of them. There are traces of his work in Vels, Tiers on the Breitenberg and the Ritten, Leifers, and many other places.

Brethren assembled in Klausen from mountain districts on both sides of the river which flowed through the picturesque little town. Places "beyond the bridge" were considered a bit safer because they were in territory ruled by the secular magistrate of Guffidaun. That part of Klausen on the west side of the river was under the bishop of Brixen, bitter enemy of all heretics. On the east side—"beyond the bridge"—there were flat natural terraces on the heavily wooded hillsides which furnished suitable places for secret meeting. As numbers grew, however, Blaurock realized the increasing danger and moved meetings to more remote and secluded areas far beyond town limits and changed location frequently.

The Voice of Strong George Silenced at Last

There could be no doubt about the fate of Blaurock's predecessor, Michael Kirschner. He lay in the Kräuterturm prison in Innsbruck. For weeks he was questioned under torture, but he steadfastly refused to surrender his faith or betray his brethren. He was burned at the stake on the Schiesstätte just outside Innsbruck on June 2, 1529.

An edict of the Diet of Speyer in April 1529 confirmed previous mandates of death for Anabaptists, and authorities redoubled their efforts to root out the heresy. Innsbruck government officials threatened to dismiss Hans Preu, chief magistrate of the Guffidaun district, if he were not more vigilant in apprehending and punishing Anabaptists. They would replace him with an "able and responsible" man, they threatened, who would understand that the false teachers and their followers were enemies of church and state.

Thus motivated, this official succeeded in laying hands on George Blaurock and Hans Langegger about the middle of August 1529. He put them into the tower prison of the Guffidaun castle and proudly sent his report to Innsbruck authorities. The latter were delighted. They hoped to get much more information about other Anabaptists than Preu had extorted from the two men. Magistrates and judges in nearby districts were instructed to assist Preu in the investigation. The two Anabaptists were to be kept under close guard day and night. If Blaurock escaped, Innsbruck warned, Preu would "suffer for it in body and goods."

The charges against Blaurock were quite different in this last trial from those which had been pressed in Zurich and other Swiss towns. In the Protestant areas he was punished for disregarding mandates against rebaptizing and for causing disorder among the people. Here in Catholic Austria charges were that "he had forsaken the priestly office, rejected infant baptism, taught a new baptism, would have nothing more to do with the mass, and did not believe that Christ was bodily in the wine and bread." He was further charged with opposing "confession to the priests and maintaining that one should not call upon the mother of Christ and pray to her."

After Blaurock's captors had tried in vain to extort a confession from him or at least some information which might lead them to other Anabaptists, the inevitable sentence was pronounced: death by burning. It was carried out September 6 on the Holzschranne near Klausen, where "Strong George" gave the ultimate witness to his faith.

What was that faith? Staunch belief in a loving heavenly Father, salvation through his Son's sacrifice, a church of believers committed to sharing this gospel. Baptism signified for him enrollment in this church, and the Lord's Supper was a service of fellowship and thanksgiving. The true Christian was he or she who trusted in Christ alone and was trying to obey his commands. A consistent Christian would avoid oath-taking or serving as a magistrate and endure persecution if necessary. Jesus said, "Resist not evil," and his followers must abjure use of force even in self-defense.

George Blaurock was not a theologian but a pioneer evangelist. His methods were sometimes crude and his remarks impolite. But surely he was sincere, untiring, and courageous in spreading the gospel as he understood it. He was the apostle of the Anabaptists to the common people.

Blaurock's Hymns

In the *Ausbund,* a collection of Anabaptist hymns already published in the sixteenth century, there are two hymns which are attributed to Blaurock. With the first of these—which begins, in free translation, "God judges justly"—there is the following notation: "This hymn was written by George Blaurock, one of the first Brethren, burned in the Etschland in the year '27." (The date is in error.) The tune to be used with this hymn is then indicated. There are thirty-three stanzas, the first of which follows:

Gott führt ein recht gericht und niemand mags ihm brechen.	(God is in charge of a righteous court— No one is able to overturn it.
Wer hie thut seinen willen nicht,	Whoever does not do his will on earth
dess Urtheil wirt er sprechen.	Will receive God's final judgment.)

Other stanzas praise God for his grace and accessibility, manifold blessings, redemption through the work of Christ, the responsibility of the sinner to repent or face terrible judgment and hell, the privilege of God's people to be freed from the power of sin and to follow his teachings, proclaim his Word to all the world, baptize the converted, observe the fellowship of the Supper, endure suffering for the faith even as the Savior suffered and died for us and who will come again to claim his own.

The second hymn, entitled "Forget Me Not, O Lord," bears the following superscription in the *Ausbund:* "This hymn was written by George Blaurock, who was burned at Clausen in Etschland, along with the person known as Hans von der Reue, in the year 1528." The tune is then indicated. (Date of Blaurock's death and the name of his associate are in error.)

This is a death hymn *(Sterbelied),* evidently written by Blaurock during his last imprisonment as a farewell to the Brethren. There are thirteen stanzas, beginning once again with praise to God for his truth made known and for the giving of himself through his grace, as Father and Savior, at a time when the writer as a younger man was in despair with the heavy load of sin.

"Strengthen mightily my faith," he implores, "else the whole structure will be rubble, if you are not there to help." The thought is continued in the next stanza: "Forget me not, O Lord, but be always beside me; may your Spirit protect and teach me, that in my sufferings I shall always be comforted and win nobly the victory in this fight."

Suffering has come, the enemy has attacked with sharp weapons "so that all my body quaked before false teaching and coercion." But stanza eight brightens with hope, "You, Lord, did have mercy, and by your grace and power helped me, your poor son, and made me victorious."

The last three stanzas sound again Blaurock's note of victory, as he finishes life's course: "In the hours of the last day, as our turn must come, help us, Lord, to bear the cross out onto the battlefield. Attend to us with all grace, that we may be able to commend our spirit into your hands.

"With all my heart I pray to you for all our enemies, no matter how many of them there be, that you, O Lord, as is your wont, lay not their misdeeds to their charge. I pray you, may it come to pass according to your will, O God.

"And so I take my leave, together with my companions. May God lead us by his grace into his kingdom, that we may be in the faith, undoubting, his holy work completing, and may he give us strength to the end."

• MICHAEL SATTLER •

4
• MICHAEL SATTLER •
Holiness in the Church, in Life, and in Death

Like most Brethren leaders of the early sixteenth century, Michael Sattler had very little time for his Anabaptist ministry before being done to death by established church and state. He was born about 1490 in the town of Staufen, district of Breisgau, in the extreme southwestern part of Germany. He became a diligent student, mastering the Latin language and other subjects offered in Latin and monastery schools. He took vows at the monastery, St. Peter's of the Black Forest, just to the northeast of Freiburg. He rose to the office of prior, second in authority only to that of the abbot of the monastery.

Michael, unlike those monks who had their mistresses, took his vows seriously. It is likely that his revulsion at the immorality and hypocrisy of others would have itself in time been sufficient to drive him from the cloistered life. His study of the Scriptures, particularly in view of what he had heard of Martin Luther's reformation and of the gospel-based claims for justice by revolutionary peasants, hastened the process. Brought to decision by these influences, and perhaps by the insistence of peasants occupying St. Peter's on May 12, 1525, Michael left the monastery.

Ferdinand of Austria, younger brother of Emperor Charles V of the Holy Roman Empire, ruled parts of Germany including Breisgau. Under the influence of Cardinal Campegio, Ferdinand had ordered the extermination of heresy in his realm. The peasant troop that took over St. Peter's included Anabaptists from Waldshut and nearby Hallau—the latter town lying between Waldshut and Schaffhausen, Switzerland. It may be that their ideas joined with those which had already begun to alienate Michael Sattler from monastery life. As a seeker for the truth he went to the north-border regions of Switzerland, about fifty miles distant from Freiburg and St. Peter's. He resided for some time in the home of the Anabaptist Hans Kuenzi in Oberglatt, north of Zurich; and Michael learned the weaver's craft from his host so that he would be able to support himself.

He probably attended the November 6-8, 1525, baptism disputation in Zurich. The questions involved in the discussion interested him greatly. By this time he was closely associated with Swiss Brethren even if he had not yet joined them. With their leaders and others in the Zurich area he was arrested, tried, then released from prison on November 18, after agreeing to renounce Anabaptism, pay court costs, and permanently leave Zurich territory. After his banishment he evidently returned to his Anabaptist friends in the more northerly areas of Switzerland. He must have reached a firm decision about his faith and joined the Swiss Brethren in the summer of 1526.

Michael married Margaretha, evidently a former member of the Beguine community; its members gave themselves in charitable service, but did not take vows as nuns. Referred to later as "a talented, clever little woman," she proved to be a faithful and courageous helpmate in Michael Sattler's meteoric life.

Seeking His Way and His Work

About eighty miles northward was the city of Strasbourg, which appeared to be quite open to evangelical doctrine, and Sattler made his way there. The leading reformers in the city, Martin Bucer and Wolfgang Capito, received him cordially. The two reformers, especially Capito, minimized infant baptism, emphasizing love and tolerance. Sattler made friendly contact with Brethren in the Strasbourg area. He spent long hours in talks on the issues with Bucer and especially with Capito; the latter said these discussions took place "in a brotherly and friendly spirit."

Also involved in these matters in Strasbourg at the time were Ludwig Haetzer, young Swiss radical who worked on the fringes of the Anabaptist movement but never joined it, and Hans Denck, who did so but had mystical and spiritualist leanings. The Strasbourg reformers had little regard for these others; they respected Michael Sattler, who represented the quiet, pacifist evangelical faith of the Swiss Brethren. They called him a "co-worker in Christ."

Bucer arranged a disputation on the views of Denck, which resulted in the latter's expulsion. A number of the Strasbourg Anabaptists were imprisoned. Haetzer, defamed in further disputes with the reformers, left Strasbourg.

This must have been a soul-searching time for Michael Sattler. He had made no progress really, either in drawing the reformers to toleration for the full Anabaptist faith or in bringing about the release of some of his brethren who had been imprisoned. They asked for him to accept "in love" the shortcomings of a national church. They would certainly continue the practice of infant baptism, but simply as a symbol. The reformers opposed vigorously the idea of a separatist church of believers that renounced all use of force for the Christian, who was thereby disallowed any participation in government. Sattler saw no further purpose for his remaining in Strasbourg, and he slipped quietly out of the city at the turn of the year 1526-27.

After he arrived in the Würtemberg area, across the Rhine River from Strasbourg, Sattler assembled his notes from the talks he had had with the Strasbourg reformers and penned a letter to them explaining why he had left. He listed twenty points of doctrine; mostly they were quotations or paraphrases of New Testament passages. The listing begins: "Christ came to make holy all those who believe in him alone" (1 Timothy 1:15ff.). "He who believes and is baptized will be saved," the second point reads, "but he who does not believe will be condemned" (Mark 16:16).

Further points included (omitting Scripture references):

"Faith in Christ Jesus reconciles us with the Father and gives us access to him. Baptism seals all believers into the body of Christ, of which he is now the head.... Those fore-known, called and believing, should be conformed to the image of Christ.... Sinners of the world are against his kingdom. Those who are believers have been chosen out of the world, therefore the world hates them.... The devil seeks to destroy; Christ to make holy.... Christians are fully at peace and confident in their heavenly Father, without any outward or worldly armor.... Christians are the family of God and fellow citizens of the saints, not of the world. But they are the true Christians who practice the teachings of Christ.... Flesh and blood, pompous display, worldly honor and the world itself cannot understand the kingdom of Christ. To sum it up: Christ and Belial have nothing in common."

In his accompanying letter Sattler addresses his "beloved brothers in God," Capito and Bucer "and others who love and confess Christ from the heart." He writes of his depar-ture from their city: "I could remain no longer without doing real dishonor to God. For the sake of my conscience I have to leave the field to the opposition. I pray that you will under-stand this is an act of Christian humility. The Lord will ulti-mately dispose."

He pleads for the incarcerated Brethren, "Be mercifully considerate of those who are in prison. Those in error ... are not to be coerced.... Christians admonish charitably.... Do not legalistically coerce people this way or that. May the Lord God have mercy on us all and give us his Spirit to lead us in the way of Christ Jesus."

William Reublin, banished from Zurich as an Anabaptist in January 1525, worked in northern Switzerland, then in Germany. He probably influenced Sattler to join the Brethren and seems now to have invited him to share the work with him in Reublin's native area of Hohenberg. The main town was Rottenburg on the Neckar, some sixty miles east of Strasbourg, with another important town, Horb, just north of there. We note one ominous fact: it was Austrian-controlled territory, ruled by Ferdinand, the strongly

Catholic persecutor of "heretics." Under the ministry of Reublin and Sattler, Brethren work took on new life.

Tracts on Doctrine and Christian Living

It was perhaps during this period that a series of five Anabaptist tracts appeared, either from the pen of Michael Sattler, or from one of the other Brethren. They varied from seven hundred to four thousand words each in length and reflected some of the same concerns indicated in the twenty points of Sattler's communication addressed to the Strasbourg reformers. The treatment of subjects also bore remarkable resemblance to parts of the Schleitheim Confession, which would appear some months later. The tracts would be published in the years following, along with writings by Sattler.

The first and longest of the tracts, *Concerning the Satisfaction of Christ*, deals with the atonement, not just as the means for forgiveness of sin as Lutherans were inclined to emphasize, but for deliverance from sin to newness of life. It chastizes Catholics as "work saints," and Protestants as "scribes," who are regarded as avoiding the former error by eliminating works and Christian character as essential for Christian life. Sattler quotes from the words of Christ, the epistle of James, 1 John, and many other biblical writers to support the Brethren's view that the true Christian must be a disciple, that faith to be real must issue in a worthy life.

"And when Paul prays, in Romans 3, that those who are justified through Christ are justified without any merit or without the works of the law," the writer states, "he does not mean that a man can be saved without the works of faith (since Christ and the apostles demand such) but without those works which are done outside faith and the love of God, such as circumcision and the like, which the Jews did that they might thereby be justified." Potentially, the atonement is universal in scope, the Anabaptist holds, but it is not operative in those who reject it or deny the Lord by an unchristian life.

The second tract, *Two Kinds of Obedience*, opposes legalism and begins with an explanation of the title: "Obedience is of two kinds, servile and filial. The filial had its source in the love of the Father, even though no other reward should follow, yes even if the Father should wish to condemn his child; the servile has its source in a love of reward or of one's self. The filial always does as much as possible, apart from any command; the servile does as little as possible, yes nothing except by command." The exposition continues, "As one administers death, the other administers life. The one is of the old covenant, the other of the new." This principle is applied to gross crimes, but also to anger, divorce, swearing and the use of force against any evil.

Concerning Divorce goes further into one of these problems, and it reflects the usual Anabaptist principle of elevating New Testament authority above that of the Old. These people held to the inspiration of the entire Bible, but not with a "flat book" theory of inspiration. Moses permitted divorce, but Christ did not, except for adultery—and neither should his faithful followers. Disregard of this teaching would lead to expulsion from the fellowship. After divorce for the allowed reason, the person might remarry, but only to a believer. In a mixed marriage, the unbeliever might live apart from his or her believing spouse if desired, but in itself this would not constitute grounds for the believer to divorce.

Concerning Evil Overseers, the shortest of the tracts, treats further the problem of being unequally yoked together with unbelievers—at worship, in this case. "It is said," the writer accuses those who oppose his view, "that one can without harm hear papist or Lutheran sermons, since it is expected of people and they do not want to offend anyone. Nevertheless, in Matthew 24 Christ earnestly commands us to flee from such desolation and abomination." Various references are given from the Old Testament and the New—occasionally also from the Apocrypha. Believer's baptism marks the point of separation for those withdrawing from established churches.

Speaking again of those opposing his view, the writer continues: "Since they say ... that infant baptism is an unimportant matter and that one can baptize infants without harm to the truth, it is certain they are in league with the Lutherans, that they might perhaps escape the cross in the future.... Infant baptism is exactly opposite from the baptism of Christ (Matthew 17) and belongs to the antichrist or hireling (John 10).... We want to warn all you brothers and sisters in the Lord ... in order that you may not be led astray from the hope placed before you by the falsehood, deceit, and fickleness of overseers—and pray the Lord of the harvest that he may send forth faithful laborers into his work."

The last of the five tracts, *The Hearing of False Prophets*, treats in general the subject of the previous writing and was sometimes published with it. It treats further the question whether a true believer should submit himself to the teachings and leadership of those who fall short of the full truth God has for his people. The Strasbourg reformers stressed love as the predominant principle of Christianity, as we have seen: pious and conscientious believers should not insist on lesser doctrines and practices and separate themselves from others but rather join with them in love and work together. Sattler and other Anabaptist leaders insisted on the importance of obedience to Christ as Lord and the observing of his other commands as well as that of love.

In this tract he applied the principle to the subject at hand: "Love commands one (Matthew 7 and 16) to beware of false prophets who come to us in sheep's clothing (that is, attached to the letter [of the Law]) and who will indeed not allow people to follow in freedom but will bring them into subjection through the hypocrisy they cause ... both papists and Lutherans, yes and all others also of their kind, preachers who proclaim the letter for the spirit, yes, human commands for God's commands.... You generation of vipers, how can you speak that which is good when you are evil, for out of the abundance of the heart the mouth speaks? (Matthew 12; Mark 12; Philippians 3).... Apostles of the angel of darkness are speaking everywhere and presenting themselves as the apostles of Christ to all those who wish sincerely to walk in the true way (2 Corinthians 11).... They are beginning to show their fury in open attack against the unhappy flock of the Lord so that they may be recognized and known by their fruits before all the world."

Shall the just live by faith, regardless of the character of their life? Sattler refers to Ezekiel 18 and asks, "If the righteous man turns away from his righteousness and lives in iniquity so that he practices all the abominations of the ungodly, shall that man live?" Then he concludes the tract, "The God of peace and the Father of mercy shall graciously deliver both you and us from the present power of darkness and of the antichrist through the revelation of his Son, our Lord Jesus Christ. Amen."

The Gathering in Schleitheim

What would become probably the most important of all Anabaptist meetings took place in Schleitheim (or Schlaten, as the local dialect has it), a Swiss town just north of Schaffhausen, on February 24, 1527. It was in the general area to which Sattler had retreated, after leaving the monastery, as Paul the apostle to his "Arabia," to find direction for his new life as an evangelical. Decisions made at this gathering, the size of which is unknown, helped unify Brethren groups and, according to Mennonite scholar John H. Yoder, decided "whether the movement was to live or die." This gathering seems to have been mainly under the leadership of Sattler.

Differences in faith and life had emerged among the various Anabaptist groups, and this caused confusion. Most Anabaptists, like the Swiss Brethren, emphasized biblical authority (to such a degree that some would accuse them of bibliolatry and legalism, which they strongly denied), a church of committed believers, baptism on profession of faith, support for government, except that true Christians were not to take part in it because this inevitably involved using force or waging war.

State church leaders differed sharply with the Anabaptists, especially regarding baptism and the church's relationship to government; on the latter point Anabaptist theologian Balthasar Hubmaier also was at variance with most other Anabaptists. Hans Denck had looked upon Scripture in a manner which set him apart from his fellow Anabaptists; he differed also in the importance given to baptism and the church. Ludwig Haetzer, who was generally lumped with the Anabaptists by many contemporaries, had been immorally involved with a young woman in Basel. "Brethren" such as these were regarded by the majority of Anabaptists as "false brethren." Michael Sattler understood the great need of drawing the lines more precisely and of giving guidance to sincere Brethren groups who wanted to be congregations of faithful Christian disciples. In contrast to his seemingly broader views in his early days of Anabaptist associations, Sattler was now convinced of the need for very clear principles and (reflecting his monastic days, perhaps) strong discipline.

Sattler had apparently drawn up the draft of a document focusing on these needs, based on the main emphases in his letter to the Strasbourg reformers, and had circulated it among some German and Swiss Brethren believers. This, with changes made during discussion, was adopted by the assembly. It did not constitute a full theological statement, being more like a manual for church development that concentrated on disputed points. It dealt primarily with matters of faith that, although basic to Anabaptism, were questioned not only by state church leaders but also by some persons more or less regarded as part of their movement. Originally called "Brotherly Union of Some Children of God Concerning Seven Articles," it became known as the "Schleitheim Confession."

It affirms that God requires obedience to his will, which has been faithfully recorded in the Bible. It records agreement by the assembled Brethren on seven matters: baptism, excommunication, the Lord's Supper, separation from the world, pastors, a government's use of the sword, and oaths. The statement, originally sent out as a letter in handwritten copies to congregations of believers, was in the German dialect common to the area; eventually it came to be printed in several languages.

The Schleitheim Confession

The introductory section begins: "May joy, peace, and mercy from our Father through the atonement of the blood of Christ Jesus, together with the gifts of the Spirit who is sent by the Father to all believers to give strength, consolation, and constancy in all tribulation until the end, be with all those who love God and are children of the light scattered everywhere as it has been ordained of God our Father, wherever they are with one mind assembled, in unity of spirit, in one God and Father of us all: grace and peace of heart be with you all, Amen. . . .

"A very great offense has been introduced by certain false brethren among us so that some have turned aside from the faith, thinking that they are observing and practicing freedom of the Spirit and of Christ," the introductory section continues. "Such persons, however, have missed the truth and to their own condemnation are given over to lasciviousness and self-indulgence of the flesh. They think faith and love can do and permit everything and nothing will be of harm to them or cause their condemnation since they are still 'believers.' "

The introductory section of about 550 words is followed by the body of the document, four times longer, setting forth the seven points that had been discussed at the assembly; a concluding section of about 340 words completes the document. Articles on separation, the sword and oaths are treated at greater length than are those on baptism, excommunication, and the Lord's Supper—on the latter three subjects Anabaptists could generally agree. The former three, as we have seen, fomented great differences in teaching and in practice.

"Baptism should be administered to all those who have been instructed regarding repentance and amendment of life, who truly believe that their sins are taken away through Christ and who desire to walk in the resurrection life of Jesus Christ, having been willing to die with him and be buried, that they might be raised with him." So begins the brief section on this subject. A few lines further on: "This excludes all infant baptism, the highest and chief abomination of the pope."

The ban, or excommunication, is for believers "who, being inadvertently overtaken, sometimes slip and fall perhaps into error and sin. They should be admonished, then at the second offense likewise secretly disciplined, and the third time the same, openly before the entire congregation according to the command of Christ in Matthew 18."

Concerning the Lord's Supper: "All those who desire to break the one bread in remembrance of the broken body of Christ and who wish to partake of one drink in remembrance of the shed blood of Christ should have been previously united by baptism in the one body of Christ which is the church of God and whose head is Christ."

The fourth point, on separation from the world, takes about 365 words. "A separation shall be made from evil and wickedness which the devil has planted in the world. We should simply have no fellowship with such people of the world or associate with them in their many abominations," the confession states.

"There is nothing else in the world and in all creation than good and evil, believing and unbelieving, darkness and light, the world and those separated from the world, the temple of God and that of idols, Christ and Belial—and one can have no part with the other."

That from which absolute separation is to be made is exemplified: "all popish and anti-popish [Protestant] works and idolatrous services, gatherings, church attendance, winehouses, civic affairs, commitments made in unbelief and other such things that are held in high regard by the world but are practiced in flat contradiction to the commands of God according to the pattern of total unrighteousness that is the world."

A pastor "should be, as Paul prescribes, one who entirely and absolutely has a good report from those who are outside the faith. This office shall be to read, admonish, teach, warn, discipline or to ban in the congregation, lead out in prayer for the edification of all sisters and brothers in prayer, lift up the bread when it is to be broken and take care in all respects for the body of Christ that it be built up and developed, that the name of God be praised and honored by us and the mouth of the slanderer stopped."

As for the pastor's remuneration, discipline where needful, and replacement, the statement specifies, "This one should be supported, where he has need, by the congregation that has chosen him, so that he who serves the gospel may also live therefrom as the Lord has ordained. But if a pastor should do something requiring discipline, he shall not be dealt with except on the word of two or three witnesses. If they [pastors] sin they should be disciplined in the presence of all, that others may fear. But if this pastor is banished, or through his cross brought home to the Lord [i.e., in martyrdom—this may have been added in recollection of the arrest of eight Anabaptists in Rottenburg a week before], from that very hour another should be ordained in his place so that the little flock and people of God not be destroyed but rather through admonition be sustained and comforted."

Relationships with Government

As for the use of force the Schleitheim document affirms that "the sword is ordained of God, outside the perfection of Christ. It punishes and puts to death the wicked, guards and protects the good. In the law [of Israel] the sword was ordained for the punishment and death of the wicked, and the same is ordained to be used by worldly magistrates. In the perfection of Christ [the church] the ban alone is used, for warning and excommunication of the one who has sinned, without the putting to death of the flesh, only the warning and the command to sin no more."

Further, the confession reads: "It is asked, in regard to use of the sword, whether a true Christian should be a magistrate if he is chosen for some office. To this the answer: People tried to make Christ a king, but he fled and did not see in that the ordinance of his Father. Thus should we also do as he did and follow after him; then shall we not walk in darkness. He himself says, 'Whoever would come after me, let him deny himself and take up his cross and follow me.' . . . Christian weapons are spiritual, against the ramparts of the devil. Worldlings are armed with steel and iron, but Christians are armed with the armor of God, with truth, righteousness, peace, faith, salvation, and the Word of God." Further, on the same point (which takes, in all, 570 words), it is declared on magistrates, "Their citizenship is in this world, the Christian's in heaven."

The last section proscribes taking an oath: "The oath is a confirmation among those who are quarreling or making promises [vows]. In the law [of Israel] it is commanded to be made in God's name alone, truthfully and not falsely. Christ, who teaches the perfection of the law, forbids to his own all swearing whether true or false, by heaven or earth, by Jerusalem or our own head." In answer to the argument that God swore by himself to Abraham, or through his servants to others later, the statement declares that although God had the power and authority to perform what was promised by his oath, man does not—a person can never be sure that he can keep the oath or perform it. "Therefore, we should not swear at all. . . . Christ said, 'Let your speech be . . . yes, yes, and no, no; whatever goes beyond this is of the devil.' "

In the conclusion the readers are admonished: "Take care about all those who do not walk according to the simplicity of divine truth as presented in this letter . . . in order that every one of us be governed by the rule of the ban and henceforth be freed from the entry of false brothers and sisters among us. . . . Separate yourselves from what is evil; thus the Lord will be your God and you will be his sons and daughters. . . . May the name of God be forever hallowed and greatly praised, Amen. May the Lord give you his peace, Amen. Done at Schlaten am Randen, St. Matthew's Day, the year MDXXVII."

A brief tract of a page or two on congregational life often circulated with the Schleitheim Confession within Anabaptist circles, and some scholars have attributed it to Michael Sattler. It is an appeal for loving relationships and Christian order in the congregations, with seven points: "Brothers and sisters should meet at least three or four times a week. . . . They should take up something to read together. The one to whom God has given the best understanding should explain it. . . . Let none be frivolous in the church of God, either in words or actions. . . . When a brother sees his brother erring he should warn him according to the command of Christ and admonish him in a Christian and fraternal way.... Christians in the time of the apostles ... stored up a common fund; from such a fund aid can be given to the poor according as each has need.... All gluttony should be avoided among brethren gathered in church. Serve a soup or a small amount of vegetable and meat, for eating and drinking are not the kingdom of heaven.... The Lord's Supper should be held as often as brethren are together, thereby proclaiming the death of the Lord ... that we might also be willing to give our bodies and lives for Christ's sake, which means for that of all the brethren."

Ever the Pastor, Even in Prison

Michael Sattler proceeded to Horb after the Schleitheim conference to take up his pastoral work there, apparently unaware that authorities had discovered the Anabaptists in that immediate area. The trap was set for them. A number of men and women of Rottenburg and Horb were arrested, including both the Sattlers and Reublin's wife and child. A complete copy of the Schleitheim articles was found on Sattler's person. Also (from the standpoint of the authorities) there were incriminating notations about activities and plans of the Brethren. Horb officials feared an uprising in sympathy with the Anabaptists and they found also that their prison was too small for the rather large number of "heretics" that had been arrested. They engaged fourteen mounted guards to take the prisoners to the more secluded town of Binsdorf. There the prisoners, Michael Sattler in particular, were kept under heavy guard and questioned interminably.

Meanwhile, higher-ups planned the trials, which were to take place in Rottenburg. King Ferdinand favored the immediate drowning of Sattler, but district authorities wanted to give at least some show of legality. The trial was first set for April 12, 1527, but had to be postponed to the middle of May because the University of Tübingen refused to send two doctors of law as requested. They mentioned that they were too busy, and that Rottenburg was in another diocese, but the real reason seems to have been that participation in a trial sure to render the death sentence would disqualify them for priestly functions; they might desire ordination later. Tübingen suggested the University of Freiburg, which was in any case closer to Rottenburg. Two non-university prosecutors, two Tübingen doctors (not of the law, as requested, but of the arts, where there was no interest in ordination) and two from Freiburg eventually came. Ensisheim, along with two or three other towns, sent representatives to sit on the court, including the bloodthirsty Ensisheim city clerk Eberhard Hofmann.

The Anabaptists remained eleven weeks and three days in the Binsdorf jail. Sattler realized that the authorities fully intended to put him to death, but his chief concern remained—to render what service he could to the churches. He wrote a moving letter of pastoral consolation, over two thousand words, to his now leaderless little flock in Horb. Characteristic of his courage and unselfish concern, he said less of his own perilous position than of their spiritual needs, and their need for comfort.

"My beloved brothers and sisters in the Lord," the letter begins, "may the grace and mercy of God the heavenly Father through Jesus Christ our Lord and the power of the Spirit be with you brothers and sisters beloved of God." From the pastor's heart came the admonition to "walk in the sure-footed and living way of Christ, namely, through the cross, distress, imprisonment, denial of self, and finally through death; thereby you may certainly present yourselves to God your heavenly Father as a pure, God-pleasing, upright church of Christ which is cleansed through his blood that it may be holy and irreproachable before God and men, separated and purified from all idolatry and abominations, in order that the Lord of all lords may dwell there and it may be for him a tabernacle."

The writer warns against those who turn from full commitment to the Word and way of Christ and urges his people "not to forget love, without which it is impossible that you be a Christian congregation." He quotes from 1 Corinthians 13, then continues, "Certain brothers (I know who they are) have come short of this love and have not wanted to build up one another through love but are puffed up and have become useless in vain speculation, [seeking] knowledge of those things God would keep secret unto himself.... You have seen what such puffed-up speech and ignorance has produced and daily you see the false fruitage."

"Dear brothers, do not be surprised that I deal with this matter in such seriousness," the farewell letter continues—as Sattler finally gives some attention to his own situation. "Brethren have doubtless made known to you how certain ones of us were taken as prisoners ... and brought to Binsdorf. During this time we have experienced many attacks of the adversaries against us. Once they menaced us with cords, then with fire and afterward with the sword. In such dangers I have surrendered myself entirely to the will of the Lord and am, with all my brothers, my wife, and some other sisters, prepared for witness to him even unto death."

Sattler states that "few faithful workers are in the vineyard of the Lord," and that "this letter serves as a farewell to you all who truly love God and follow him (the others I do not recognize), and also as a testimony of my love toward you.... I would have desired that I might have still a little time to do the work of the Lord, hoping to be useful; but it is better for me personally to be released and with Christ to await the hope of the blessed. The Lord can surely raise up to himself another laborer to complete his work. Pray that reapers may be driven out into the harvest, for the time of threshing is near.... And if something [some teaching] is forgotten, pray the Lord for understanding. Be generous to all among you who have need, especially those who work among you in the Word [as pastors] who are hunted down and cannot eat their own bread in calmness and peace."

Toward the end of the epistle Sattler refers to himself again briefly: "If I am to be offered up as a sacrifice to the Lord, let my wife be commended unto you as myself. The peace of Jesus Christ and the love of the heavenly Father and the grace of the Spirit keep you unsullied by sin and present you joyful and pure at the demonstration of divine glory in the coming of our Lord Jesus Christ.... Beware of false brethren.... I wait upon my God; pray without ceasing for all those who are imprisoned. God be with you all. Amen. In the tower at Binsdorf. Brother Michael Sattler of Staufen, together with my fellow prisoners in the Lord."

Saints in the Dock

Under the guard of twenty-four armed men the prisoners were moved to Rottenburg, where the trial opened on Friday, May 17, and continued the next day. It seems there was a large panel of "judges." Chairman of the court was the district government head Count Joachim of Zollern; nominal attorney for the defense was Jacob Halbmeyer, mayor of Rottenburg. The sly legal expert from Ensisheim, clerk Eberhard Hofmann, made himself the most prominent prosecutor and pressed brutally forward toward his goal of securing the most cruel sentence possible. The people of Horb and others expressed displeasure at such tactics, and the authorities were amazed at the number of appeals for mercy toward the Anabaptist prisoners that came from every side.

On the bench of the accused sat Michael Sattler, his wife, Margaretha, nine other men, and eight other women. Sattler, by their common agreement, spoke for the group. Offered a defense attorney, he declined, holding that the real charges against them were theological and ecclesiastical; state authorities should have nothing to do with such things. True Christians, he felt, were forbidden by the Word of God to go themselves the way of worldly law in these matters. He indicated his readiness to be persuaded otherwise, but only from the Word of God. He spoke throughout in a respectful, reasonable, and forthright manner.

Count Joachim had the charges read out. Seven applied to the entire group, the last two to Michael Sattler alone. The first accused the Anabaptists of violation of an imperial mandate, evidently a reference to the Edict of Worms against Luther, May 1521, which of course had nothing to do with Anabaptism. The second charge said the Anabaptists had rejected the Catholic doctrine of transubstantiation, the real presence of Christ in elements of the Eucharist. The next charges were that they rejected infant baptism and extreme unction. The fifth that Anabaptists were said to break bread into a dish of wine and take them together. Another charge was "despising the mother of God and the saints," and still another, refusing to swear an oath before authorities.

The two charges solely against Sattler were that he had abandoned the monastic order and married; and he had taught that if the Turks came into the land, no resistance should be offered. Indeed, he had allegedly said that if war could conceivably be justified, he would rather fight against Christians than Turks.

Placing last the charge about not resisting the Turks was a stroke of genius on the part of those who planned the trial. Turks had been for many years the foremost enemy of the empire and of Christendom, the scourge of Europe and symbol of horror. Ferdinand with great effort had raised money and troops to save civilization and the church from invading Turkish hordes. Was he now to be told that he and his faithful Christian warriors were to be regarded as worse than the Turks! This charge against Sattler, of advocating high treason, struck home to almost everyone, for all feared the Turks. It seemed to elevate the trial from petty questions of church polity and doctrine to a crime against society.

Discussion of the charges and their elaboration seems to have continued for quite a long while. Various participants in the proceedings felt free to speak out in mockery and hatred against the accused. Little effort was made to maintain order and dignity such as might be expected in a court of law. Due perhaps to such diversions and delays, Sattler could not remember the order and wording of some of the charges. He asked that they be read again. In reply the clerk from Ensisheim mocked: "He has boasted that he has the Holy Spirit; it would therefore seem to me unnecessary to grant him this. If he has the Holy Spirit as he boasts, the Spirit can tell him what is in the indictment."

Sattler, ignoring this stupid and unworthy comment, quietly renewed his appeal to the court. "You servants of God," he said, "I hope this request will not be denied me, for not all the articles of accusation concern me. I do not remember them exactly." Eventually the indictment was read again. Then the courageous Anabaptist leader, after consulting with his codefendants, began to answer the charges with modesty, reasonableness, and skill. Regarding the first, he said the imperial mandate outlawed Lutheran teaching, not that of the Brethren; the mandate required that the gospel and the Word of Christ be followed, which believers sought to do. In respect to the second charge, Sattler did not deny that the Brethren rejected the teaching that the actual body and blood of Christ were in the communion. He argued, as had Luther and Zwingli, that Christ had ascended to heaven and therefore that his body could not be in the material elements and could consequently not be eaten.

Sattler admitted to the third charge as well, the rejection of infant baptism; he insisted that faith must precede baptism. The fourth, that of rejecting anointing with oil in extreme unction, was likewise admitted, on the basis that this was the pope's oil only and not in the spirit of biblical passages about anointing with oil such as James 5:14. Sattler denied the charge of despising Mary and the saints but insisted that Mary was not mediatrix or intercessor; saints, he said, were living believers. He defended the Anabaptist position against oaths with several passages, including Matthew 5:34, 37, reporting Jesus' words: "Do not swear at all. . . . Let what you say be simply yes or no." He ignored, as did the court, the insignificant and unjustified charge of mixing elements in communion.

In regard to the charges against himself alone Sattler explained his departure from the monastery as resulting from his study of the writings of Paul and other Scripture, as well as his observation of the unworthy life of many monks and priests. "I considered the unchristian and perilous state in which I was," he said, "beholding the pomp, pride, usury, and great whoredom of the monks and priests; I went and took unto myself a wife, according to divine ordinance," referring to 1 Timothy 4:3.

On the fateful last point, about the Turks, Sattler emphasized the teaching of his fellow believers that even the worst of evils should not be resisted with armed force; they felt this was entirely outside the "perfection of Christ" and the Lord's will for his followers. He admitted having taught that "if the Turks should make an invasion, they should not be resisted, for it is written: You shall not kill. We ought not to defend ourselves against the Turks or other persecutors but earnestly entreat God in our prayers that he be our defense and our resistance. As for my saying that *if* war *were* justified, I would rather march forth against so-called Christians than against the Turks, I give this reason: the Turk is a true Turk and knows nothing of Christian faith. He is a Turk according to the flesh; but you, claiming to be Christian and making your boast of Christ, persecute faithful witnesses of Christ and are Turks according to the spirit." Numerous references were made to Scripture, as usual, to support the defense.

A Verdict of Infamy

Sattler declared to the court as a principle of Anabaptist faith that magistrates are ordained of God, called to punish the wicked and protect the good. He and his brethren had done nothing against God and the gospel, he insisted. Nor had they ever opposed government by word, act, revolt, sedition, or in any other way. He requested that theological experts be called; he would debate with them, using the Bible as authority. If proved from Scripture to be in error, Anabaptists would gladly accept their punishment. "But if we are not shown to be in error," he said, "I hope to God that you will repent and change your minds." This remark evidently provided comic relief for the callous court. The idea that the august judges might be instructed and converted by this simple preacher struck them as highly amusing. They put their heads together, exchanged muted comments, and burst out laughing.

"Yes, you rascally desperate and villainous monk," snapped the Ensisheim clerk. "You think we should debate with you? As a matter of fact, believe me, the hangman will debate with you!" Not one of the lawyers found a word to say in defense of any of the accused. Sattler, miraculously maintaining his calm, said, "Whatever God wills, that shall come to pass." This self-control on the part of the accused excited the city clerk even more. "Indeed, it would be good if you had never been born," he declaimed. Sattler responded quietly, "God knows what is good." The clerk then cried out, "You arch-heretic! You have seduced pious people. Oh that they would only give up their errors and ask for mercy!" Sattler responded, "Mercy is with God alone." The clerk could not bear for the accused Anabaptist to make rational comments and he exclaimed, "Yes, you desperate rascal, you arch-heretic, I tell you this, if there were no executioners here I would dispatch you myself and be sure I would thereby do God a service."

Evidently the Ensisheim clerk was not getting the popular support desired for his scurrilous remarks, and he spoke for a time with Sattler in Latin so that the people in the courtroom would not understand. Then he called upon the chairman for the verdict. Asked whether he rested his case, Sattler replied, "You servants of God, we are not sent to defend the Word of God in court. We are sent to testify to it. We cannot therefore approve of this as a legal trial; we have no such command from God. We are ready to suffer, however, for the Word of God—whatever be laid upon us to suffer—all because of our faith in Christ Jesus our Savior, as long as we have in us a breath of life, unless we are convinced otherwise from Scripture."

The judges withdrew to deliberate on the verdict. Evidently they were not of one mind to the extent imagined by the Ensisheim clerk and others prominent in the trial. They deliberated for about an hour and a half. Meanwhile, soldiers guarded the accused. One of them mocked Sattler, "When I see you get out of this, I'll believe in you." Another grabbed a sword from the table, unsheathed it, and cried out, "See here, with this we will debate with you!" Someone asked Sattler why he had not remained in the monastery, where he had occupied the high position of prior. The accused man answered, "I could have been a lord according to the flesh, but it is better as it is." Seemingly, nothing could shake his calm faith.

Finally, judges returned to the courtroom and the terrible verdict was read. It directed that Michael Sattler "shall be given into the hands of the executioner. The latter shall take him to the square and there cut out his tongue, then forge him fast to a wagon and with glowing iron tongs twice tear pieces from his body, then on the way to the site of the execution five times more as above, then burn his body to powder as a heretic." Even this dire development failed to upset Sattler. His wife, Margaretha, remained composed as well, speaking comfort and encouragement before the entire court assembly. Michael comforted his wife, and the others, against whom sentences were spoken later. An eyewitness wrote afterward of the awful event, "All this I saw and heard myself. May God grant to us also to testify of him as bravely and as patiently as this. Amen."

Before the Anabaptists were led back to their prison cells, Sattler spoke privately with the mayor of Rottenburg, whom he regarded as responsible for the conduct of the trial. "You know that you with your fellow judges have condemned me contrary to justice and without proof; therefore, take care and repent. If you do not, you and the others will be condemned to eternal fire in God's judgment." Saturday night, Sunday, and probably on through Monday night, Sattler and the others remained in their cells, buffeted surely by powerful emotions. On Tuesday, May 21, the terrible execution took place.

Death Not the Last Word

Preliminary torture, as prescribed in the sentence, began in the marketplace. The executioners cut a large part from Sattler's tongue, but he was still able to speak enough to be understood; he prayed for his tormenters. Then they tore pieces from his body with red-hot tongs. After that he was fastened to a ladder that was thrown into a cart, which began its mile-long journey to the place of execution. On the way, the glowing tongs tore at the poor victim's flesh five times more. The procession arrived at the previously chosen site and Sattler, lashed still to the ladder, was tied to the stake and the fire was lighted. During this process, he appealed again to the officials, his judges, and the people to fear God, repent, and be converted. Then he prayed, "Almighty, eternal God, you are the way and the truth; since no one has been able to prove this as error, I shall with your help on this day testify to the truth and seal it with my blood."

Even after the fire was burning his body, his voice could be heard in prayer and praise. When the ropes on his hands burned through, he raised the forefingers of both hands, thereby giving the signal he had agreed on beforehand with his fellow believers to indicate that such a dying was bearable and that he remained firm in his faith. Then he cried out, "Father, into your hands I commend my spirit."

Three other Anabaptists tried with Sattler were also executed. Several eventually recanted publicly and were banished. The wife of Count Joachim von Zollern tried to persuade Sattler's wife to give up her faith and live with the countess as part of her court, but the courageous woman affirmed that she would be faithful to her beliefs and to the memory of her martyred husband—that she would have preferred to die with him in the fire. Margaretha was drowned in the Neckar River a few days after the execution of her husband.

Wolfgang Capito of Strasbourg wrote to the burgomaster and council at Horb interceding for the remaining Anabaptists in prison, and he wrote a letter of comfort to the prisoners. He said Sattler had "always shown a commendable zeal for the honor of God." Martin Bucer wrote, "We do not doubt that Michael Sattler, who was burned at Rottenburg, was a dear friend of God, although he was a leader of the Anabaptists, but much more skilled and honorable than some others . . . so we have no doubt he was a martyr of Christ." This seemed to be a widespread view. People were repelled by the barbarity of the execution and attracted by the victim's gentle, loving, and unsullied character. Wilhelm Reublin—who had escaped arrest, although his wife remained eighteen weeks in prison—wrote an account of Sattler's trial and death which was widely circulated; so did the Reformation supporter Klaus von Grave-neck, who was an eyewitness of the events, and others.

A sixteenth-century *Selection of Beautiful Christian Hymns* is still in use, in more recent editions (e.g., *Ausbund ... schöne christliche Lieder*) by the Old Order Amish Mennonites (Anabaptists). It has a thirteen-stanza hymn of Sattler's (in a later German than that of his time) which begins:

Als Christus mit sein'r wahren Lehr
Versammlet hatt' ein kleines Heer,
Sagt er dass jeder mit Geduld
Ihm täglich's Kreutz nachtragen sollt.

(As Christ with his teaching true
Had gathered a little flock,
He said that each one,
patiently,
Must daily bear his cross.)

The last two stanzas reflect Sattler's pastoral concern:

O Christe hilf du deinem Volk,
Welch's dir in aller Treu nachfolgt,
Dass es durch deinem bittern Tod
Erlöset werd aus aller Noth.

(Do help, O Christ, your people,
Who follow you in all faithfulness
That they through your bitter death
May be redeemed from all distress.)

Lob sey dir Gott in deinem Thron,
Darzu auch deinem lieben Sohn;
Auch dem Heiligen Geist zugleich,
Der zieh noch viel zu seinem Reich.

(Praise to you, God, on your throne
And also to your beloved Son;
Likewise to the Holy Spirit also,
May he yet draw many to his kingdom.)

Sattler's "Farewell Hymn," composed probably during the Binsdorf imprisonment, comprises six stanzas:

Muss es nun seyn gescheiden,
So woll uns Gott beleiten,
Ein jedes an sein Ort;
Da wollend Fleiss ankehren
Uns'r Leben zu bewähren
Nach Inhalt Gottes Wort.

(The time has now come for a parting,
And God will go with us,
Each one to his own post,
Where we betake ourselves valiantly,
Our life to prove the truth
Of the message of God's Word.)

Das solten wir begehren
Und nicht hinlässig werden,
Das End kommt schnell
    herbey:
Wir wissen keinen morgen,
Drum lebend doch in Sorgen
Der G'fahr ist macherley.

(That we should be eager for,
And not hold back supinely.
The end approaches rapidly;
We know for sure of no
    tomorrow,
So still we live in sorrows
And dangers are manifold.)

Betrachtend wohl die
    Sachen,
Dass uns der Herr heisst
    wachen,
Zu seyn allzeit bereit:
Dann so wir würd'n
    erfunden
Liegen und schlaf'n in
    Sünden,
Es würd uns werden leid.

(Look well to those matters
The Lord has told us to
    attend,
To be prepared at all times
Lest we be found to be
Prostrate, asleep in sin,
It would be grievous for us.)

Drum rüstend euch bey
    Zeiten,
Und alle Sünd vermeiden
Lebend in G'rechtigkeit:
Das ist dass rechte Wachen,
Dardurch man mag gerathen
Zur ew'gen Seligkeit.

(So equip yourselves in time
And shun all sin,
Living in righteousness
Which is the true
    watchfulness
Whereby one can attain
Unto eternal blessedness.)

Hiemit seynd Gott befohlen,
Der woll uns allzumahlen,
Durch seine Gnad allein,
Zur ew'gen Freud erheben,
Dass wir nach diesem Leben
Nicht kommen in ewigs Leid.

(Herewith be commended to
    our God
That he might, all of us to-
    gether,
Through his grace alone
Raise us up to eternal joy,
That we, after this life
Come not into eternal
    torment.)

Zum End ist mein Begehren
Denckend meiner im Herren,
Wie ich auch g'sinnet bin:
Nun wachend allesammen,
Durch Jesum Christum,
    Amen,
Es muss gescheiden seyn.

(At the end, what I long for,
Keeping my thoughts upon
    the Lord,
As I always try to do,
Now, just watching, alto-
    gether,
Through Jesus Christ,
    Amen,
A parting there must be.)

• HANS DENCK •

5
• HANS DENCK •
God Speaks His Word in Everyman's Heart

In the fall of 1519 Hans Denck, whose name appears also in many other forms, received his "baccalaurcus" degree at the University of Ingolstadt in South Germany and made preparations to leave. About nineteen years of age at the time, he had previously been awarded the "scholasticus" at the same university. Tall, quiet-spoken, and personable, he shone in humanistic studies, Latin, and Greek; and he made friends easily.

He had grown up in Heybach (Habach), Upper Bavaria. His parents seem to have taken the Christian faith somewhat more seriously than most did in a time of all-pervading Roman Catholicism in that part of Europe. Hans later testified that he was taught the faith by his mother and father. They evidently detected quite early the boy's intellectual acuteness and had him trained for scholarly pursuits; he never learned a trade.

For this reason one may imagine that the youth departed from Ingolstadt with uncertain steps out into the world; but the youth surely glowed with hope, even in the dark. Hans made his way to the larger city of Augsburg, thirty-five miles to the southwest of Ingolstadt. He had some contacts there; perhaps he would be able to secure a position as tutor for children in some wealthy family or as editorial assistant in a printshop.

Hans did not find opportunities for lasting employment in Augsburg. He did make new friends, as was usually the case wherever he went. One close friend in Augsburg, with whom he later corresponded, was Veit Bild, a monk in the monastery of St. Ulrich. The monk's interests lay predominantly in the realm of classical literature and general science. An eager humanist scholar, his learning was declared by some, extravagantly, to embrace "all knowledge" of the time. He excelled in music and writing, including poetry—and even astrology fascinated him.

Hans Denck was also an enthusiastic humanist. Men of this ilk tended to revolt against or at least minimize medieval religious authority and restraints while drawing on ancient classical ideas in a spirit of scholarly freedom. The University of Ingolstadt still had something of a reputation for positive humanism while Hans was there, although the institution's fame had declined since earlier years. Under the lead of Professor Johann Eck, Martin Luther's staunch antagonist, the university was turning to ultra-Catholicism. This was a different emphasis from that which had prevailed when Hans first registered as a student there, two days before Luther tacked his ninety-five theses on the church door in Wittenberg, about two hundred miles to the north.

Hans does seem to have returned to Ingolstadt some time after graduation for studies in Hebrew with one of Europe's outstanding Hebraists, Johann Reuchlin. Maybe he would have stayed longer if it had not been for Eck's increasing influence as a reactionary. Certainly the latter's legalistic approach was diametrically opposed to that of the brilliant young Denck, who not only embraced humanism but imbibed deeply from the springs of medieval mysticism.

The Wandering Humanist Scholar

Although Hans had not succeeded in obtaining a suitable position for providing a livelihood in Augsburg, influential friends there secured for him a post as tutor of children in Stotzingen near the city of Ulm. During this period he wrote several times to Veit Bild. The communications, in Latin, included versified epigrams in that language and in Greek; all reflected the humanistic spirit.

Evidently the tutoring arrangements did not satisfy Hans. In March 1520 he wrote to Veit Bild again, asking for the latter's help in getting a position in Augsburg. All was arranged, and Hans planned to return to that city at Whitsuntide 1520. Evidently he did, but soon left again. He was precentor and teacher in Donauwörth, north of Augsburg, for a while. By the fall of 1522 we find him in the imperial city of Regensberg, about seventy-five miles northeast of Augsburg—unemployed, discouraged. Here again influential friends aided him in securing a teaching position in the Hohes-stift, a college-level school.

Reformation influences were working deeply in the mind of the young humanist; these were strong in Regensberg, perhaps due partly to the presence there during part of this time of an emerging radical reformer, Balthasar Hubmaier. These influences seemed to be even stronger, however, in Switzerland, to which Hans felt strangely attracted. Ulrich Zwingli of Zurich was leading the reform in that confederation, with recently arrived Professor Johannes Oecolampadius already prominent in Basel. A contemporary described Hans Denck as being so "deluged in the Lutheran spirit" that he left for Basel to visit Oecolampadius; Hans had known the latter in Augsburg.

He arrived in Basel the end of January or beginning of February 1523 and Oecolampadius, who was living in the house of the printer Cratander, received him cordially. During his time in Basel young Denck worked as a "corrector" in the printing house of Cratander, then that of Curio. For the latter he edited the last three volumes of the widely used Greek grammar by Theodor Gaza, the first of which had been prepared in this way by the Catholic humanist Desiderius Erasmus. As was customary in those days, editor Denck included in the published volumes very brief literary contributions of his own—a couplet in Greek and a six-line poem in Latin praising in humanistic fashion the liberating power of Greek learning.

Hans attended some lectures at the university in Basel,

notably a course by Oecolampadius on Isaiah. He joined in religio-humanist discussions with the great Erasmus, who then lived in Basel, and with Oecolampadius and others. Erasmus deeply desired church reform, not through revolt and schism as Luther and Zwingli seemed to but through knowledge of the Greek New Testament and suitable interpretation, along with serious application of Jesus' teachings in the Christian's life.

Among many scholars and reformers with whom Oecolampadius corresponded was Willibald Pirkheimer of Nürnberg, Germany, who was a close friend of the famed Nürnberg artist Albrecht Dürer. In the course of this correspondence Oecolampadius learned of an opening for the headmastership of St. Sebaldus School in Nürnberg, and he recommended his gifted young humanist friend Hans Denck for the post. The Nürnberg city council forthwith employed him, and Hans went there to take up his new work in September 1523.

An Independent Thinker Is Born

Nürnberg, a "free imperial city"—northwest of Ingolstadt and Regensburg—enjoyed a high reputation as a center of cultural renaissance in Germany. Lutheranism was openly preached, and shortly before Denck's arrival the council formally voted for church reform. Their chief instrumentality for implementing the program was Andreas Osiander, young pastor of St. Lorenz Church. He enthusiastically promoted, in word and deed, the movement of reform.

Humanists of Nürnberg had been instrumental in the establishment of St. Sebaldus School. They welcomed Denck in their midst. The council, notified at the beginning of the year 1524 that the new headmaster had married (probably to a young woman of the humanist circle), voted a supplement to his salary so that he could set up a home. Denck's wife evidently assisted with family finances by taking in students as boarders. Hans Denck must have made a good director of the school academically. He was, however, becoming more and more interested in theology and church reform; with his free spirit, this got him into trouble. The various reformers and their local government supporters demanded the right to differ with the traditionally established church, but they felt no inclination to grant this right to those who questioned their own teachings.

Denck, as headmaster, disagreed with the utilizing of some students from his school in the church service during the observance of the mass, and he forbade their "ministering" in this way. That brought forth a strong censure from the council on June 13, 1524, along with a mandate that Denck's order to the students be rescinded. The young headmaster felt obliged to acquiesce, but the incident demonstrated that after less than nine months in Nürnberg, the waters were already troubled for him there.

The climax came in connection with artists of the Albrecht Dürer circle who had freely criticized the new order, speaking specifically "in a disrespectful manner about baptism and the Lord's Supper." On November 10 the city council reprimanded Hans Greiffenberger for scandalous paintings and unorthodox views. A few weeks later the brothers Barthel Beheim and Sebald Beheim, along with Jörg Benz, were put on trial. They not only expressed doubts about the sacraments and various dogmas but denied the full divinity of Christ. Sebald Beheim mentioned Hans Denck as one with whom they had spoken about these things. The council forthwith summoned him to appear before them, then turned him over to the Lutheran ministers, under Osiander's lead, for full examination.

Denck defended himself so cleverly at this hearing that pastors and council gave up on settling the question in oral discussion and demanded a written statement of his beliefs. They indicated that he should treat specific topics: Scripture, sin, the righteousness of God, law and gospel, baptism, and the Lord's Supper. The council recessed the trial of "the godless painters," as they were called, until Denck's views could be examined. Denck wrote out a statement and turned it over to the council January 14, 1525.

"I, Hans Denck, confess that I truly find myself—really feel it and sense it—a person poor in spirit, subject to every infirmity of body and soul," the statement of almost twelve hundred words begins. "However, I feel at the same time also within me something that gives strong resistance to my inborn rebellious nature and points me to life and blessedness, which it seems as impossible for my soul to come to as it would be impossible for my body to ascend into the visible sky." Here is Denck the serious and honest seeker, but also the budding theologian. Although he does not yet claim to be even a fully believing Christian, he hints at some fundamental points for all his future work—human sin, the need for supernatural grace, hope of salvation, the consciousness of an inner witness and power.

The Theologian Emerges

So just where did Denck stand at this time? He certainly did not want the kind of Catholicism that Eck represented. He appreciated the courageous stand of Martin Luther in rejecting papal and ecclesiastical authority in the dispensing of God's grace, returning to the Bible and personal faith as bases for the Christian life. As he read much concerning Protestant doctrine, however, and observed its outworking—especially in the cities where he had lived, which were rife with immorality—he saw that something was lacking.

The Reformation mottoes of faith alone, grace alone, and Scripture alone were fine, Denck felt, but what about people who did not take them seriously or did not understand them? What about those who could not read the Bible? Preaching to them was fine, but was this enough, by itself, to get the gospel to everyone and bring a needed response in life? The young thinker found within himself, and believed to be in the heart of every person, a witness of the Spirit of God which "gave strong resistance" to the inborn tendency to sin. This conclusion had come as the result of extensive reflection in the spirit of practical mystics, especially as found in a little book written anonymously decades before, which had influenced Luther greatly. The latter called it the *German Theology.*

"It is said that one comes to the life through faith," Denck continues in his statement for the Nürnberg authorities. "I accept that. But who gives me this faith? If it were inborn, I should have the life naturally by birth; it is not so." He refers here to his Christian upbringing: "From my childhood I learned the faith through my parents and I spoke regularly about it; later on, I also read many books and I boasted of having the faith. In truth, however, I never did take a good look at that which is the opposite of faith, my natural portion by birth.... The above-mentioned poverty of spirit certainly rebukes this false faith.... the inborn sickness or poverty of spirit basically does not diminish; the more I clean and spruce myself up, the more it is sure to increase. It is like a bad tree with rotting roots; it will become worse the more one cultivates and tends it."

In his eager stumbling toward spiritual ground, Denck continues: "I should earnestly desire to have faith, which is life. Since it is basically not to be found in me by nature, however, I would not deceive myself or others. Indeed, if I should today declare, 'I believe,' tomorrow I could well prove myself a liar—not I really, but the truth which I sense to some degree in my inward being. I certainly know this in myself that it is truth, and I shall, God willing, listen to it, whatever it will say to me; and if anyone wants to take it from me, I shall not permit him to do so.... Wherever it points me, there shall I go ... from whatever it drives me, I shall flee.

"So long as I just take up the Scripture myself, on my own, I understand nothing. Insofar as that inward truth drives me, just so far also I comprehend, not because of merit but of grace.... That which is within me, not my own ... that which drives me on, without the aid of all my willing and doing ... is Christ, to whom the Scripture gives witness that he is the Son of the Most High.... I dare not say that I have this faith, even though I know that my unbelief cannot endure in his presence.... 'Lord, I believe, help my unbelief.' So ... I hold with Peter that Scripture is a lantern which shines in the darkness."

Further on, Denck deals with other theological questions. "The righteousness of God is God himself," he writes. "Sin is whatever rebels against God, which in truth is 'nothing'.... Of course all believers were at one time unbelieving. Those who have become believers had to die first so that thereafter they would no longer live to themselves as unbelievers do but rather live for God in Christ."

The Mystic Tries to Be Practical

Denck had dealt with only five of the topics assigned to him, and these quite in a free way. Mainly he was concerned to get across to his challengers the basic conviction that genuine truth, witnessed to in Scripture and manifested in Christ, has a further witness, available to every person, in his or her own heart. The greatest sin, for Denck, is unbelief. All sin is seen as rebellion against God, the righteous one; since such rebellion is a futile undertaking, sin may be defined, ultimately, as nothingness.

Denck did not complete the assignment by the due date, but, as already noted, forwarded the parts he had written to the council. It allowed him a few days more to write on the remaining topics: baptism and the Lord's Supper. Regarding baptism, he opines, "All things which by nature are impure become even more so the more one tries to wash them. . . . Who would undertake to wash off the redness of bricks or the blackness of coal, whose very nature is what it is?. . . Also in the same way a person who by nature is unclean, in body and soul, will be washed in vain outwardly if he has not begun to be softened and changed from within. The almighty Word of God can alone descend to and penetrate into the hardened abyss of man's uncleanness, as a driving rain can soften arid ground."

"This water of baptism saves," Denck says, commenting on 1 Peter 3:21, " 'not because it removes the filth of the flesh but rather because of the covenant of a good conscience with God.' This covenant means that whoever is baptized into the death of Christ is baptized in order that he might die to the old Adam as Christ died and that he may walk in a new life with Christ as Christ was raised (Romans 6). . . . Outward baptism is not essential to salvation. . . . Inward baptism . . . is essential. Thus it is written, 'He who believes and is baptized will be saved.' "

Regarding "the Supper of Christ" Denck emphasizes the

inner experience as well. "This is the work of Christ ... if I place my will under the will of God in Christ the Mediator, as was suggested above in the case of baptism. Whoever is of this mind and eats of the living invisible bread will be strengthened and confirmed in the right life." The same holds true with the cup. "One can live without material bread by the power of God ... without the inward bread, no one can live. For the just person lives by faith (Habakkuk 2, Romans 1). He who does not believe does not live."

Driven Hither and Yon

The council accepted the statement from Denck; but its members were much irritated, as were the pastors, when they discovered that he had already shared his writing with friends in the city. The council turned Denck's papers over to the pastors, who studied them and then wrote for the council a lengthy evaluation of Hans Denck's confession. This evaluation begins with the customary obsequious address to the lords of the council. There follows then the description of the views of those questioned as "errors of their faith which they expressed and spread about in a careless and scandalous manner." Zooming in on their most formidable adversary, they continued, "Hans Denck, schoolmaster at St. Sebaldus School, proved to be so skillful that we considered it to be useless to argue with him orally.... He does not give straightforward answers ... [and] attempts to elaborate and color the thoughts and ideas of his mind (Scripture never speaks as pointedly as he does), so that one can readily perceive that another than the Spirit of Christ drives him."

"He comes with cunning and discards Scripture as if it were useless just because not everyone understands it," the Nürnberg preachers complain, "yet it is clear enough." Regarding belief he "maintains that God alone gives faith and anyone who derives it from Scripture has it from himself and not from God; that is a deception typical of this kind of prophet.... Denck has said ... there is something in him which offers resistance to his badness.... To the end he insists that it is Christ. Yet at the same time he denies that he has any faith.... If he insists on calling his faith no faith until it is entirely perfect (which never happens, in this life), he acts contrary to Christ and to all Scripture."

The writers, primarily Osiander, no doubt, state at the close of their own composition: "Therefore, worthy, honorable and dear lords, we have herewith not sought to answer him but have written rather for your information. . . . However, we desire nothing less than that you, honorable lords, continue to deal with him. . . . If it does not help, it will then be your duty, worthy lords, for the sake of divine order and your office, to see . . . that this poisonous error . . . be not spread any further among the people."

The recommendation of the pastors pleased the council, which forthwith voted on January 21, 1525, without giving the accused a chance to reply, to banish Denck and the "godless painters." Schoolmaster Denck was to be notified, "since he has brought in certain unchristian errors concerning our holy faith, circulated and dared to defend them, has conducted himself in connection with this in an entirely unworthy and contemptible manner before the pastors and scholars, in the presence also of council members, would accept no instruction from Scripture, rather trusts himself more and his own knowledge . . . it is not right to tolerate his person here. . . . Rather, he should swear an oath to submit himself to leave the city, be ten miles away before nightfall, and for all his life long not come any nearer to this city than that. Otherwise, he will be sought out and punished bodily."

Denck received the decree of the council with great consternation. He had not imagined that he would be expelled without any further chance to discuss the matter. He accepted it, however, as the will of God for him at this point and took the oath required of him. He made hasty arrangements for his wife and their child to remain in Nürnberg for the foreseeable future, gathered a few personal belongings, and departed. Thus began a period of wandering which would end with his death in the not-very-distant future.

During the following weeks and months the unfortunate young scholar, supporting himself somehow by occasional tutoring, received one or more offers of permanent employment as a teacher, one of these in Mühlhausen, a few miles northwest of Basel. If he actually taught there, it was for quite a short period. We soon find him, if our interpretation of town records is correct, across the border in central Switzerland, imprisoned in Schwyz for his negative views on infant baptism. By early or late summer of the same year, 1525, he appeared in St. Gall.

A Committed Christian but Ever the Seeker

Denck continued to hold to his views concerning the Spirit's witness in the human heart, the importance of commitment and living the Christlike life. In St. Gall, where Anabaptists numbered perhaps a thousand, he lived with one of these and probably attended Anabaptist meetings but did not join the group. Although now doubtless a committed Christian, he remained in some respects a seeker.

The Anabaptists may have placed too much emphasis on biblical literalism for him and he may have been too much of a universalist for them. He evidently hoped, on the basis of his belief in a good and loving God and the suggestion of several Scripture passages, for the salvation of everyone eventually. He insisted that Christ's atonement was sufficient for all humankind, but there is no evidence—except for the charges of his opponents—that he ever declared that everyone would be saved. Most of the Brethren would not understand Denck's philosophical and sometimes mystical way of expressing himself; but they should have known, from his emphasis on the call to commitment, freedom of choice, and human responsibility that he could hardly be a thoroughgoing universalist. He never seems to have made speculations about the future life.

Two leading churchmen in St. Gall, layman Vadian (Joachim von Watt) and reformer-historian Johannes Kessler, both accused him of universalism, as did several other contemporary opponents; but Denck's own writings do not support the charge. In the process of condemning him, the two St. Gall leaders do accord some praise. Denck was to Kessler "a learned, eloquent, and humble man ... tall, very friendly, and of modest conduct. He would otherwise be praised very much, had he not defiled himself and his teaching with terrible errors.... He was exceedingly trained in the word of the Scriptures and educated in the three main languages.... His opinion was that no man would go to hell ... for Paul said, God desires all men to be saved.... Although the Scriptures prophesy everlasting things, it means [to Denck] nothing else than for a long time; as God commanded his people to keep circumcision forever and yet in the New Testament it was displaced. His teaching was quite similar to the fantasies of Origen."

Vadian, principal civic leader in St. Gall, wrote, "Denck was in every respect excellent, even to the degree that he surpassed his age and seemed greater than he was. He, however, so misused his mind that he defended with great effort the opinion of Origen concerning the liberation and salvation of those who are condemned. He could cite Scripture passages sharply and above understanding. The bountiful love of God was praised so much—as he did for instance in a certain meeting—that he seemed to give hope even to the most wicked and most hopeless people that they would obtain salvation, which would be granted to them someday, however distant it might be."

In the latter part of September 1525 we find Denck quietly settled in the city of Augsburg. Two noblemen friends had succeeded in securing for him a position tutoring the children of well-to-do families in Latin and Greek, as he had done in other places. He lived as a rule in the homes of those whose children he instructed.

Ministry of Writing Discovered

Augsburg, at this time, was divided religiously. The Protestants had the upper hand, but they were not of one mind, theologically. Some were loyal followers of Martin Luther; many others held to Zwingli's view of baptism and the Lord's Supper as being symbolic only. No Anabaptist congregation existed as yet in the city, but there was a small group that was questioning infant baptism, as well as opposing Luther's view of the Supper.

Word got around that Hans Denck was a man with a court record; somebody reported to the city council that he had been expelled from Nürnberg because of disobedience toward city authorities. He was asked for an explanation.

"I was schoolmaster there for a year and a half," Denck wrote of his time in Nürnberg. "Afterward I got into an argument with Osiander, a preacher there, concerning certain words of the sacrament." Denck lists the seven topics on which he had been required to respond and suggests to the Augsburg councilors that they could "clearly perceive therefrom whether this had anything to do with obedience or disobedience.... I was ordered to leave the city within a week, without any reply from Osiander. However, I am grateful to God if it pleased him so."

Denck expresses his appreciation to the noblemen who had made possible his employment in Augsburg and hints to the councilors that they might use their good offices to secure more such assignments for him: "Perchance it might happen, by your gracious and kind permission, that I could be given more of this desired work to do." He begs the "honorable gentlemen" ("lords") that they not "lend a ready ear to idle accusations against me which can never be substantiated by sound evidence." He concludes: "With this I humbly commend myself to you, begging of you to permit me to carry on what I have begun with your kind leave and hoping that I can conduct myself in such a manner that you, worthy gentlemen, will have no cause for displeasure. In case I have done something unwittingly or should do anything in the future that may displease you, honorable gentlemen, I humbly beg you to let me know of it. I shall be found most obedient. God preserve you, worthy gentlemen. Amen."

Without further question, officially, Denck was allowed to remain in Augsburg to teach. He must have spent a great part of his spare time in writing, for several of his booklets were published during the thirteen months he spent there. One of these was *The Assertion that Scripture Says God Practices and Produces Good and Evil.*

In this work of about 9,200 words the author apologizes, at the outset, for going public on the issue and speaking dogmatically about God. The latter "impelled me," he says, "so that I cannot remain silent.... There are certain brothers who think they have the gospel all figured out, and whoever does not give an all-inclusive yes to what they say is branded the worst of heretics." The introductory paragraph ends prayerfully, "O Lord, my God, let me be pleasing unto you and then you do unto me as you will, through your most-beloved Son Jesus Christ, through whose Spirit the world should and must be judged. Amen."

The purpose of the little book was to counter the doctrine of rigid predestination taught by many Lutherans, of which Denck believed resulted in much irresponsible living. If one were irreversibly destined for a certain fate into all eternity, people said, what difference would one's conduct make? Nothing one could do would change it. In his writing Denck emphasizes God's universal gift of the freedom to choose, to serve Christ, and to live a life of devoted discipleship. Evil was not created by God, he says, but God uses even sin—which is still to Denck a futile "nothingness," ultimately—to punish or redeem and make things right. The author employs the literary device of having the imaginary reader ask questions or make assertions, twenty-three of them, to which he gives answer.

"If God does not cause sin but permits it," the reader is made to say, "in any case his will must be involved, . . . he is still responsible for it. Answer: It is better that God allow sin than that he should have caused it, which he could not have done without forcing and driving people like a stone or a block of wood. In that case his name could not be known or praised by human beings." Denck states the sinner's hope: "The Word of God is with you before you seek it; the Word gives to you before you ask, opens the door before you knock. No one comes of himself to Christ unless the Father draw him, which he in his goodness faithfully does. The Mediator is Christ, whom no one can truly know unless he follow him in life."

God's Purpose and Human Response

Again the "reader" protests: "You say: 'Still I would like to know what hinders me from being saved, since God wants to give this blessedness to me, as you assert, and I can indeed say that I should like to receive it.' Answer: Exactly this hinders it, which has hindered all the elect, that your will, and God's will, although they indeed seem to be one, are not.... You seek your own self and not God, for himself. That is shown by your unsubmissiveness; you always seek some hiding place, to escape the outstretched hand of God.... We must always be attentive to hear what the Spirit in us says.... This witness is in all people and preaches to each one individually, whoever listens for it. And whoever gives excuse that he doesn't hear it is a liar and has blinded himself.... For the Lamb has existed from the beginning and remains until the end a Mediator between God and humankind."

While emphasizing the inner witness so that none may find excuse, Denck says, "One should not discard completely any outward witness [e.g., Scripture] but hear and test all things in the fear of the Spirit.... Then day by day the understanding will become clearer until we hear God speaking with us most clearly and become certain of his will, which is that we give up all of self and give ourselves over to the freedom which is God."

Denck meets a further questioning statement. Reader: Christ surely died out of love for humankind, " 'but not for all; rather, just for many.' Answer: Since love was perfected in him ... although we were his enemies, he would not exclude anyone. If he had excluded anyone his love would be a mockery and a respecting of persons, which it is not.... This sacrifice was pleasing to the Father, and if there were a thousand more worlds of people, there would still be satisfaction to him for all sin. When Scripture does indeed say 'he died for many' and, again, 'for all' it is not contradictory but is there because not all will receive the light although it has shined on all; many will deny the Lord although he has paid redemption's price for all, as Scripture abundantly testifies."

Although Denck rejects predestination as an arbitrary and exclusive act of God, he admits divine foreknowledge of sin; but this does not make God responsible for it. "If a child were inclined to thievery and his father laid out a penny to test whether the child would steal," and the child did, "is the father to blame for this sin because he laid out the penny—although he had often forbidden it and warned the child not to steal? No one can affirm such a thing. So it is with the Father in heaven."

Humankind is in dire need of Christ, Denck says, still, "God will have no one forced but each one must come voluntarily into his service.... He desires to hold no one against his will. It is no less true that it is pleasing to him, as he determined from all eternity, that he wishes all persons to be saved. Therefore he prepared from all eternity the means by which people should be saved, in which they were created, namely, his Word. Even the receiving of the Word is of God ... in order to reconcile the unrighteous with the Father ... God will not force anyone.... The fault is with those who will not respond."

For all his philosophy and mysticism, Hans Denck in his writings was a missionary at heart. With reference to the loving Father who sought the obedience of the people of Israel and then later of others, he says: "O that the entire world would so come to the Lord, who would be wonderfully ready to show grace toward it. He calls all people and offers his mercy to everyone.... Not that he says, 'Come,' thinking and wishing to himself that this one or that one remain there where he is. Not that he gives his grace to someone and desires secretly to take it back, not that he works repentance for sin in us and secretly prepares hell for us—for in all his gifts he is constant and true."

The author makes it personal for the reader: "I testify and plead with you, in light of the coming again of Jesus Christ, our Lord, to all who hear, see, or otherwise come to know the truth of God.... accept it ... as Christ taught and proved by his own life.... [Accept] the denial and loss of self, that you may stand before his judgment seat guiltless and secure; otherwise the truth is and will continue to be for you a blatant lie, due to your perverted nature."

That one who takes these words to heart "can and should pray to the merciful and true God to remove from us what is shameful ... not for our sakes but in order that his name be praised among all the heathen and all peoples. This he promised us through his servants the holy prophets and his Son Jesus, the Anointed One, whom he has placed as a King above all kings and Lord over all lords. [This is the one] whom the whole world fears and still does not believe but soon will experience in truth on that day toward which all saints look forward with joy. Amen."

Obviously, Denck's primary concern was to invite everyone to be obedient to God as he is revealed in his Son, Jesus Christ. He repudiated the excuse of those Lutherans and others who protested that if they were not of the elect they could not believe and be saved. Denck insisted that by God's grace everyone has the enlightenment and power within him or her to respond, obey, and be blessed of God in this life and the next.

Anabaptism Espoused, Writing Continued

The Anabaptist congregation in Augsburg probably developed out of the small group of radicals mentioned earlier. Balthasar Hubmaier, a native of the area, discussed the issues at length with Denck when the former stopped in Augsburg on his way from Zurich to Moravia in the early summer of 1526. Hubmaier appreciated the sound scholarship, deep earnestness, and Christian commitment of Hans Denck. He evidently felt, however, that the younger man was too philosophical and too optimistic theologically—he really should give more respect surely to the written word of Scripture, the ordinances, and the everlasting wrath of God against the adamantly rebellious.

Hubmaier apparently convinced Denck that the latter's ministry would be more effective in the structured fellowship of the Brethren. In any case, Denck was baptized about this time, possibly by Hubmaier. The congregation in Augsburg grew, and Denck became its leader. This group, however, was not a part of the Swiss Brethren movement. It was rather the beginnings of a South-German Brethren movement, influenced greatly in its early stages by Denck and his ideas. "Hans Denck's activities spread the thing like cancer, to the deplorable harm of many," a pastor of the established church complained.

Hans Hut, a traveling bookseller who had long opposed infant baptism, came to Augsburg and visited Denck—as he probably had during the latter's time in Nürnberg. Denck and an Anabaptist from Tyrol, Austria, persuaded Hut that he should join the Brethren movement. He finally agreed and Denck baptized him at Whitsuntide 1526. The convert was about as different from Denck in temperament and preaching as could be imagined. The most appealing doctrine to Hut was the second coming of Christ—which he proclaimed regularly and emotionally as an imminent event. He agreed, however, to submit in a loose way to the discipline of the Anabaptist community; he evidently expected to use that movement to promote the cause as he understood it. He worked zealously as an itinerant Brethren evangelist. It is a credit to Denck that, considering Hut's personality, he was able to work harmoniously with him. Hut should be given such credit, too, for working with Denck and others.

One of Denck's most important literary compositions was *The Law of God*. The subtitle hints at his message: "How the law is abrogated and still must be observed." It is not the easiest of Denck's works to read. He was writing for fellow Anabaptists now, as well as Lutheran opponents and others, and he seems to have tried sometimes to speak to the arguments of all at once; this can be confusing. *The Law of God* represents an effort to face the moral and ethical problems which had been alluded to in a previous book—problems occurring in the lives of those who were flocking to Lutheranism and other reform movements without any claim to a personal experience of God's grace and without any sense of obligation to live a consistent Christian life.

In *The Law of God* Denck uses the same device as in his previous book—the "reader" raises the issues, in this case, eighteen questions, to which Denck then replied. One hundred twenty-two scriptural (and apocryphal) references are cited. Denck did not enjoy controversy and advised his readers against it. "Most dearly beloved," he admonishes, "do not cause any quarreling when there is no need for it.

Let each one suffer wrong so long as there is no harm to him in regard to the kingdom of God. In this manner, we shall be able to stand before the wrath of God. I am always worried about the great sin people commit in uttering so many useless words on both sides." On the other hand, Denck writes, "Whenever I can show someone his error and point out to him the right way, this I do very gladly. This concern for him is not of myself; God has put this in my heart. If it bear fruit, this is his work too."

Denck explains the different senses in which he employs the word "law." "There are three kinds of law: Scripture calls them commandments, customs, and statute law. Commandments are those that flow from the love of God and neighbor and can never be transgressed without sin; the consciences of all reasonable people testify to this.... Customs are external ordinances directed to the natural and daily habits of people in order that they be reminded of those things that are divine and eternal ... sacraments or signs.... Statute laws are judgments that are established between brothers to protect the innocent and punish the guilty."

Law and Gospel

In reference to Jesus' teaching in Matthew 5:17, Denck comments: "He whom the whole world acknowledges with the mouth and denies by its deeds says, 'I am not come to abolish the law but to fulfill it!' Carnal wisdom of the world ... tears these words out and says, 'Christ has fulfilled the law so that we do not need it.'... The words are thereby explained in such a way as to serve perverted human nature, to which everything that comes from God is pus and poison—the way everybody lives proves that.... If this interpretation were true, it would be all the same, no matter how one lived after conversion. The world is full of people whose lives and fruitfulness were better before they began to glory in their faith than afterward."

The writer affirms that Christ "has fulfilled the whole law, not placing us above it but giving us an example that we follow him.... You say: 'If he has done nothing else than

prepare the way ... he is no more, then, than Moses.'...
Answer: ... Christ has done so much more.... He speaks
and writes it for all, from the beginning of the world to its
end, in their hearts. He who has it in his heart lacks neither
the path nor feet [to walk with], neither light nor eyes [to
see], or anything else that is necessary to accomplish the will
of God. Neither path nor feet are any good for one who does
not have it in his heart."

Referring to Mark 9:23 and the power available through
faith, Denck has the reader exclaim, " 'Hey, nobody is able
to fulfill the law.' Answer: True, this is possible to no one,
merely as a person; to believers, on the other hand, all things
are possible ... as those who are one with God, freed from
the creaturely world and also [freed] in part from their own
selves.... The understanding, the will, and the powers of all
created beings are God's and one with him."

Explaining the overcoming power of love to fulfill the law
the author makes a comparison: "Whoever fulfills the law of
love fulfills all ceremonies, even if he never gives a thought
to them. Whoever takes in plenty of large gold pieces could
let all small coins pass by; it would actually be difficult for
him to carry the latter around—not that he despises them,
but that he not miss having the better ones. Whoever
possesses enough gold pieces has enough and to spare, even
if he hasn't a penny in coin.... Whoever keeps God's commandments holds his law in deep affection and gladly hears
talk about it ... where there is no faith, fulfillment will
never come about.... We are all fallen because of sin....
He who has once truly repented of it is born of God and is no
longer sinning" (1 John 3:6).

Denck leaves no doubt as to the source of regeneration.
Again he has the reader speak, "You say: 'What good is it if
one repents all he likes, for if Everyman has sometime
broken the law, no one will be saved, according to you.'
Answer: If God has once made something and someone
breaks it, God can make it good again. If God does not will to
remake it, it is and always remains broken. What he has re-
made is as if it had never been broken; a damage mended is
no damage at all."

The author summarizes and explains the proper use of Scripture: "All commandments, customs, and statute laws, so far as these are written down in the Old Testament and the New, are abrogated for a true pupil of Christ (1 Timothy 1); that is, he has one Word written in his heart, that he loves God alone.... He despises no witness of Scripture; rather he searches it with all diligence.... He withholds judgment on what he does not understand and awaits revelation from God.... All Scripture is given for the purpose of correction, teaching, and comfort.... Scripture and law are in themselves holy and good; in a perverse heart, however, everything will be perverted, and nothing can help such a person except God himself, without any intermediary."

Referring to Ezekiel 3:17ff. and 33:1ff., Denck says, "He who rightly proclaims God's wrath is the one who can proclaim his grace effectively.... However fully such a one knows God, he still rejoices at every witness ... [and] every admonition, written or spoken in truth. He gives himself day and night to the law of God.... Such a one cannot hold Scripture higher than his level of obedience to its teaching— namely, loving God alone with all his heart. He who honors Scripture and is cold in the love of God, let him beware lest he make an idol of Scripture—which is what the learned scribes do who are not learned regarding the kingdom of God.

"You say: 'Is it wrong for one who does not know God to regard Scripture highly, since he may thereby come to knowledge?' Answer: If someone were to give you a letter promising great possessions and you did not know the writer—how upright and rich he is, and whether he is as you hoped—it would be utter folly to rely on his letter.... The letter is of no use to someone not in God's house; a person in God's house knows even without the letter how good the Lord is....

"You should not discard the letter, however faithfully you may be serving the Lord, for it is also established as a testimony against you in case one day you should wander from the way. If you do not keep to the letter, you cannot use it for assurance.... He who does not come to know God through God himself has never known him."

Use and Misuse of Scripture

The misuse of Scripture, as Denck understood it, continued to bother him; he regarded it as one of the chief causes of divisions among Christians. Some of the reformers seemed simply to substitute the Bible for the papacy. He felt that some Anabaptists treated it as a legalistic code. To show the Bible's higher spiritual unity as interpreted through the Holy Spirit—and the impossibility of always taking it in a literal way—Denck drew up a list of forty "paradoxes" from the Old and New Testaments, including the Apocrypha. The long title to this little publication begins *He Who Truly Loves the Truth* and ends with the words *The Fear of God Is the Beginning of Wisdom*.

In his introductory paragraph to the reader, Denck—insisting that he is "speaking without malice"—describes the rise of "many sects and so-called heresies" both in days gone by and in his own time. Even the various members of a single party disagree sometimes, he observes, "and this would not happen if one gave attention to the one true teacher, the Holy Spirit. To his teaching Scripture gives clear testimony ... but to those in whom this is not sealed by the Spirit of God himself, it appears to be contradictory in many places....

"Two opposing Scripture passages must both be true. One will be contained in the other as the lesser is in the greater, as time is in eternity, finitude in infinity. He who gives up on opposing Scripture passages and cannot find their unity lacks the ground of truth. We ... should bemoan our poverty, and hunger after the bread of life.... Our Father ... tends to give only to the hungering. This is then the reason these paradoxical Scriptures are brought together (many, many more of such could have been found). May God use them to the edification of his own people! Amen."

The seventh paradox contrasts "I am not come to judge the world but to save it" (John 12) with "I am come to judge the world" (Romans 9). The eighth, "If I give testimony of myself, my testimony is not true" (John 5) with "If I give testimony of myself, my testimony is true" (John 8). The eleventh, "For who can resist his will?" (Romans 9) with "You always resisted the Holy Spirit" (Acts 7). The twelfth, "Everyone who asks receives" (Matthew 7) with "You ask and receive not" (James 4).

The fourteenth paradox contrasts "Preach the gospel to all creatures" (Mark 16) with "Cast not pearls before swine" (Matthew 7). The sixteenth, "I will not be angry forever" (Jeremiah 3) with "These will go to eternal punishment" (Matthew 25). The next, "God wills that all should be saved" (1 Timothy 2) with "Few are chosen" (Matthew 20). And the next, "God does not tempt anyone" (James 1) with "God tempted Abraham" (Genesis 22). The twenty-second, "No one has seen God" (John 1) with "I have seen the Lord face to face" (Genesis 32). The twenty-fifth, "Judge not that you be not judged" (Matthew 7) with "Judge righteous judgment" (John 7). The last one, "God says, I will to harden Pharaoh's heart" (Exodus 4) with "Pharaoh hardens his heart" (Exodus 8 and 9).

For all his learning, Hans Denck was, of course, still a man of his time, and the way he treated Scripture, seen in his selection of paradoxes, seems on occasion to be almost as arbitrary as that of his opponents. Two such examples are the thirty-third paradox, "The bars of the earth have encased me forever" (Jonah 2) contrasted with "And God spoke to the fish, and it spewed Jonah onto dry land" (Jonah 2) and the thirty-seventh, "With whatever measure you measure, it shall be measured out to you" (Matthew 7) contrasted with "In the cup which she has mixed, mix for her double" (Revelation 18).

Persona non Grata in Augsburg and Strasbourg

Denck seems to have worked quietly in Augsburg even after becoming an Anabaptist. Urbanus Rhegius, leading Lutheran pastor in the city, protested toward the end of Denck's time there that the latter, despite contacts they maintained, had not mentioned his controversial views. Once discovered, however, these were brought into the open by Rhegius and resulted in Denck's departure from Augsburg. The Augsburg pastor was a bitter antagonist of Anabaptist teachings in general, but with Denck he zeroed-in—as other reformers did—on the latter's hope for the eventual consummation of all things within the purposes of God. Among those emphasizing election and predestination, this was his most vulnerable point.

Rhegius had conversations with Denck, trying to convert him, then called in his pastor-colleagues in the same effort. Since these talks were ineffectual, he suggested a disputation before the city council. Even if this should be just as fruitless, at least it would demonstrate the pastor's Lutheran orthodoxy and Denck's failure to measure up to it. Denck agreed to a disputation, even one before the whole city, which then was arranged. As he reflected in private on the matter, however, Denck decided that nothing good could be gained by public argument; so, early on the day when it was to take place, he quietly left the city.

He made his way to Strasbourg, where more religious toleration prevailed at the time than almost anywhere else in Europe. Martin Bucer and Wolfgang Capito were the two leading reformers there. They gave a serious hearing to the Anabaptist position and opposed really severe persecution against them. These two would have perhaps favored believer's baptism as more scriptural, but due to traditional usage they retained infant baptism as an outward symbol.

Capito may have seriously considered going over to the Brethren—certainly some of the latter thought that he was close to this; he was a good friend to Michael Sattler and other Anabaptists. Capito shared many of the ideas of Hans Denck, honoring Scripture as the "outer Word," but warning lest the dead letter be made into an idol. He also held it not as ultimate truth, but as a witness to that truth—the ultimate source being God, known through his Holy Spirit. Capito, like Denck and others, pointed out apparent contradictions in the Bible which could be resolved only through spiritual understanding. Despite these similarities Capito, and Bucer even more so, turned against Denck and other Anabaptists because of their separatism, church discipline, and minimizing the doctrine of predestination.

Denck had fairly close relationships with the little group of Anabaptists in Strasbourg, including Michael Sattler. He also met the antipedobaptist Ludwig Haetzer, who was engaged in translating the prophet Isaiah. Capito had been helping in this project and now Denck also was cooperating. There were theological conversations with Capito, Ludwig Haetzer, and others, which Denck later declared to have transpired in an orderly and harmonious way.

The reformers, however, were anxious to be rid of Denck. Not only was Bucer unhappy with Denck's theology, but he also felt this learned Anabaptist had a harmful influence on people in the city generally. Bucer arranged a public disputation, in which he took the leading part; the populace indicated its interest by attending—about four hundred in number. The outcome never lay in doubt, however. Bucer convinced the council to banish Denck, who had to leave on Christmas Day, 1526.

Evangelist, Translator, and Author

About two weeks later we find Denck in the town of Bergzabern, where he conversed with the Lutheran pastor. Then, for three days he entered into formal discussions with some Jews residing in the town about the law. These efforts remained without perceptible result; we read of no converts, and know of no congregation of the Brethren to have been established there.

Next we hear of Denck in Landau, where there was indeed a small Brethren congregation. To this group he evidently brought a letter of recommendation from fellow believers in Strasbourg. Denck had private talks with the Lutheran pastor, Johannes Bader, then he participated in a public disputation. As usual, this unique Anabaptist proved himself an effective debater. The positive impression made in these discussions strengthened the position of the Brethren there. Bader later published a book, *Fraternal Warning*, which included, amid violent attacks on the Anabaptists, what Bader claimed to be Denck's own writing on baptism. It reveals rather typical Brethren teaching concerning this ordinance.

On Bader's recommendation the city council banished all Anabaptists and threatened with serious punishment anyone who harbored a person even suspected of leanings toward their beliefs. Denck left this place about the beginning of February 1527. He surfaced in the city of Worms, north of Landau.

In this small but important city on the Rhine River near Mantz, Martin Luther had been required to appear before the imperial diet in April 1521. He had refused to recant and was placed under imperial ban. Since that time Reformation ideas had gained strength in the area, but powerful Catholic leaders of church and state made progress difficult. Two leading pastors, Jacob Kautz and Hilarius, were Lutheran, but they were interested in more radical reform. They discontinued infant baptism, probably under the influence of a wandering Brethren preacher Melchior Rinck, and they became Anabaptist just before Denck arrived. Another who reached Worms at about this time was Ludwig Haetzer. He had enjoyed labors with Denck on the translation of Isaiah in Strasbourg and suggested they work together on a translation of the remaining prophetic books. Denck agreed.

The Anabaptist movement seemed to be advancing rather rapidly in Worms. Denck doubtless participated in it but not prominently. He and Haetzer practically hibernated, giving themselves without reserve to the translation work. Within eight weeks the job was done—the first translation of the Old Testament prophets into German from the original Hebrew—a work generally regarded as excellent. Its use is reflected in both Zwinglian (1529) and Lutheran (1534) translations of the Old Testament. The first edition of the Haetzer-Denck *All the Prophets* was published in Worms, and it had ten reprintings in two years' time. Over the next five years, there were eleven further editions.

Two of Denck's best writings, *Concerning True Love* and *God's Order and the Work of His Creatures*, were also published in Worms. The latter, just over six thousand words, includes three hundred Scripture references. It repudiates the old idea of many Lutherans that theology starts, so far as man is concerned, with God's secret order of predestination—the elect to blessedness and others to damnation. In his introductory section Denck has these antagonists quoting Romans 8:29, "Whom he foreknew, he also predestined" for salvation—and no others.

In way of answer, Denck warns, "Look well to the words, beloved, that you not misuse them to your own condemnation (2 Peter 3). For although the words of God are in themselves clarity and light, (Psalm 19), our darkness does not comprehend them (John 1), while we are self-seekers (Matthew 10). . . . We shall therefore most briefly contrast here, starting with the beginning of creation, the ordering of God [his purposes and plan] and the work of his creatures."

God's Good Plan and Man's Fateful Choice

God's Order is divided into twelve brief chapters. The first one begins, "We know that God in truth is good. . . . He also made and created all things good. Insofar as man is evil, however, this he is apart from God, (Psalm 10), and not one of God's own. Although man himself is to blame that he has cast himself into death. . . . God remains no less than what he is, which is good, Exodus 3. . . . He gives everyone the motivation, grace, and power to be converted [six Scripture references are given here]. . . . He causes no one to sin (Ecclesiasticus 15). The light, God's invisible Word, shines in the hearts of all people born into this world. . . . To him who does not desire it, it shines in judgment and damnation (John 3, 9); but he who desires willing service . . . would not allow himself to force anyone against his will to serve him; similarly, he forces no one to do evil (Ecclesiasticus 15). God desires that everyone be saved (1 Timothy 2, 4; 2 Peter 3), but knows full well that many condemn themselves (Romans 9)."

Chapter two is on "the two paths people may take, one unto life, the other unto death (Matthew 7)." The third chapter deals with hell, which to Denck is the state of a person who renounces God and is allied with evil; and it starts already in this life. "God prepares the way for salvation . . . and makes us aware of our own misery so that we may call upon him in our despair, and he shall help us. . . .

Then salvation begins.... We become poor in spirit (Matthew 5) ... and see the one God truly, entirely as he is.... God is good, from the beginning. We recognize and trust him only after going through great tribulation.... The more one sins, the more a person is separated from God (Isaiah 59; Luke 16).

"There are two wills, that of man and that of God; the great divine purpose is that they become one.... The more a man resists ... the more unrest it causes him.... The closer a person is, and the more similar he is to his created origin, the freer he is; the closer he is to damnation, the more he is enslaved (Matthew 5, 18).... Whoever says he has no grace from God to become a godly person is a liar, since everyone does (Psalm 116)."

The eighth chapter begins, "To believe is to obey the Word of God ... with the certain confidence that it points to the best (Hebrews 11). Whoever does that cannot possibly go astray, even though he may err.... He seeks the godly way in all things ... so he doesn't have law anymore (1 Timothy 1); he is rather the law in himself (Romans 2).... This does not mean that he is perfect ... he still prays daily for forgiveness of his sins (Psalm 32).... The Lord has therefore accepted him and elected him (2 Corinthians 1), so that he can fearlessly and truthfully say, 'You are my Father, and I am your son' (Romans 8; Psalm 89)."

The writing closes with the quotation of Isaiah 55:1-3: "Ho, all you who thirst, come to the water; and he who has no money, come.... Why do you spend your money for what is not bread and your labor for what does not satisfy? Do this one thing and hear me and you shall live abundantly ... so shall your soul live."

Needs Never Greater Than Divine Love

Jacob Kautz, although he certainly must have worked in consultation with Denck, Hilarius, and Haetzer, did not avoid publicity as these others did during the time they were together in Worms. In his preaching he decried formalism in faith and worship, calling people to union with God and to consistent Christian living. He challenged his opponents to public disputation and he tacked on the door of the Prediger (Preachers') Church a summary, in seven "theses," of his beliefs. These, which show Denck's influence, stress the inner spiritual life and deprecate outer forms such as infant baptism and communion; even the spoken and written Word are suspect until confirmed by the inner spiritual reality.

Following the disputation Kautz and Hilarius were banished. Denck and Haetzer were not mentioned in the city council's mandates. Denck continued his literary activity. One of the five small books he wrote at this time remains to be mentioned. Perhaps his best work, it strikes the keynote of his life and ministry.

It is somewhat shorter than *God's Order* and is entitled *Concerning True Love*. It begins: "Love is a spiritual power by which a person is united, or longs to be united, with another. Where there is perfect love, the one who loves does not withhold himself from the beloved. Rather, he denies self, as if he no longer existed, and counts all injury and loss as nothing if he suffers for the sake of the beloved.... Wherever it might be possible (and it is possible) the loving one would give himself willingly and gladly in death if that could benefit the loved one."

Bringing in again at this point his doctrine of the inner spiritual reality, Denck says, "In some persons just a little spark of this love may be detected, more in one and less in another. In our time, unfortunately, it has been extinguished in almost all people.... This little spark, however small it might be in a person, comes not from men but from perfect love. This love is God.... Flesh and blood cannot comprehend such love.... Therefore it pleased eternal love that the person in whom love was most perfectly demonstrated be called Redeemer of his people.... This man is Jesus of Nazareth ... [in whom] God had such compassion for the world that he would give up all real justice, which condemns our sin.... A person should stand in the highest degree of love toward God and insofar as he can he should aid and help his neighbor toward this also, so that he too may know and love God ... through Jesus Christ."

Insisting that all law of the old covenant is comprised in

the new, Denck says, "He who daily grows in love does not thereby add anything to the law but simply fulfills it. Love consists in this, that one knows and loves God and learns to give up and give over to him all that is created in the world, although these things might be pleasing to him as carnal man. On the other hand, he should accept and bear everything, albeit distasteful to the flesh, in the love of God. . . . The sign of the covenant, baptism, is to be given, and never denied, to those, and those alone, who through the power of God are invited to it through the knowledge of true love. . . . Holiness means to have separated oneself once for all from the evil world and filthiness of the flesh to serve the Lord God only. Water baptism denotes this and testifies to it. Such a person recognizes the old life as evil and desires henceforth to walk in newness of life."

In "a summary of the teaching of Jesus Christ," Denck finds the way "by which all quarreling that might arise as to what is true can be settled for anyone who understands it thoroughly or desires with all his heart to understand it. The one who teaches something which he has not received through love, that is, which is not grounded on this foundation, should not try to justify it as being above love. . . . That infant baptism is wrong the truth amply testifies, in that the first and most needful business for messengers of Jesus Christ is that they teach and make disciples for the Lord and seek the kingdom of God above all things. This we should do. Whoever baptizes someone before he is a disciple testifies by this that baptism is more essential than teaching and understanding, which is an abomination in the sight of God."

In the latter part of *Concerning True Love*, Denck takes up points which were evidently of lesser importance in his thinking but which he taught as an Anabaptist during this period—oaths and nonparticipation in government. "Oaths and vows are not within human power to keep," he insisted, and he based the prohibition on this idea, more than on the literal injunction of Jesus, "Swear not." "What a friend of God recognizes as right he should do, so far as is possible for him, even without an oath or solemn promise. . . . One will say, 'Does not God himself swear oaths?'. . . If we could be certain that we would be able to keep them, as he is, we could also swear oaths. It would be the same with killing, and with dominion over others [as in government], if we could do these things, like God, without revenge and self-seeking. But this is not the case." Thus, one is to respond with a simple yes or no, as Jesus indicated, and not utter empty oaths or take God's name in vain.

Government is recognized as ordained of God. However, "To use force and to rule is not allowed for any Christian who wants to boast in his Lord alone. The realm of our King is in the teaching and power of the Spirit. . . . This is not to say that force per se is wrong, within the center of the evil world, for it serves God in his wrath; but love teaches something better to all its children, namely, that they are by his grace to serve God. For it is the nature of love that it does not will or desire harm to anyone, but serves everyone for one's growth so far as this is possible. If government could treat everyone as its members would desire God to treat them, it could be truly Christian in its position. . . . Since the world would never tolerate this, however, a friend of God should not and cannot enter the ranks of government but rather should leave it. . . . Whoever loves the Lord . . . should never forget what befits a true lover, namely that he forego all force for the sake of the Lord and not oppose being subject to others [rulers] as to the Lord."

In the final appeal of this writing Denck says, "O, all of you who long for love, seek love while it may be found, for the Lord God offers it free of charge to all who long for it with all their hearts."

Difficulties in Active Mission

The uproar caused by Kautz and his Anabaptist supporters drew deep criticism. Even the moderate reformers in Worms were castigated. Although the influence of the Reformation continued there, it was officially renounced. The Brethren began to be cruelly repressed. It was no longer fruitful soil for a peace-loving Hans Denck. He wandered among congregations in South Germany, then in Switzerland. It was reported that in some areas he won many converts. On August 10, 1527, the Zurich council wrote letters of warning about him to Strasbourg and Worms. They called Denck an "arch-Anabaptist."

In August he went to Augsburg, where there was still a rather strong Anabaptist congregation. It was swelled by refugees from areas of severe persecution. Hans Hut had built up congregations in several of these areas, and many of the refugees held his chiliastic views. A number of wandering preachers were also converging on Augsburg. Hut, Denck, and others felt it would be good to have a conference to discuss matters on which they differed in emphasis. Hut desired also that some mission strategy should be agreed on in view of the imminent return of Christ (probably at Whitsuntide in 1528, he figured). Meetings began on August 20 and continued several days, with perhaps from fifty to sixty persons attending. Problems were discussed and mission assignments made.

This gathering has since been called the Martyrs' Synod, because Hut later referred to one of the meetings as a "council" and because so many of the principals were put to death for their faith soon afterward. It was not, however, a well-organized and official conference, where participants represented the various Brethren churches and made decisions for them. Besides inspirational services, there were long discussions of the differences of approach, especially perhaps between Hut and Denck, and harmonious decisions seem to have been reached. Hut's eschatology was not condemned, except where he tried to be too specific in details and dates; but he was asked not to preach on the subject except when requested to do so. As for mission assignments, teams from among those participating in these meetings were asked to work in various districts of South Germany, Austria, and Switzerland. Hans Denck, along with Gregor Maler and Hans Beck, was asked to "comfort and teach" Brethren congregations in the Zurich and Basel districts of Switzerland. However, after these meetings, Denck turned up in Nürnberg, where he aroused the antagonism of authorities, then later in Ulm. Finally he proceeded to Switzerland.

In late September or early October 1527 he arrived in Basel, disillusioned about his effectiveness as evangelist and minister, harried by opponents of the establishment, exhausted, broken in spirit and unwell. There he was admitted into the home of a friend who worked for the printer Cratander. After he had time to rest a bit, he penned a letter to Oecolampadius, the Basel reformer, asking for the latter's mediation in the securing of permission for residence.

"I have lived so much in exile," the poor refugee writes, "that I wish, God willing, I could have permanent and secure residence somewhere. With strangers this is not possible, for I am unable to do almost any kind of work. With friends and acquaintances, it is impossible because of their suspicion that I favor sects and create perverse dogmas. God is my witness that I desire the welfare of only one sect, which is the church of the saints, wherever it may be.... I do not deny that in questions of dogma I have erred at times and still may err.... I have expressed myself in such a manner that I should better have been silent.... Exile is hard, really difficult for me, but more difficult is the fact that results and fruitage do not correspond to my zeal. No other fruit do I desire, the Lord knows, except that as many people as possible—whether circumcised or baptized or neither—glorify the God and Father of our Lord Jesus Christ with one heart and mouth."

Oecolampadius accepted Denck's appeal, but the Basel reformer still seems to have wanted from him a formal statement about his beliefs and how they had changed. Denck obliged. Oecolampadius published this statement two years later under his own (inaccurate) title, *Hans Denck's Recantation*. The subtitle, *Protest and Confession*, comes nearer to describing the statement. It comprises about 2,400 words and represents that faith in which the mature Denck had lived and served, stated in as conciliatory a way as he could conscientiously make it. The statement reflects fatigue and disillusionment with an aggressive ministry. Denck returns as it were to his own quietistic approach, resting the great cause on this earth to an all-wise and loving heavenly Father. It treats of Scripture, the recompense of

Christ, faith, free will, good works, sects, ceremonies or rites, baptism, the Lord's Supper, and oaths.

Hans Denck's Last Words

"I am heartily willing to have every disgrace and shame, deserved or undeserved, fall upon me, provided only that God shall be honored thereby, for he is worthy of all honor and love," Denck begins his statement of faith. "However, when I began at first to love him, I fell into disfavor with many people.... As I increased in zeal for the Lord, people increased in their zeal opposing me.... I have been so strongly maligned and accused by certain ones ... that it is difficult, even for a man of tender and humble heart, to restrain himself.... I pen the present writing ... to answer that which is unjustly attributed to me and to confess wherein I have found myself lacking or in error.... It pains my heart that I should be in disunity with many persons, each of whom I must acknowledge as my brother, since he worships the same God I worship and honors the Father whom I honor, namely, that one who sent his Son as Savior into the world.... So far as it lies within me I would be reconciled with all my adversaries."

Regarding the Bible, he writes, "I prize holy Scripture above all human treasures, but not so highly as the Word of God which is living, mighty, and eternal, free of all elements of this world [such as paper, ink, human frailty]; since it is God himself, it is not letters of the alphabet, but Spirit, written without pen and paper so that it can never be destroyed.... Scripture cannot possibly make a bad heart better, although it may become more knowledgeable.... Holy Scripture therefore serves believers for good and unto salvation, unbelievers unto condemnation.... Therefore a person who is elected by God can be saved without preaching and Scripture. Not that preaching should not be heard or Scripture read, but to make clear that otherwise no unlearned people could be saved because they cannot read, and many whole cities and countries could be lost because they have no preachers."

On the recompense of Christ Denck writes: "The suffering

of Christ was adequate to make satisfaction for the sin of all people.... He who believes that Christ has redeemed him from sin cannot be a slave to sin." On faith, he says: "Faith is godly obedience and confidence in God's promises through Jesus Christ. Where this obedience is absent, the confidence is false and deceptive. Obedience must be righteous, that is, heart, mouth, and deed must go along with one another." On free will, he believes: "He who surrenders his will to God's will is truly free.... God compels no one who is not compelled by love to stay in his service; and the devil cannot force anyone who has once known the truth to stay in *his* service. Thus it is the same, whatever it is called, free or captive will.... The name itself is not worth quarreling about."

Denck says of "good works": "God will reward everyone according to his works, to the evil person eternal punishment according to his justice, to the good person eternal life according to his mercy. It is not that anyone has earned anything from God or that God owes anyone anything.... He looks upon faith and good works, delights in them and rewards them. These do not originate with us, rather we accept his grace.... Happy is that person who despises not the gifts of God."

Of divisions and sects, he testifies: "One should know that all areas of faith should be voluntary and uncoerced. Therefore I separate myself from certain individuals, not because I consider myself better and more just than they, but rather that it seems to me they have great shortcomings in such matters.... I seek to keep peace with everyone so far as it is possible for me. From others, persecution (and fear of the same) have separated me.... With such a conscience I await joyfully and unafraid the judgment of Jesus Christ, although, because of my faintheartedness, I fear men greatly."

Regarding ceremonies or rites, Denck comments: "Those who disregard them too much alienate the unlearned; those who esteem them too highly diminish the honor given to God.... He who energetically involves himself in ceremonies gains little; even if all ceremonies were lost, there would be no great harm. It would indeed be better to underemphasize them than to misuse them. . . .

On baptism, Denck now writes cautiously: "Baptism is registration into the fellowship of believers. . . . Infant baptism is not according to the command of Christ, for with children one cannot tell which is a Jacob and which an Esau. . . . Infant baptism is a man-made institution and available to Christians. No believer will suffer harm for having been baptized in infancy, and God asks about no other baptism so long as one holds to the order that is fitting for a Christian congregation. Otherwise, I do not know what God will do. Let him who baptizes anew take heed that he is not laboring before he is hired. He who is not called and sent out to teach undertakes in vain to baptize. For this reason I would, God willing, discontinue baptizing forever unless I have another call from the Lord. What I have done, that is done; what I shall do will be of no harm to anyone. Zeal for the Lord's house sent me out and has called me home again in my thinking. To do what is right in the house of God is always good, but not everyone is called to do the work of an ambassador among strangers."

The Lord's Supper should in fact be observed, Denck writes, but the spiritual significance, "a remembrance of the body and blood of the Lord," is what matters. "For as this bread sustains the body when broken and eaten," Christ indicated, "so shall my body through the power of God enliven your souls when it is given up, killed, and partaken of in a spiritual way—which means to know and believe."

On oaths Denck held a moderate view: "The Lord Christ says: you shall swear not at all. . . . One who has the mind and spirit of the Lord promises, vows, or swears nothing beyond that he can do with a good conscience, namely, that which he is obligated to do by the teachings of Christ."

Still residing in his friend's house, Hans Denck died of the plague in the middle of November 1527, aged about twenty-seven.

A brief writing of about three pages, attributed to Denck and entitled *Fundamental Articles*, was published as appendix to an edition of the *German Theology* in 1528. It lists basic theological points on the nature of God, perfection of

Christ, and the freedom of man to submit his will to that of God through the Holy Spirit.

A commentary on the prophet Micah, running in the original printing to over two hundred pages, has also been attributed to Denck. It appeared in 1532. The translated biblical text of the prophetic book might well be primarily the work of Denck, and much of the commentary reflects his spirit. Micah 4 begins: "In the latter days, the house of the Lord shall be established . . . the peoples shall flow to it. . . . No nation will draw the sword against another. . . . Everyone will sit under his vine and fig tree and no one shall frighten him." A subtitle reminds the reader of Denck's tolerance: "One should never cause another to suffer because of his faith." The conclusion of this same section is also a fitting conclusion to the story of Hans Denck: "Even in outward things . . . as the prophet says . . . among all peoples each should be able to walk in the name of its god. . . . No one should deprive any other of this freedom—be he heathen, Jew, or Christian. . . . In this manner, may we enjoy the gifts of God in peace."

• BALTHASAR HUBMAIER •

• BALTHASAR HUBMAIER •
Truth Is Immortal

Balthasar Hubmaier, outstanding reformer and Anabaptist leader of the early sixteenth century, attracts our sympathetic interest not only by his important achievements and strengths but by his failures and weaknesses as well. He did not consistently match with courage the fierce persecution that fell his lot; but he worked hard, dared much, suffered greatly to find and follow the truth as best he was able to discover it—and he sealed that faith finally with his blood. An honest and adventurous thinker for his day, practical-minded and determined, eloquent and creative, he must surely rank among the most modern in spirit of the great church reformers of the sixteenth century.

The fields of his evangelical activity were relatively small and sometimes remote from the centers of reform, the forces arrayed against him overwhelming, the time for bringing his program to fruition very brief. One marvels, not that he sometimes stumbled and fell, but that he could hold as persistently as he did to the search for right ways in the service of God and his people. Hubmaier was able to organize large numbers of people into new congregations, holding to New Testament patterns as he understood them.

Balthasar Hubmaier matriculated at the University of Freiburg in Breisgau, extreme southwestern Germany, on May 1, 1503. He must have been eighteen or nineteen years of age at the time. He had been born in a family of modest circumstances in Friedberg, Bavaria, six miles east of Augsburg. Intending tentatively to enter the priesthood, he probably secured a basic education in Friedberg, and then in the cathedral Latin school in Augsburg. So advanced was Balthasar in his studies that he received the bachelor of arts degree after his first year at the university. Continuing his work there, he considered entering the field of medicine but then remained, after all, in theology. His major professor was Dr. Johann Eck, soon to become the flaming defender of Catholic orthodoxy against the Lutheran reformation. Eck was evidently a year or two younger than his favored student, Balthasar.

Pressed by financial need, Balthasar withdrew from the university in 1507 and took a position as schoolteacher in Schaffhausen, just over the border in Switzerland. His time there was short, for "at the first favorable opportunity," Eck related later, "he returned to his accustomed studies, which were under my guidance." Balthasar further mastered Latin, studied Greek, and Hebrew, and was ordained. Then he served on occasion as priest and popular preacher while in Freiburg. One of his fellow students—and lecturer for a time—was his later persecutor, Johann Faber. Eck moved to the University of Ingolstadt in 1510, and Hubmaier succeeded him as rector at the University of Freiburg. In the following year Balthasar was honored when the university bestowed upon him the *baccalaureus biblicus*. One event which took place during his Freiburg years was his leadership of a disputation on the question as to whether the number of church festivals might be increased. Hubmaier took the negative side in this debate.

A year and a half after the departure of Eck for Ingolstadt, forty-five miles northeast of Hubmaier's birthplace, Hubmaier followed him there. In Ingolstadt the latter received, after six months of further work, a doctorate in theology. He was immediately made a professor in the same field at the university and a preacher in the city's largest church. Soon he became prorector, the chief executive officer of the university, but he served in that capacity for less than one full session, 1515-16. Ambitious, no doubt, for advancement in other ways as well as academically, and conscious of his abilities as a popular speaker and leader, he found himself unable to pass up an opportunity to become cathedral preacher in the nearby city of Regensburg. He moved there in January 1516.

Prominent Priest, Preacher, and Leader

A bitter campaign was raging against the Jews in Regensburg, and the cathedral preacher was expected to take the lead in it. Hubmaier accepted the role with enthusiasm. The general economy of Regensburg was steadily declining; but the Jews there, manifesting solidarity and initiative, continued to prosper. They lent money to less fortunate citizens at high rates of interest. Church law considered even moderate interest as usury and generally forbade it; Hubmaier also held to this principle, even in later years. He preached vehemently against the Jews. Receiving interest on loans was simply not regarded as a valid business to be engaged in. Hubmaier later characterized it as a "godless and shameful way of living."

What was happening to the Jews in Regensburg had occurred earlier in many large cities of Germany. In the end they were generally driven out, their homes and businesses destroyed; but in Regensburg they managed to survive. They were important to the overall economy and had powerful support, especially in the imperial house. The Jews in Regensburg enjoyed the direct protection of the emperor. Their ghetto was separately administered. Earlier, an emperor had ordered citizens of Regensburg to pay fair interest to Jewish lenders, and priests who had unjustly opposed the Jews were ordered punished. The emperor at the time, Maximilian I, continued this policy; his representative in Regensburg threatened Hubmaier for preaching against Jews. Before an imperial commission, he defended himself as best he could by splitting hairs: he had not preached against usury, he said, but against Christian judges trying usury cases.

The Regensburg city council sent its mayor, accompanied

by Hubmaier, to the imperial diet in Augsburg in early July 1518 to present Regensburg's position on the Jewish question. The issue was considered to be of such importance that the emperor himself was there to hear the arguments. After about three weeks the mayor wrote home that the cathedral preacher had defended himself in an impressive way before the imperial court against the charge of the Jews that he had stirred up the city against them. This appearance of Hubmaier before the emperor furnished material for folk songs that were later sung in the streets of Regensburg. It was finally decided that the cathedral preacher should be allowed to remain in his position if he would promise to respect privileges guaranteed by the emperor to the Jews. He made the promise, but then resumed anti-Jewish activities upon return to Regensburg.

Within six months after the hearing in Augsburg the emperor Maximilian was dead, and the interregnum that followed affected greatly the situation in Regensburg. The Jews now had little recourse in high places. On February 21 the synagogue in Regensburg was demolished, the ghetto ravished and the entire Jewish population driven from the city. In the tearing down of the synagogue a master stonemason was injured, fatally, it appeared. A few hours later he revived, and the people said it was a miracle of the virgin Mary—manifesting her glory in the very place where she had been dishonored by the Jews. On the site of the demolished synagogue a Catholic chapel was erected and, at Hubmaier's suggestion, named Beauteous Mary *(zur schönen Maria)*. Hubmaier was appointed priest of the chapel and he preached there. Various miracles were soon reported at the images of Mary in the chapel and outside, and he used these events as topics for sermons.

People came from far and wide seeking some miracle or to hear the sermons. The Beauteous Mary became the focal point of a pilgrimage movement, and a larger and more elaborate chapel was built. A papal bull of June 1, 1519, declared a hundred days remission of punishment in purgatory for penitents who visited the shrine on certain holidays. The influx of pilgrims, sometimes several thousand on a single day, brought new prosperity to the economically troubled city. The episcopal administrator in Regensburg competed with the city council as to which side should profit most from the windfall income. Handling unruly crowds at the shrine was itself no easy task with, as Hubmaier himself described it, "a huge throng of men and women dancing and screaming like cattle."

As chapel priest, Hubmaier tried to exercise some restraint in judging which of the miracle claims were genuine, but he became unhappy with this business and the disputes about income. He began to seek another place of service. He urgently requested the city council to transfer to him the benefice of a church in an area where a priest was retiring, but this came to nothing. Plague was spreading in the district and Hubmaier desired even more earnestly to leave. He learned of an opportunity in the town of Waldshut on the Rhine at the Swiss border, where a brother of his friend Faber was living, and decided to try that. Upon his departure from Regensburg he received a cordial send-off by the episcopal administrator and the city council; the latter provided a letter of recommendation and a generous going-away gift of forty guilders.

Seeking, Far and Wide, for Right Ways

Waldshut, a border town of Hapsburg hereditary lands under Austrian administration, had imperially-guaranteed rights and privileges, although it claimed only about a thousand inhabitants. It lay in the diocese of Constance, where Hubmaier had been ordained years before as a priest, and comprised two parishes. Hubmaier went as chief priest in the church of the upper parish, which was larger; it boasted a staff of five clergymen. Priests were chosen by the people and the city council, and supported by the Königsfelden cloister, which was itself under the patronage and authority of the council of state in Bern, Switzerland. Hubmaier had enjoyed status as an outstanding preacher, and he surely took a large cut in salary by coming to Waldshut, but soon he was asking for a larger allowance. Bern opposed this, but since the bishop supported Hubmaier in his claim, Bern authorities gave in for the sake of peace and urged the Königsfelden nuns to grant the higher remuneration—only for this one priest, not for the others in Waldshut.

For about two years, 1521-22, Hubmaier served as a model priest in Waldshut. He celebrated mass, preached effectively, presided in ceremonies and processions, even introduced new celebrations. As always, he sought to work in harmony with state and church authority. During holy week and Easter he had two members of the council assist him at the altar. People of the town were proud of their able and eminent priest. Hubmaier himself, accustomed to bustling cities and momentous activities, had trouble adjusting to the quiet routine of small-town life. In a letter to a friend he complained of his lonely existence, which he compared to life "in a barrel." He began to cultivate contacts with learned persons and religious leaders beyond the narrow confines of his parish.

He corresponded with city physician and humanist Johann Adelphi in Schaffhausen, Switzerland (only twenty-seven miles from Waldshut), also with Christian humanists Beatus Rhenanus and Johannes Sapidus, and later the reform-inclined pastor-lecturer Johannes Oecolampadius in Basel, Switzerland, also in the general vicinity. One of Hubmaier's closest friends in this correspondence was Wolfgang Rychard, city physician of Ulm in Germany, an outstanding humanist who was very much interested in church reform and inclined toward Lutheranism. With some of these Hubmaier exchanged books, also news about literary and ecclesiastical developments. Hubmaier's thoughts and concerns ranged widely, but he continued the faithful performance of his duties as priest in Waldshut.

Reformation efforts in Zurich, about thirty miles to the southeast in Switzerland—as well as those in Basel and Schaffhausen—interested him tremendously. He had contact with humanists Desiderius Erasmus and Heinrich Glarean, and educator Konrad Pelikan, as well as Oecolampadius and Rhenanus in Basel. He visited the German cities of Freiburg, which he found still "captive" to outmoded ways in church life, and Ulm, more open to new ideas as exemplified in the liberal and Lutheran views of his friend Rychard. Hubmaier, in the spirit of humanistic openness to truth, began a study of the Corinthian letters in the Bible— then Romans, which had been so influential in Martin Luther's pilgrimage toward evangelical faith.

After a visit with Rychard in Ulm in November 1522, Hubmaier proceeded to Regensburg, the scene of his earlier labors as a popular leader and preacher. He received a cordial welcome from council members and church personalities there. The dispute about income from the chapel had been resolved, but pilgrimages to the shrine had diminished. The Regensburg people, at the beginning of December, urged Hubmaier to become chaplain again at Beauteous Mary. Surely he could revive interest, and income, at the place. Although his departure from Regensburg two years before seems to have been more in the form of a leave of absence, the thought of returning on a permanent basis does not appear to have been in his mind when he came on this visit. His thinking had begun to take new directions. He was still quite uncertain, however, just where it should all lead.

In mental conflict about these questions, he finally decided to accept the renewed appointment in Regensburg, for one year. The contract was signed on December 22. Hubmaier promised to preach at the chapel, organize processions, examine and publicize miracles occurring there, and do "whatever might be considered good and necessary for the maintenance and increase of the pilgrimage movement." His salary was fixed at fifty guilders a year, plus small extra allowances for weekday services conducted. He did not resign in Waldshut, and thus retained a way of retreat for himself in the event things did not work out in Regensburg.

Hubmaier entered energetically into the various aspects of his renewed ministry there, but his primary interest was in preaching. He began a series of sermons from the Gospel of Luke. To his friend Rychard in Ulm he wrote, "Among us in Bavaria the gospel is also being preached." This approach was not sufficiently satisfying to Hubmaier, however; the strain on his conscience was too great. He felt uncomfortable in dealing with alleged miracles and publicizing them. Within a few weeks of taking up the work again in Regensburg, he experienced what might fairly be called his most basic conversion. He became an evangelical. He had been meeting quietly with a group of Lutherans in the city, and the spiritual experience took place in that fellowship.

Still, he intended to stay the year for which he had contracted, putting greater effort into his pulpit ministry. Yet it was not to be. Hubmaier seemed by nature to be a person who would seek doggedly for the truth, according to the light available to him at the time. Once he found the way which seemed right, he felt impelled to give his all to it. He left Regensburg on March 1, 1523. Although precipitant, this move was made in full agreement with the city council, who presented the departing preacher with a cash gift (even after such a brief period of service) of fifteen guilders.

Identifying with Swiss Reform

Hubmaier settled again in Waldshut, where he felt sure he would have a better chance than in Regensburg of giving expression to his new convictions. His views were not entirely Lutheran; although his spiritual awakening had come during his sojourn among Lutherans, he always denied being one himself. He probably did not greatly value, even at this early period in his evangelical development, Luther's doctrines of the real presence of the body and blood of Christ in the Eucharist and the complete bondage of the human will because of original sin. Hubmaier still had many questions in his mind, but on one thing he was firm: his theology, when worked out, must come from the Bible.

He looked with admiration and great expectation to centers of reform in Switzerland, especially Zurich. Zwingli had led in its first public disputation on the issues in January, just about the time Hubmaier was undergoing a fundamental personal change of commitment in Regensburg. Following the disputation the new direction of reform was adopted officially in the city and canton of

Zurich. The Waldshut pastor was attracted more and more to Zwingli's approach—gradual change, with the cooperation of the civil authorities, emphasizing Bible preaching. Leading pastors in several other Swiss areas were taking the same approach.

Almost immediately after his return to Waldshut, Hubmaier set about preaching against abuses in the Catholic Church. His bishop in Constance, months later, entered a formal complaint against him for a holy day sermon of April 19, 1523, in which he was said to have slandered the priesthood by calling priests soul murderers and priests of Satan who preached falsehoods, dreams of monks, and of the Fathers of the church—and who withheld the gospel from the people.

Hubmaier took the initiative in establishing closer connections with reformers in Switzerland. He preached on two different trips in Appenzell. With a colleague who was prior of a nearby monastery, he made a trip on horseback to St. Gall, in northeastern Switzerland. The two men were impressed by the leadership there of Joachim von Watt, known as Vadian, formerly professor at the University of Vienna. He was an outstanding scholar, physician, mayor-to-be, civic and church leader. During the three days in St. Gall Hubmaier preached in church and out on a hill in the open air. The people were so pleased with what they heard that a large number gathered in and around the house in which he was staying, and he led them in a Bible study on the book of Galatians.

Hubmaier's main purpose for the trip was to meet with Zwingli in Zurich. He had been influenced already by the latter's *Sixty-Seven Articles,* which had served as basis for discussion at the public disputation three months earlier. The two men spoke several times about church reform, baptism in particular, and other questions. They agreed that the New Testament gave no real support for the practice of infant baptism and Zwingli said, Hubmaier reported later, that children should not be baptized until they had been instructed in the faith. Zwingli admitted in one of his later writings that he had held for a time "the error that it was advisable to wait in baptizing children until they should come to a good age." Other reformers were, at about the same time, questioning the validity of infant baptism. These included Luther, Carlstadt, Oecolampadius, Wolfgang Capito and Martin Bucer in Strasbourg—but almost all of them held to it in the end.

Zwingli's preaching against images in the church and popular agitation against such things led to the calling of a second public disputation October 26-28, 1523, and Hubmaier attended. The discussion dealt with images and the mass. The chairmen were Dr. Sebastian Hofmeister of Schaffhausen, Vadian, and another person from St. Gall. Ludwig Haetzer, as a young Swiss cleric and not yet the controversial figure he later would become, took part and wrote up the official report of the disputation. Hubmaier, as one of the ten academic doctors present, occupied an honored seat beside Zwingli. The latter, along with his associate in Zurich, Leo Jud, were principal speakers. In the course of his own comments Hubmaier referred to these others as his "dear brothers in Christ." As for his own standing there, the Zurich council later adopted a resolution for Hubmaier certifying that "our special good friend the worthy and learned Dr. Balthasar Friedberger" (Hubmaier) was highly honored in Zurich. While there, Hubmaier preached in churches of the city, with acceptance and appreciation as usual.

At the disputation, he spoke five times. On both the subjects under consideration his opinions corresponded with those of Zwingli and most other participants. "In all disputes concerning faith and religion," he said, "Scripture alone, proceeding from the mouth of God, ought to be our level and rule. . . . Scripture is the sole light and true lantern by whose illumination all fictions of the human mind may be discovered and all darkness dispelled." To support this approach he quoted both from the Old Testament and the New. "Wherefore," he continued, "those errors too that have sprung up concerning images and the mass should be examined and corrected by the sole rule of the Word of God." In another speech he said, "It is blasphemy if we teach that images call, move, and draw our souls to piety. For it is

Christ who calls the sinner, who moves him to what is good, and invites him to the heavenly marriage feast. God the Father draws those who come to Christ."

Regarding the other main topic of discussion Hubmaier declared, "Although there are still several abuses left in the mass (which I prefer to call Christ's testament, or the memorial of his death) . . . the chief cause of all these is that we celebrate mass as a sacrifice. . . . I cannot proclaim it in any other way than Zwingli and Leo [Jud] have by saying the mass is no sacrifice but rather a publishing of Christ's testament, in which is celebrated the memorial of his death through which he surely offered himself once for all on the altar of the cross and cannot be offered again."

He presented numerous Scripture references to support this view, then said in regard to the language of the ordinance, "The mass should be read in Latin to the Latins, in French to the French and in German to the Germans. There can be no doubt that Christ used a language at the Supper with his disciples that could be understood by all of them. . . . It is ridiculous to recite Latin words to a German who knows nothing of the Latin language. What else is this than to hide the Lord whom we ought to proclaim? He who undertakes to celebrate mass truly ought to feed not only himself but also others hungering and thirsting in spirit, and that under both kinds," that is, both bread and wine.

There were two participants at least in the discussions who were prepared to go further than a theoretical disposition of the questions under consideration—layman Conrad Grebel, later to become the Anabaptists' first leader, and Simon Stumpf, a pastor in the canton of Zurich. They wanted some specific action taken, but were overruled. The city council forbade removal of images at this time, or a change in the mass. At Zwingli's suggestion, they did add an admonition that pastors should preach the Word of God clearly.

Threats from High Places Fail to Intimidate

As Hubmaier attempted to introduce Reformation ideas and practices in Waldshut, he met tremendous opposition from imperial and Austrian authorities. This was all the more true since these ideas seemed to come primarily from church leaders in Switzerland. The ruling house of Hapsburg was represented at this time in Austrian-controlled lands by Archduke Ferdinand, younger brother of the Holy Roman Emperor Charles V. Ferdinand resided in Innsbruck. The Hapsburgs were uncompromising Catholics and they bitterly opposed the reformers. They resented Switzerland, which had long before wrested its independent autonomy from the Hapsburgs. In 1468 Bern had tried to annex Waldshut to its canton and to the Swiss confederation. Waldshut had defended itself successfully, thus retaining an honorable place in Hapsburg realms. There were suspicions that, at the least provocation, Switzerland would still have designs on Waldshut.

Hubmaier became, in the eyes of Austrian rulers, a marked man. Just over a month after the disputation in Zurich, a government delegation from Ensisheim, in whose district Waldshut lay, appeared in Waldshut. It charged Hubmaier with violation of an imperial mandate against anyone joining the "Lutheran sect," with falsely expounding Scripture, and with having presented himself at the Zurich disputation as the representative of three Hapsburg cities of the area, in addition to Waldshut. The delegation demanded that Hubmaier be handed over to the bishop of Constance for trial on these charges.

The Waldshut council, comprised of the mayor and eight members, rejected the demand and denied as false all charges against their pastor. Ensisheim officials gave Waldshut fourteen days to meet their demand.

The council did not wait that long. Within a week they wrote to authorities in Ensisheim formally rejecting the charges and declaring unreserved support for their pastor. He had in no way violated imperial mandates, they wrote, and certainly had not claimed at the disputation in Zurich to represent any towns other than Waldshut.

The Ensisheim delegation then reported to Archduke Ferdinand, recommending the arrest and punishment of Hubmaier along with his close supporters. Even before he received this report, the archduke, who was behind the action against Hubmaier, had proposed to the Austrian government that this "Lutheran heretic" be arrested by forces from outside the town and delivered to the bishop of Constance. Austrian officials accused Waldshut of trying to merge with the Swiss confederation. Waldshut stood firm, denying all charges. Their pastor was loyal to the government, they said, and he had often preached in a "beautiful and thorough" way about obedience to civil authorities. His only "crime," they said, was that he preached God's Word in a pure and clear manner. They added that he was so highly regarded by the people as a spiritual leader that there would be great danger of dissension and uproar if he should be taken from the town by force.

The controversy between Waldshut and the Austrian government continued. It might seem like a struggle between an ant and an elephant, except that the Hapsburg superpower found itself rather powerless at the time. Available imperial forces were embroiled in a war against France and its Swiss mercenaries in Italy. Little Waldshut took full advantage of this situation, and church reform under Hubmaier's leadership advanced unabated. Defying Catholic tradition concerning fasts, the pastor and the mayor, along with others, ate meat during the New Year's festival at the beginning of 1524. Hubmaier had been preaching vigorously against obligatory fasts, images, mass, interest, and church taxes. Images gradually disappeared from the church, and other changes were introduced.

At this point Hubmaier received a call from Regensburg to return no later than April 4 to take up duties at the Beauteous Mary Chapel again. He still retained this benefice. Toward the end of March he wrote, making known his evangelical views and revealing his profound desire to preach the pure gospel in Regensburg. He gave serious consideration to the opportunity but declined it in the end and gave up the benefice. In his letter he took the occasion, however, to testify to his present faith and apologize for earlier shortcomings.

"I hear with great sadness," he wrote, "how in your city of

Regensburg more men preach vanity than the pure Word of God. That makes my heart ache; for, under God, what does not flow from the living Word is dead. Therefore, says Christ, search the Scriptures. He does not say to follow the old customs—although I did nothing else when I was with you the first time. However, I did it in ignorance. Like others, I was blinded and possessed by the doctrine of men. Therefore I openly confess before God and all men that I then became a doctor and preached some years among you and elsewhere and yet had not known the way to eternal life. Within two years Christ has for the first time come into my heart to thrive. I have never dared to preach him so strongly as now, by the grace of God. I lament before God that I lay ill so long of this sickness. I truly pray him for pardon."

The latter part of the writing makes a straightforward evangelical appeal: "Yield yourselves to God, trust him, build on his Word, and he will not forsake you. Whether he gives a short life or a long one, you will have eternal life beyond. And should people call you heretics, be joyful, for your reward will be great in heaven." The letter closes with a long list of cities and districts in Germany and northern Switzerland which had, like "heretic" Hubmaier and "foolish" Waldshut, espoused evangelical teaching.

Reform in Waldshut Given a Manifesto

Hubmaier's first published writing, *The Eighteen Articles*, 860 words in length, defined what he felt reformation should mean in Waldshut. It was circulated widely and came out in four editions during 1524. Prepared in the first place for discussions with the clergy of the town, and for a public disputation, it stresses authority of the Bible and salvation by faith that shows itself in Christian works. Mass should be celebrated in the language of the people, the document affirms, and it is not a repetition of the sacrifice of Christ but a remembrance. Catholic practices regarded as abuses or worse are openly condemned. "Faith alone makes us right before God," the first article asserts, and the second explains that this faith is an "acknowledgment of the grace of God which he has showed us in giving his only begotten Son. This excludes all nominal Christians who have nothing but a historical faith in God." Further articles develop this same idea: "Such faith cannot remain dormant but must reach out to God in thanksgiving and to people in all kinds of works of brotherly love. Thereby all works of pretense are cast down such as the burning of candles, use of palms and holy water.... Images are good for nothing."

There seems to be a foregleam of the future Anabaptist in the first part of the eighth article: "Just as every Christian believes and is baptized for himself, so should each one judge from Scripture whether he is being properly nourished by his pastor." Christ alone is to be called upon as the only intercessor and mediator; "thereby, all pilgrimages fall away." Services are to be in the language of the people of each country. "Here vanish matins, primes, terces, sexts, nones, vespers, complines, and vigils.... Church members are responsible to support and take care of those who clearly preach to them the pure Word of God.... Whoever seeks purgatory ... looks for the grave of Moses—it shall never be found.... To forbid priests to marry while overlooking their carnal lewdness is to release Barabbas and put Christ to death. To promise chastity in the strength of man is nothing else than to promise to fly over the ocean without wings."

The last two articles assert, "Whoever for worldly advantage denies or remains silent concerning the Word of God sells God's blessing as Esau sold his birthright and will also be denied by Christ, and whoever does not earn his bread by the sweat of his brow is condemned and unworthy of the food he eats. Herewith are all idlers accursed, whoever they may be." The statement closes with the motto which Hubmaier was to use at the end, and sometimes also at the beginning, of future publications: *Die warheyt ist untödlich:* truth is immortal, or unkillable—truth cannot be killed (as "heretics" can).

The season of Pentecost, or Whitsuntide, in mid-May 1524, proved to be a decisive time for reform in Waldshut. Hubmaier had meetings with the clergy of the town; eight or nine of the twelve disagreed with his principles and his program and were obliged to leave Waldshut. On Corpus

Christi Day, Bible texts were read in German during the procession, and the sacrament of the Supper was simplified. Among the populace, lines were strictly drawn. At a public meeting someone suggested that, for the sake of peace, Hubmaier be given over to the Austrians as Archduke Ferdinand was demanding. Many others opposed this vociferously. Two hundred citizens took a vow "in spite of everyone and in all justice to keep the doctor [Hubmaier] with them." Women of the community, some of them armed, are reported to have marched at this time to the council hall in support of their pastor, demanding assurances that he would be permitted to remain; and their demands were satisfied.

In mid-June, Hubmaier was called again to Regensburg! This time it was not to Beauteous Mary, but to a church in the city whose benefice, according to arrangements made years before, he had a right to; the pastor there had just died. The city council was now inviting Hubmaier to take up duties in this parish by July 25. The council, overwhelmingly Catholic, would certainly have known by now of his reformed position—from his own letter to them of more than two months earlier, if not otherwise—but the member who conducted this correspondence in the summer of 1524 was the one on the council who was strongly evangelical. Other members who joined in the invitation to Hubmaier were probably encouraged by the pastor's strength in standing up to the Hapsburgs and hopeful he could help gain more independence for Regensburg. Hubmaier was tempted by the offer, but he finally resigned all claims in the larger city. He would stay with Waldshut.

In mid-July the Austrian government in Innsbruck advised a military attack on the town to enforce orders that Hubmaier be expelled or delivered to Constance for ecclesiastical trial; at the same time they expressed fear that such an attack on Waldshut might possibly cause the Swiss to intervene on its side. On August 3 Archduke Ferdinand ordered the government in Ensisheim to proceed with force against the disobedient town. Still uncertain about Switzerland, the district government sent imperial secretary Veit

Suter to a conference of the Swiss confederation in Baden. He was assured there that Swiss authorities would forbid their people to support Waldshut; most Swiss cantons were still strongly Catholic. However, representatives of Zurich, Schaffhausen, and one or two other cantons were said to be in secret consultation on the question of whether Waldshut might be admitted to the confederation.

Waldshut Seeks Allies and Hubmaier a Refuge

Besides the relationship with Switzerland, another development came to be regarded as vital for the survival of Waldshut in its independent course—the peasant uprising in southern Germany. On June 23 peasants in the territory of Stühlingen, northeast of Waldshut, rebelled against their ruler, Count von Lupfen. In the early negotiations between ruler and peasants, there were representatives from the Black Forest and four Rhine towns, including Waldshut. The peasant movement was directed against servile treatment and social injustices imposed by unscrupulous rulers. For their own reasons a few nobles and others allied themselves with the peasants, who cited evangelical teachings in support of their claims to minimal rights and decent conditions of life.

After intermittent negotiations, Count von Lupfen and his rebellious peasants reached an agreement on July 24 for an armistice lasting a month. The discussions were held in Tiengen, just east of Waldshut, and after these were concluded six hundred Stühlingen peasants entered Waldshut and remained three days, according to official reports. This was obviously done with the consent of the Waldshut council. The insurgent peasants made a flag for themselves and chose a strong leader, Hans Müller von Bulgenbach. By the time the armistice ran out, both sides felt ready for war. Waldshut had been seriously threatened with attack since the beginning of August, and the reason it had not taken place was that Austria and the ruling nobility did not have funds available for the campaign.

Hubmaier felt, with considerable justification, that he himself was the only real cause for Austrian hostility against Waldshut. To make matters worse, the rulers were looking upon him as a ringleader of the peasants' revolt. He regarded peasant demands as being just—the abolition of forced labor and of oppressive tithes and taxes, freedom to hunt, fish and take fuel from the forests, the right to choose their own pastors. He could also affirm their willingness that all demands be tested by the Word of God. Hubmaier had indeed preached to the peasants while they were camped in and around Waldshut and had counseled with their leaders about the wording of documents and proclamations. He did not wish, however, to become embroiled in purely political and socioeconomic struggles. He wanted, primarily, to free Waldshut from the threat of destruction or serious losses, if this could be done without sacrifice of the truth as he had come to understand it. He decided, therefore, to leave Waldshut, for a time at least, and departed for Schaffhausen on August 29.

After Hubmaier left, and apparently with no counsel from him, Waldshut's alliance with the Stühlingen peasants reached its climax. The two sides concluded a treaty of mutual assistance. For Waldshut there simply seemed to be no other way of survival. Armed peasants, in a show of solidarity, entered Waldshut more than eight hundred strong. This alliance lasted apparently only a few days, when the peasants, feeling it was essential for them to come to terms with their lords at this time, concluded a treaty with them on September 10, and the cooperation with Waldshut came to an end.

On the occasion of Hubmaier's absence those who had been dissatisfied with the reform reasserted their views and seemed for a period of two or three weeks to have secured control. The priests who had left in May returned two months after that, and they were most likely part of this reaction, as was the former mayor who had previously supported Hubmaier. Evangelicals soon regained the upper hand. Meanwhile, the pressures from outside had not lessened. Austria had demanded not just that Hubmaier leave but that he be handed over for punishment and that the town restore the old order entirely in its churches. The archduke called again upon his territorial rulers to bring Waldshut to heel by armed force. This was more easily said than done, since these rulers had their hands full with the peasants. They saw this latter problem as separate from the Waldshut issue, even though Ferdinand and the Austrian authorities did not.

Schaffhausen officials would certainly have preferred that the controversial pastor Hubmaier had chosen some other place of refuge, but they felt not the least inclination to turn him over to the bloodthirsty Austrians. Imperial secretary Veit Suter met with representatives from Catholic cantons in Baden two days after the fugitive's arrival in the northern Swiss town and extracted a commitment that they would "bring Hubmaier down." They in turn pressed leaders in other parts of Switzerland and South Germany to help secure the arrest of the heretic. The four "forest cantons" of Switzerland, strongly Catholic, joined in a letter to Schaffhausen urging that Hubmaier be imprisoned. The council of the little city then informed other cantons that the doctor from Waldshut had disappeared "into freedom." This evidently referred to the fact that he had taken up residence in a priory, which was ordinarily regarded as sanctuary where a fugitive might be immune from arrest. This was simply their excuse; the real reason Schaffhausen authorities did not arrest Hubmaier was that they did not wish to do so.

Schaffhausen followed a middle course in regard to the Reformation, which would not be formally adopted until 1529. During Hubmaier's time there, councilors gave partial support to reform as it was being promoted in Zurich, but priests continued mass and the seven daily offices. Some traditional church ceremonies had been suspended. The larger council favored reform, but the smaller council (which was generally the one to give ecclesiastical directives) held mostly to the old faith. This necessitated compromise. Placing all hope in almighty God and his Son was essential, the Schaffhausen councilors wrote in a letter to the confederation. Over and beyond that, each person should be allowed to believe as he thought best to secure the salvation of his soul. The result was that Schaffhausen probably showed as much or more tolerance in matters of faith during this period than did any other canton of Switzerland. To be sure, the confederation conference—without the support of Zurich, Basel, and Appenzell—had the Schaffhausen council closely guard Hubmaier to be sure he did not escape.

Petitions to Schaffhausen and a Polemic to Eck

A day or two after his arrival in the northern Swiss city, Hubmaier addressed a petition to the city council asking for protection against any violent action his enemies might seek to perpetrate against him. When he did not receive a reply immediately, he wrote the council another, then a third. These were later published as *An Earnest Christian Petition*. With a preface, it comprises about 2,765 words. Following the title and byline came the already familiar "Truth is immortal" motto and the date, 1524.

In the first petition Hubmaier mentions having heard that he was to be arrested. He knows of no reason why he should be, although he has tried to find out. He professes his willingness "to appear before your honors to give and receive justice and rights and to abide by the same through weal and woe." He continues, "In the meantime I shall not remove person or property and I shall do everything that is right in such a matter. May your honors, however, be so gracious to me as to do me no violence or allow me to be arrested until there has been a fair and legal trial." Anticipating possible outcomes, Hubmaier declares, "If I am found to be in the right, just let me have the satisfaction of being acquitted; if it is discovered that I am guilty, I should be punished in person and property according to the severity of the offense."

In the second petition Hubmaier suggests that a disputation be arranged between him and opposing pastors and priests from various parts of Switzerland, including those strongly Catholic. The points at issue would be discussed on the basis of "holy Scripture and divine truth." Again he offers, "If I am wrong, I should be punished. But if the above-mentioned pastors lose the argument I now request for God's sake that they might be induced to acknowledge their error, then dismissed without punishment." Recognizing the difficult position of Schaffhausen, Hubmaier says, "The hardest thing of all for me is that your honors should be involved with me in this matter. A closer look would show, however, that it is not my affair, but God's. He has brought it about in this way; to him in heaven be praise. Let your honors have no fear for me; neither shall I myself fear, for divine truth is immortal and although it may for a time be imprisoned, scourged, crowned with thorns, crucified, and laid in the grave, it will arise victorious on the third day to reign in triumph throughout all eternity."

In the third and most lengthy of the petitions Hubmaier gives extensive biblically based arguments why he should receive a fair hearing and then continues: "I am often called a disturber of the people, one who stirs up strife, a Lutheran, a heretic and similar calumnies. Because of my teaching the pious, honorable city of Waldshut is terribly slandered—this especially pains my heart."

Hubmaier repeats, "I am ready and willing to give to everyone an account of my teaching, my faith and my hope which I have preached these two years past. If I have taught truth alone, why am I, and others because of me, abused? If I have erred and taught falsehood, I call and cry out to all Christian believers that they testify about this evil and point me with God's Word to the right way again. . . . I can err, for I am only a human being but a heretic I cannot be, because I ask for instruction." The threatened pastor continues, "Should this serious and heartfelt petition of mine find no acceptance ... and I should be forced rather to endure prison, suffering, sword, fire or water ... in an attempt to force me to speak or testify other than I am now minded in the illumination of God, I hereby protest and testify before my heavenly Father and before all people that I intend to suffer and die as a Christian."

It was not at all sure that little Schaffhausen, in protecting Hubmaier, would be able to hold out against Catholic cantonal governments and Austrian authorities. In this perilous situation, the beleagured pastor was still able to do some writing. His former professor and benefactor, Johann

Eck, was now perhaps Germany's leading theological defender of popes and ecclesiastical custom. He had written bitter denunciations of reformers in Germany and Switzerland and once or twice the name of Hubmaier appears in his attacks. The latter now joined Zwingli in answers to Eck. During his first two weeks in Schaffhausen he wrote *Theses Against Eck* or *Axiomata*—twenty-six articles, about 750 words in all. It was published both in the original Latin and in German translation. The byline on the title page describes the writer as "pastor in Waldshut, a brother [in Christ] of Ulrich Zwingli."

Hubmaier refers to Romans 10:10: " 'With the heart one truly believes unto righteousness, but with the mouth confession is made unto eternal salvation.' If you will not believe, you will not understand. . . . Search the Scripture, not papal laws, not councils, not church fathers, not schoolmen—unless they speak as Christ spoke. For although these talk, Christ has spoken already and he will judge all things. . . . The dark places of Scripture should be explained by those that are clearer. . . . Obedience is without doubt the church's due in such matters as quarrels or brotherly love, but matters of faith must be judged by Scripture alone." Hubmaier sent the *Axiomata* to Eck, along with his challenge to a disputation—which was ignored—and forwarded a copy to Zwingli for his approval before publication; the latter was pleased with it.

Striking a Blow for Toleration

Adelphi was no longer in Schaffhausen, but a new friend of Hubmaier's there was the city's leading pastor and reformer, Dr. Sebastian Hofmeister, who also published a polemic against Eck, using harsher language than Hubmaier had. Zwingli appreciated all this support from Schaffhausen. Eck had ridiculed Hubmaier for calling himself a "brother in Christ of Ulrich Zwingli." Hofmeister counters, in his writing, "Balthasar is not at all ashamed to be a brother of Zwingli's, of mine and of others who stand up for the divine Word and hold to it. We would like to keep him in our brotherhood."

The most important writing of Hubmaier's from the period of his Schaffhausen exile, especially for the cause of religious tolerance, was a thirty-six-article document of about 1,200 words, *Concerning Heretics and Those Who Burn Them*. It was addressed to "Brother Antony" Pirata, provincial vicar of the Dominican order in Constance. Pirata zealously defended Catholic tradition and called evangelicals heretics. In the middle of the writing Hubmaier refers to Antony and his order: "So unholy and so very far off from evangelical doctrine is the entire order of preaching friars, those two-colored birds [referring to the black and white robes of Dominicans] of which our Antony is one, that up to now the heresy hunters have all come from [this order]."

Hubmaier begins, in this writing, by giving his own definition of the group under discussion: "Heretics are those who wickedly oppose holy Scripture . . . and those who cast a veil over Scripture and interpret it in a different way from that which the Holy Spirit requires." As for the proper treatment of real heretics, the writer continues, "Those who are such should be overcome with holy knowledge, not in a quarrelsome way but quietly—although holy Scripture does contain wrath. This scriptural wrath is really a spiritual fire and loving zeal—not burning [at the stake], contrary to the Word of God. If heretics will not respond positively to carefully presented truths or evangelical reasoning, leave them alone and let them continue to bluster and rage." Amid many scriptural quotations Hubmaier drives home his point: "Heresy hunters are the greatest heretics of all when they, against the teaching and example of Christ, condemn heretics to the fire. . . . They are not excused when they babble that they are giving over the ungodly to the secular authorities [for punishment]; whoever gives them over in such a way sins even more greatly than they (John 19)."

The writer does not oppose use of the sword by authorities to punish the lawless. "The secular power rightly and properly puts to death evil persons who injure the bodies of the defenseless (Romans 13). But the ungodly cannot [by their beliefs] injure anyone. . . . The secular power judges criminals, not the ungodly. . . . To burn heretics is, according to appearances, to testify to Christ; in truth, however, it is to deny him monstrously (Titus 1). . . . If it is therefore a great outrage to put heretics to death, how much greater to burn to ashes faithful heralds of the Word of God, unconvicted and even unheard so far as the truth is concerned." Hubmaier concludes, "Now it should be clear to everyone, even the blind, that a law for the burning of heretics is an invention of the devil. Truth is immortal."

Threats against Waldshut increased. It sought aid from nearby towns, in vain, then from the insurgent peasants of the Black Forest. An attack was planned on the town for October 19, 1524, and fully expected. The peasants promised to serve Waldshut as mercenaries for a month. They came, but the rulers against whom they were rebelling persuaded them to leave earlier. Deserted even by the peasants, Waldshut pled again for help from Zurich. The latter responded, although not officially.

Evangelical citizens of Zurich assembled a band of armed volunteers which went to Waldshut's aid, arriving on October 3. This kind of action corresponded to that of individuals or groups of mercenaries from Switzerland that had traditionally gone to fight on their own in various European armies, but these in Waldshut served without pay. The number varied greatly, occasionally reaching a hundred or more. It was probably their presence which held off the Austrian attack for two or three months. In addition, the Austrian army which was intended for the attack on Waldshut had to be diverted to put down a peasant uprising in Hegau. On October 26 imperial forces were defeated at Milan and all available troops were needed in Italy. Although Catholic Switzerland vociferously opposed the intervention in Waldshut of men from Zurich, and it was embarrassing (as well as dangerous) for Zurich officially, the action of the volunteers was popular among evangelicals. Zwingli said Waldshut was simply trying to uphold Reformation principles and in Strasbourg Wolfgang Capito praised the courage of the people of Waldshut.

Hubmaier realized full well the problem he was making for Schaffhausen by remaining there. It was quite evident also that the Hapsburgs had not at all let up on the pressure against Waldshut because of his absence. At the end of October, therefore, after two turbulent and busy months, Hubmaier left Schaffhausen. On his way to Waldshut he went, by way of Zurich, for talks with Zwingli and to arrange for the publication of his *Axiomata*.

Struggle of Waldshut for Freedom of the Word

The returning pastor received an enthusiastic welcome upon entering Waldshut on October 27, 1524. According to an unsympathetic contemporary, it was "as if God himself had come down to them from heaven." The people, said this commentator, celebrated with drums, pipes and horns, and with great pomp "as if he were the emperor himself." People observed the return of their church leader also by attempting to complete the reformation in Waldshut. From both churches they removed tablets, images, sanctuary lamps, and chalices. These were destroyed or melted down, while church banners and altar cloths were cut and sewn into trouser bands. On a further raid into the churches people destroyed a silver monstrance which cost two hundred guilders. These actions, surely more precipitous and violent than Hubmaier would have desired, effectively albeit crudely demonstrated his teachings about abuses.

Writing later against holding the consecrated host in the monstrance, he quotes Acts 7:48, "The Most High dwells not in temples made with hands." From that principle Hubmaier deduces that "in behalf of Christ one cannot construct for Christ housing of wood, stone, silver, or gold, as in the great churches or expensive monstrances." He then makes a word play on monstrances, calling them "monsters." He condemns these things as earthly objects, created things being worshiped instead of the Creator.

Hubmaier introduced evangelical changes into the liturgy of worship gradually. As he explained in one of his letters to the council of Schaffhausen while there, he had not always preached and practiced to the full extent of his understanding, feeling that he should feed his flock with milk until they could take stronger food. Now in the services he began to read the Gospels and New Testament epistles in German. Sometime later he put other parts of the liturgy in the language of the people rather than intoning it all in Latin, altered the canon of the mass, and administered the sacrament to the people in both elements.

A conference was held in Reinfelden, beginning on November 3, called by nobles attempting to mediate the dispute between the imperial rulers and Austria on one side and Waldshut on the other. Representatives came from various cities and provinces of the area, but also—in support of Waldshut—from Zurich, Schaffhausen, and Basel. Waldshut had its own representatives there and, believing their position to be strong, they presented four demands: (1) that the gospel might be preached freely and unhindered in their city by their "present doctor" or by someone else, (2) that the city have the freedom to choose its own pastors—insisting here again that they would not allow Hubmaier to be taken from them "unconquered," (3) that Waldshut receive no punishment as a result of the present controversy, and (4) that it be recompensed by the ruling house for heavy expenses—set at approximately six thousand guilders—to which it had been driven through the unlawful and unjust threat of war.

One swells in pride at the courage of the little town, but they were obviously overplaying their hand—unless they really expected to be allowed to join the Swiss Confederation. The Austrian delegation at Rheinfelden rejected Waldshut's demands, insisting once more that the town dismiss both Hubmaier and the remaining Zurich volunteers. Waldshut for its part rejected this, and the conference closed on the third day with no evident results. Archduke Ferdinand sent a message to the conference that there should be no further negotiations with Waldshut until he gave the word. The reason was that he hoped for military support from the Swabian League to bring Waldshut to heel. This league had promised to take up the Waldshut problem.

The Swabian League was a loose and widespread federation of European states including Austria. Constituent members were (1) electors and princes, (2) prelates, earls, barons, and other nobles, and (3) the cities. Its principal purpose was to preserve peace among its members. The league was strongly Catholic; it opposed Lutheran and other reform movements, including the one in Waldshut. Until a general church council should be called, however, the league had ordered princely and city authorities to install pastors and keep a watchful eye on their preaching. Waldshut felt it was following these instructions exactly. It received much support from representatives of cities in the league, for they were suspicious of infringements on cities' rights anywhere. The Swabian League offered to mediate the dispute between Waldshut and Austria and called a conference in Constance for that purpose. It met at the end of January 1525.

The conference was attended by representatives from Waldshut and the Austrian government, as well as from each section of the Swabian League. The usual demands, claims, and defenses were made. League representatives suggested that Waldshut dismiss the Zurich soldiers still in their town, so that they would no longer be charged with rebellion as they had been, and the Waldshut representatives agreed to this. Since Austria held Hubmaier to be the cause of all the trouble, the league suggested that Waldshut dismiss him and choose a pastor who would preach in the traditional way and restore earlier religious practices.

The Waldshut men replied that up to that time Hubmaier had instructed them in the holy Word of God as a true spiritual leader. There was no proof, they said, that he had preached contrary to imperial mandates, and his frequent request that he be examined for error had gone unanswered. Nor had he ever, as alleged, incited the people to insurrection. It would therefore be unjust to dismiss their preacher. Unjust or not, this was exactly what the Austrians were determined to have carried out. They brought such pressure to bear, and issued such threats, that the Waldshut delegates, to save their little city, finally declared themselves willing to dismiss their beloved pastor.

They also agreed to give up the claims for reimbursement, which they had made again at the beginning of the Constance meeting. They promised, in addition, that all who had felt obliged to leave the town during the disturbances would be allowed to return, and would receive back their property and civil rights. Despite Waldshut's concessions, the conference failed because its representatives held steadfastly to the principle of freedom for the Word of God in their churches. They felt a further conference, as was suggested, would serve no useful purpose. They did present, at the close of the Constance meeting, the humble request that his highness the archduke take "no violent action" against their town.

Reform Marches on, Despite Increasing Peril

Hubmaier, who was not at the Constance conference, wrote later of events in Waldshut: "It was on account of the Word of God that they wanted to oppress us with force, and this, beyond all proper bounds. That was our only complaint. I here defy all people on earth and all devils in hell to show that they had any other cause against Waldshut except alone, alone, alone the Word of God.... Those from Waldshut publicly promised that they would act loyally toward Prince Ferdinand, and all others, as they had done previously, and as their forefathers had done, and even more; also to sacrifice their bodies, lives, honor, goods, and blood for the sake of the noble house of Austria. If there were a stone ten fathoms under the earth at Waldshut which was not good Austrian, they would scratch it out with their fingernails and throw it into the Rhine. They had always been the first to pay their obedience and tribute to the prince. They asked with weeping eyes, simply for God's sake, that they be allowed to continue to hold to the pure and clear Word of God. But the councilors of the prince in Constance gave this answer: 'It simply cannot be done. If such a favor were granted, it would be the same as if one fire were put out and another lighted. Other cities afterward would desire to have the same.' "

Among the original Zurich volunteers in Waldshut at the end of October 1524 was Heinrich Aberli. He had a close relationship with Conrad Grebel and others in Zurich who desired to go beyond the reform that was officially sanc-

tioned. Probably other volunteers with whom Hubmaier was in contact after his return from Schaffhausen held similar views. Hubmaier evidently maintained some contact with this radical group even after an Anabaptist church had emerged from it on January 21, 1525. None of these events pleased Zwingli and councilors in Zurich—nor did Waldshut's helping the peasants in Klettgau (partially a protectorate of Zurich) who were rebelling against their oppressive masters in Germany. Deprived of all other support, Waldshut made a mutual-assistance agreement with the Klettgau peasants, and a large contingent marched into Waldshut on Sunday, January 29. Waldshut gratefully opened its gates to admit the troops, and Hubmaier preached to them while they were in the vicinity. In any case, no further help could be expected from Switzerland. Waldshut proceeded apace with its reformation.

The Swabian League held another conference, this time in Ulm; but Waldshut—fearing for the lives of anyone it might appoint to the meeting—sent no representatives. The archduke's delegates, at his express command, denounced the people of Waldshut as "aggressors," ringleaders of rebellion, instigators of the peasants' revolt. The archduke was still seeking military support to bring Waldshut into submission. The council of the town had sent a letter to the conference, but it arrived by messenger ten days after the meetings began. The letter affirmed Waldshut's desire for the pure Word of God to be preached without disturbance in their city, and they again renounced earlier claims for damages.

In one point this letter was different from commitments made in Constance: It stated that the people of Waldshut could not, without disregard for imperial mandates and their own traditions, dismiss their "unvanquished doctor." At the very least, the letter stated, Hubmaier should be granted his request that he be examined by learned men appointed by the bishop and they should point out his errors on the basis of Scripture. Again they asked that force not be used against their city.

The league wrote the archduke suggesting that the

peasants' revolt be crushed by force immediately and that negotiations with Waldshut be continued. But the archduke continued to work toward a military solution to both his problems; he did not yet have the power, however, to apply force. The situation changed considerably when on February 24 imperial forces defeated the French, with their Swiss mercenaries, at Pavia in Italy. Archduke Ferdinand's hand was now strengthened to take the desired action, whereas Swiss influence diminished.

In line with Reformation principles, Hubmaier renounced the traditional Catholic idea that priests were especially anointed purveyors of divine grace and of necessity celibate. Other reformers were marrying, and on January 13, 1525, he married Elsbeth Hügline of Reichenach. It was a happy choice. Elsbeth proved herself a faithful, loving, energetic, and courageous helpmate.

Waldshut still pleaded desperately with Zurich, and to some extent with Basel and Schaffhausen also, that it be taken under their care and protection. The appeal now fell on deaf ears. Reformation in the town was going beyond what could be officially countenanced in Zurich and other parts of reformed Switzerland.

As early as January 16 Hubmaier had written to Oecolampadius in Basel that he was declaring publicly, according to the teachings of Christ, that small children should not be baptized. Instead of baptizing children in Waldshut, he was conducting a service in which a simple blessing was bestowed upon them and a Scripture passage read in German while the congregation knelt in prayer for the child. "But if the parents are still weak and insist that their offspring be baptized, then I baptize the child," Hubmaier conceded. In the letter to Oecolampadius he declared that both baptism and the Lord's Supper should be brought back to their original purity. He was still conducting the mass in Waldshut because he felt it would be confusing to people for reformers in various places to be at odds on so many things in teaching and practice. He wrote Oecolampadius that he wished very much to have discussions with church leaders in Switzerland concerning these matters.

Not very long after writing to Oecolampadius, Hubmaier published a short tract (about 875 words) *Some Articles on the Teaching of the Mass.* "The Lord's Supper is a remembrance of his suffering and a proclamation of his death, until he comes to us again," this writing begins. It emphasizes, in the observance of this ordinance, the fellowship of all believers. Therefore, "the bread and the wine in the Supper of Christ are outward signs of an inner Christian reality here on earth in which one Christian commits himself to another in Christlike love."

Anabaptism Comes to Waldshut

One of those who had taken part in events leading to the establishment of the first Anabaptist congregation, in Zurich on January 21, was Pastor Wilhelm Reublin of Wytikon-Zurich. He was among those who were expelled shortly afterward; with an associate he came, after two days in the Schaffhausen area, to Waldshut. Its town council received a notice from Zurich that these men represented false teachings and should be expelled. Waldshut replied on February 1 that they had been with Dr. Balthasar, but no one had noticed anything wicked about these men; anyway, they had left Waldshut on the previous day.

A day or so later, it seems, Hubmaier discussed the baptismal issue with other clergy in Waldshut, and at this time they apparently agreed with him in questioning the validity of infant baptism. He also wrote out a proposal for public disputation on the question, 161 words in all. It was evidently not published at the time but came out later as *A Public Invitation to All Christian Believers.* "Whoever wishes to do so," it began, "let him show, in German, with plain, clear, simple Scriptures, that small children should be baptized.... Balthasar of Friedberg pledges, on the other hand, to prove that the baptism of infants is an act without any ground in God's Word.... I will always give God the glory and let his Word alone be the arbiter ... to him I herewith submit myself and all my teachings. Truth is immortal."

Later, Hubmaier wrote of his conversations with Reublin,

whom he designates the "instigator of baptism," testifying that Reublin had told him what God had given him to say. Reublin was able to win some people of the Waldshut area, and they were baptized in a nearby village. Several of these came to Hubmaier and asked why he did not take the matter in hand himself, but he turned these people away. The situation in Waldshut was just too perilous at the time for further radical reforms.

The peasants' movement was gaining momentum, but open warfare was avoided until March 1525. Waldshut, bereft of all other support, was allied with the peasants of Klettgau and the Black Forest. Waldshut furnished one or two captains in operations outside Waldshut and occasionally sent small squads of soldiers to join peasant forces. In turn, the latter considered themselves involved in the defense of Waldshut. There were a few victories for peasants early in the spring campaigns, notably in Freiburg. Their successes were rare, however, and short-lived.

Reublin came back to Waldshut at the Easter season, while the peasants were experiencing their small victories in the Black Forest. By coincidence, he arrived on the same day the Klettgau peasants entered Waldshut. Hubmaier was convinced the time had come for him to take a public stand according to his convictions. On April 14, the Saturday before Easter, Reublin baptized Hubmaier and sixty other persons. Hubmaier himself then baptized many the next day, dipping into a milk pail of water that had been brought into the church from a town well. Each candidate knelt in turn and was asked to testify to his personal faith in Christ; then the pastor applied a small amount of water on his or her head. Others came for baptism, including most of the city council. Hubmaier later testified that during the Easter season that year he had baptized about three hundred persons.

He felt disappointment that there were not more baptisms and went so far as to say that he thought he would leave the town, since God's Word brought forth such scanty fruitage. He seems even to have accused those who held back of being "bad Christians." The Waldshut people were for the most part so attached to their pastor and had such confidence in him—according to a contemporary non-Anabaptist historian—that they chose rather to be rebaptized than to lose their pastor. The Lord's Supper was celebrated following the baptismal services, in a simple but dignified way, and it was followed by foot washing (apparently never repeated by Hubmaier) as an expression of Christian humility.

Zwingli's position hardened, on behalf of infant baptism and the all-inclusive church, and against rebaptism. He came out strongly against the radicals through new restrictive measures of the Zurich council and in literary activity. At the end of May his booklet *Concerning Baptism, Rebaptism, and Infant Baptism* appeared. Neither in this work nor in one that came out a month later was Hubmaier named, although his new teachings were attacked. He replied to Zwingli's work with his own, entitled *The Christian Baptism of Believers,* about seventeen thousand words. It was completed on July 11. Part of this (as eventually published) was a shorter work, about 2,200 words, *Summary of a Complete Christian Life,* which was dedicated "to the three churches in Regensburg, Ingolstadt, and Friedberg," where the author had, according to the words of his dedication, represented the Christian faith poorly.

"I openly confess that I sinned before God and all heaven," Hubmaier writes in the briefer work, "not only by my own sinful life that I led among you in utter vanity, fornication, and worldly pride, against the teachings of Christ and in false, ungrounded and ungodly teaching, in which I instructed, then fed and pastured you, outside the Word of God. Especially, as I well remember, I did many useless things in connection with infant baptism...." The writer lists numerous sacramental and liturgical rites and teachings of the church. These things he participated in, he says, knowing no better, and has since asked God to forgive him. Christ said, "Change your life for the better and believe the gospel.... Faith is not idle but rather active in all good Christian works."

There follows a discussion of the Lord's Supper. "The bread is not the body of Christ, only a memorial of it, likewise the wine." Then he uses a popular analogy, which he would repeat several times in later writings. It developed from the practice of wine-houses having a wine-barrel hoop, a wreath or some other symbol hung outside at the doorway notifying the public that they had wine in stock and for sale. The Supper is not a repetition of the sacrifice of Christ; the elements are not his body and blood, "just as the hoop before the wine-house is not the wine but rather a reminder, a sign of it." The writing ends with an appeal: "O dear sirs, friends, brothers, take to heart what I have said to you, and strive after the clear, pure Word of Christ. From it alone will faith come to you; in him alone must we be saved."

Believers' Baptism Is Defended

The larger work, the baptismal booklet, is regarded as Hubmaier's most significant writing. "Water baptism involves the confessing of one's own faith, by God's command, with the pouring of water, as a person is numbered among sinners by one's own acknowledgement and admission . . . and one is willing to live a new life according to the rule of Christ (Matthew 3)." Baptism may be in the name of the Trinity, the author says, or simply in the name of Christ and is "nothing other than a public confession and testimony by which one acknowledges that he is a sinner and witnesses outwardly before everyone of inner faith and commitment." It is emphasized that "the Word or the teaching must come before baptism so that one is brought to the acknowledgement of one's sins . . . and pardon of the same through the Lamb of God . . . with the intention of amending one's life by the help of God."

Later on comes the question put into the mouth of an imaginary opponent: "What or how much must I know if I wish to be baptized? Answer: This much you must know from the Word of God and do before you can submit to being baptized: that you acknowledge yourself to be a miserable sinner and confess your guilt, that you believe also that through Jesus Christ your sins are forgiven, that in firm resolve you devote yourself to amending your life according to the will of Christ in the power of God the Father, the Son, and the Holy Spirit. And if in this you later go astray, you will allow yourself to be disciplined and punished according to the rule of Christ in Matthew 18, in order that you may grow in faith from day to day like the little mustard seed that grows, up into the clouds of the sky. This, then, is what you must know, for [the content of] knowing and believing is the faith that Jesus is the Christ, which faith is necessary before baptism [can be administered] (Acts chapters 2, 8, 16, 19)."

Thinking surely of several of his friends and former friends among the reformers Hubmaier declares: "I know many godly Christians who freely admit that infant baptism has no foundation in Scripture and that infants should not be baptized. At the same time they do not believe that rebaptism, which is being practiced now, is grounded in the Word of God. Answer: Dear, devout Christians, listen: You err in the first place in calling this present baptism that is being practiced a rebaptism, for infant baptism, in truth and according to your own [previous] acknowledgement, is no baptism at all."

Dealing with particular questions and problems, the author states: "The first question: whether infant baptism is forbidden in the Word of God. Answer: Yes. Because the command is to baptize believers.... You say: 'There is no clear word in Scripture that a child should not be baptized.... There is not the word there, "Do not baptize small children" '—so, you say, they can be baptized. To which I say: Then I can baptize my dog and donkey, circumcise a maid, mumble prayers and vigils for the dead, name wooden gods St. Peter and St. Paul, admit infants to the Lord's Supper, bless palm branches, plants, salt, oil, and water—and sell the mass as a sacrifice. Nowhere in Scripture is it forbidden, in so many words, that we should do these things!... You say: 'Baptizing donkeys is forbidden, for Christ commanded that people be baptized.' Well, shall we baptize Jews and Turks? You say: 'Only believing people should be baptized.' Answer: So why do you then baptize infants?"

In July Hubmaier wrote a letter to the Zurich council suggesting it arrange a discussion on baptism, private or public, between him and Zwingli, whom he still referred to as his "dear brother." In this way he hoped they could come "to a good peace." Hubmaier felt his book on baptism could lay the groundwork for such a discussion. He was trying also to develop his contacts with Oecolampadius in Basel, but the latter sided with Zwingli; so did Hofmeister of Schaffhausen and the others. Waldshut no longer had any sure allies and the reformers all stood against Hubmaier.

Leaders of the rising Swiss Brethren movement did not accept Hubmaier wholeheartedly because of his positive view concerning state government (including oath-taking) and the responsibility of a Christian to serve it if called on to do so. Grebel made two trips to Waldshut for talks with Hubmaier about baptism; he reported then to his brethren that the Waldshut reformer held certain views with which he could not agree. This surely refers to teachings about the state; on other points Hubmaier seemed to be in full agreement with Swiss Brethren. The Brethren movement as a whole would continue for generations to use Hubmaier's writings as the best literary defense available for believer's baptism, the voluntary church, and related teachings.

No Letup in the Baptism Debate

The literary controversy between Hubmaier and Zwingli continued. In November the latter published *A True, Thorough Reply to Dr. Balthasar's Book on Baptism.* Hubmaier, after he had read this, prepared a rebuttal which, due to the disturbed situation in Waldshut, was not published until the following year in faraway Moravia. The booklet of sixty-seven pages, in the rather small format and fairly large print then used, totaled nearly 18,000 words and bore the title *A Discussion by Dr. Balthasar Hubmaier of Friedberg Concerning the Booklet on Baptism by Master Ulrich Zwingli of Zurich.* It came out in at least two editions. After a preface of several pages Hubmaier developed his writing in the form of a dialogue between himself and Zwingli—a favorite literary device of the time.

In his initial "speech" Zwingli complains that certain

people [such as Hubmaier] have opposed the baptism of everyone [in infancy], crying out that there is "nothing in the outward act which can contribute anything toward salvation." Hubmaier replies that there are two kinds of outward acts or ceremonies—those that are grounded in Scripture, such as believer's baptism and the Lord's Supper, and those that are not; he and Zwingli had both opposed, he writes, many abuses in the latter category. "Zwingli" is made to accuse the Anabaptists: "You throw out infant baptism because you have found it desirable to set up rebaptism." Not so, Hubmaier replies, but because Zwingli and his supporters have not come up with a single clear Scripture indicating that the rite for infants is Christian baptism.

In answer to Zwingli's insistence that people should not do just as they like but ask the church, Hubmaier answers, "One should ask of Scripture, not the church. . . . The church is built on the Word, not the Word on the church (Matthew 16)." Zwingli then requires some biblical word forbidding infant baptism. Hubmaier counters, "Christ does not say, 'Every planting which my Father has forbidden has been rooted out,' but he says, 'Every planting which my heavenly Father has not planted shall be rooted out.' So you must show clearly in Scripture the planting of infant baptism, otherwise this planting must be uprooted." Since Zwingli was not able to do this, yet was still determined to hold the entire community in the church, he made much of the baptizing of entire households as recorded in the New Testament and insisted these must have included small children; he also rested his case strongly on the analogy between baptism and circumcision in the Old Testament, which was administered to all male infants.

"Zwingli" confesses to having held earlier to the "error" himself, that children should not be baptized "until they come to the years of accountability." Hubmaier takes full advantage of the contrived admission. "Yes, you did so hold, write, and preach openly from the pulpit—many hundred people heard it from your own mouth." Also "in the year 1523 on Zurichgraben [later Hirschengraben] Street I personally confronted you with the Scriptures about baptism.

You said I was right, that children should not be baptized until they had been instructed in the faith."

At that time, one must realize, both men were charting their way as to how far reform should go, and even for Hubmaier the conclusion on this matter at that time was still tentative and theoretical. It reflected an attempt at consistent biblical exposition. If Hubmaier and the other Anabaptists had been willing to leave it there as a theoretical and historical matter, explaining how baptism was understood and practiced among primitive Christians, Zwingli would probably have gone along, and they all could have remained in the community churches. The problem resulted from their insistence on making theory into practice, setting up congregations of people baptized as believers.

God resides in the little child, said "Zwingli," although he did not dare to define whether it was through the Holy Spirit's presence or in some other way. Hubmaier's answer: "How God resides in the infant—whether the child has the Holy Spirit or belongs to God—is not ours to ask; it is a foolish, mischievous, and serpentine question. It is not seemly for us to try to judge in such things, for God himself knows whom he has chosen from all eternity, and we have no clear Scripture on the matter. Some are crying out, 'The children are God's, the children are God's, why should they not be baptized?' As to who are children of God, he keeps in his secret judgment.... To believe is a work of God and not of man; so we are not born of father and mother as children of God.... Whether God saves little children, or however he deals with them, I leave to him. I commend it into his hands. I have no Scripture about it, therefore I haven't the longing to know.... I do not say they are not saved, rather I leave it in the hands of God. May his will be done with them and with us all; for deep is the abundance of God's wisdom and knowledge—his judgments are beyond our comprehension and his ways past finding out."

"Zwingli" here claims Romans 6:4 as support for his emphasis that baptism is a public testimony, a sign of the commitment of the child to God and to newness of life in him.

Hubmaier rebuts: "The weeping child in its cradle knows nothing of signs, commitment, baptism, new life, or testimony. On the other hand, Paul does describe in this passage the meaning of baptism, namely that the baptized person . . . is dead with Christ . . . buried as Christ was and raised from the dead. . . . So shall the baptized person arise from the realm of sin and walk in new life. Any child who knows this significance of baptism and will make this commitment and give this public testimony, affirming faith and requesting water baptism before the church in order to be received into the church—that child should be baptized."

A further booklet, *Concerning Infant Baptism*, about 4,500 words, was started in this perilous period of change, but revised and printed later in Moravia. It was written in that favored form of an imaginary discussion—here it is between Hubmaier on one side of the question and Oecolampadius and three other pastors of Basel on the other. The usual arguments are presented for infant baptism—that Jesus loved little children, that baptism replaced circumcision, that entire families were baptized in New Testament times, and that the Bible did not forbid it. Hubmaier in this writing continues to defend believer's baptism as the only form of the ordinance that is biblically valid.

The Capitulation of Waldshut

Waldshut cautiously maintained contacts with rebellious peasants of South Germany, for it saw no other possible course except unconditional surrender. While Hubmaier was in Waldshut completing the writing of his booklets on baptism and attempting desperately to restore tolerable relationships with Swiss reformers, peasants in Hegau and the Black Forest were being decisively defeated by armies of the Hapsburgs and the Swabian League. As a part of the peasants' movement but to some extent still protected by Zurich, Klettgau peasants concluded on June 28 an armistice with their ruler, Count von Sulz, to last until September 1—the day on which Zurich withdrew its support completely. Waldshut, in similar peril as Klettgau, sent a few armed volunteers to the latter place, but enemy troops practically surrounded that town.

The Zurich council arranged a third disputation on the baptismal question, to begin November 6. Wide participation was invited. Two Zurich Anabaptists went to Waldshut to urge Hubmaier to take part. He desired to do so and set out on November 4. Unaware of the extent to which military activities were in progress in and around Klettgau, he entered the area on his way to Zurich. Austrian officials were searching for Hubmaier and almost succeeded in apprehending him. He learned just in time of this danger, as well as of the impending battle, and returned to Waldshut. Foiled in their plan to capture Hubmaier, the Austrians took prisoner the evangelical pastor of Griessen and blinded him. The army of Klettgau peasants suffered defeat and destruction that day. The Austrians then demanded the unconditional surrender of Waldshut, with Hubmaier and other "ringleaders" to be turned over to them for punishment.

A small group of citizens in Waldshut, firmly Catholic, had never gone along with Hubmaier's reform. Many others, including the mayor and a militia captain, now joined this group. They threatened to give over the town to the Austrians and their representatives had talks with Austrian negotiators in the area. Hubmaier, although seriously ill during this time, continued his preaching and writing. On November 30 he completed *A Discussion*, his reply to Zwingli's book on baptism, and he still sought to fulfill all his duties as a citizen. The majority of the people apparently still supported him, or very much desired to do so.

On December 5 Hubmaier and Hans Muller, a builder—the mayor and many other opponents having left—called the town's remaining populace together in the city hall. Hubmaier explained that the city had decided to surrender. Whoever was not agreeable to this was free in God's name to go wherever he wished. Hubmaier himself got a few things together and departed in haste from the town; his wife, it seems, followed somewhat later. Various reports give the number as from forty to more than a hundred men who fled, some with their families, to escape the wrath of those who would demolish every reform, every freedom, and restore medieval Catholicism in Waldshut. Later in the day the town was occupied without a fight, and the old order ruled once more.

Hubmaier ferried across the Rhine. He would have preferred to go to Basel or Strasbourg, but the roads to these centers lay within the jurisdiction of Upper Austria, under the Hapsburgs. He could hardly hope to reach either city in safety. Still quite ill, he made his weary way to Zurich, to the home of his Brethren friend, the baker Heinrich Aberli. A day or so later he transferred to a small inn run by a widow, recently baptized by Aberli, and her daughter.

The harried Anabaptist longed for quiet and a chance to regain his health in peace. It was not to be. Zwingli and others learned of Hubmaier's presence in Zurich. He was arrested and imprisoned on December 11, later confined in the city hall. He would not be free again for four months. Zwingli said the reason for his arrest was to prevent him from organizing an uprising. The real reason, of course, was his refusal as an Anabaptist to return to Zwingli's brand of reform. Zwingli, with the city council, determined to secure his humiliation and punishment at any cost.

"So, as a sick person, just up from my 'death bed,' hunted down, driven about, having lost all I had," Hubmaier later related, "they would now teach me another faith, according to the views of Zwingli, through the activity of the executioner—and not only me but many other devout people." Here he names Grebel, Mantz, Blaurock, Aberli, and a few other Anabaptists and describes Zwingli's methods: "Many devout Christian men, married women and maids, attacked openly from the pulpit, were declared worthy, as rebaptizers, of being beheaded in the name of imperial law. That was his gospel, his word of comfort, and his deed of mercy with which he 'consoled' and 'visited' imprisoned Christians."

Drama in the Fraumünster

Although the council had ignored his request the past July for a discussion on baptism with Zwingli and several others, this was now arranged; and those others suggested earlier by Hubmaier were now indeed included—Leo Jud, Oswald Myconius, Konrad Schmid, and Sebastian Hofmeister. Hubmaier felt he could quote these men in support, to some degree, of his own position. Four council members and a Zurich schoolmaster were also present for the discussion. Hubmaier stated at the meeting that it was in part due to earlier statements of Zwingli himself that he had renounced infant baptism. Zwingli answered bluntly, simply defending his current position. Hubmaier rejected, with full justification, the charges brought against him that he had claimed to be without sin, that he had taught property should be held in common among Christians and that a Christian should not "sit in the place of authority."

It seemed to Hubmaier that he found a bit more understanding for his position in Jud, Myconius, and Hofmeister; so he requested a private conference with them. This the council as a whole granted him, and these three counseled that he recant on the point of baptism—otherwise, they could see no hope for him in Zurich. Hubmaier then wrote out a statement confessing that he had erred in the matter of rebaptism. Hubmaier pleaded that the council take account of his "great illness, adversity, persecution, and poverty," and he begged them not to deliver him into the hands of his enemies, for, he wrote, "I am also a feeble man." Here we find the reason for his insincere recantation. The Hapsburgs were even then trying to extradite him; Archduke Ferdinand had made the formal request on December 14 and renewed it a few days later, sending his representatives to Zurich to take Hubmaier. The helpless captive realized that the only way to save his life would be by being allowed to remain, albeit imprisoned, in Zurich. Even if he could be freed and locate a haven somewhere, the poor man in his infirmity, in wintertime, would be unable to travel.

Having made his recantation to representatives of the Zurich council, Hubmaier was then informed that he must repeat it in the principal churches of Zurich—first in the Fraumünster. The humiliated Anabaptist went there under guard for the service on the morning of December 29. After Zwingli had preached, Hubmaier was called upon to read his recantation. Just before the service, it seems, he had learned about imperial representatives being in the city. He evidently decided that Zurich now intended to turn him over to the Austrians and that no recantation would save him. He hurriedly wrote down some notes on a scrap of paper for his own sincere defense of the freedom of faith. Later he said this was intended for use in his defense before the Austrians in case he were handed over to them. A surge of moral strength welled up within him, however, as he rose to read the recantation. He used the hastily scribbled notes rather than the carefully worded recantation in making his statement to the congregation.

"O what anguish and travail I have suffered this night," he began extemporaneously, "over the statements which I myself have made. I say here and now, I cannot and I will not recant." He proceeded forthwith to defend believer's baptism as a New Testament teaching. The people murmured with excitement at the unexpected development, and Zwingli stood in anger to interrupt him. Officials came forward to hustle the "criminal" to a cell in the Wellenberg prison, isolated in the middle of the Limmat River where it flows out of the Lake of Zurich. He was subjected several times to torture, and finally his tormented frame could bear it no longer. He confessed amid groans of pain what his persecutors desired—that the devil had inspired his statement in the Fraumünster. In further satisfaction to his tormentors, he anathematized the error and stubbornness of the Anabaptists. Zwingli had instructed him to call them anti-baptists, which he then apparently did.

He would languish for more than three months in the cold, damp Wellenberg, which because of its location was often called the *Wasserturm* or Water Tower. He was submitted repeatedly to harsh treatment and grueling interrogation. To give Zurich its due, it should be added that the council steadfastly refused to turn Hubmaier over to emissaries of the archduke, maintaining that it was its own responsibility to punish the recalcitrant reformer.

While in prison the suffering Anabaptist wrote out a statement, *Twelve Articles of the Christian Faith,* less than two thousand words—majoring on basic doctrines and avoiding extensive treatment of controversial points. This was not printed at the time, of course, but only the following year in Moravia. It is generally in the form of a faith-confession, occasionally that of a prayer: "I believe in God ... also in Jesus Christ ... born of Mary, pure and ever-chaste virgin.... I believe in the Holy Spirit.... I believe also in a holy catholic Christian church, which is a communion of the saints.... I believe also in the remission of sins ... resurrection of the body ... eternal life....

"O holy God, O mighty God, O immortal God, this is my faith which I confess with heart and mouth and to which I have witnessed openly before the church in water baptism. In faithfulness I pray you, hold me by your mercy in it, to my end. And though I should be, out of human fear and weakness and through tyranny, torment, fire or water driven from it, still I cry unto you, O my merciful Father, raise me up again by the grace of your Holy Spirit and do not let me depart in death without this faith. I pray this from the bottom of my heart, through Jesus Christ, your most-beloved Son, our Savior and Lord."

From Zurich to Augsburg

Another short writing, less than half the length of *Twelve Articles* but likewise composed in the Wellenberg prison and printed later in Moravia, was *The Lord's Prayer, in Brief.* Each paragraph until the last begins with a phrase quoted from the model prayer given by Jesus to his disciples, and what follows in each case is a personal extension of the prayer at that point, applying it to the current situation of trial and persecution. For example: "May your kingdom come. O merciful Father, we confess once again our perverseness, for we are in the kingdom of sin, of the devil, of hell, and eternal death; but, Father, we cry and call out to you as unto our most beloved Father, that you come speedily to us with your kingdom of grace, peace, joy, and eternal salvation." Under "Lead us not into temptation," the battered believer prays, for himself and his persecuted brothers and sisters: "May we not be tempted beyond that which we can endure. We are weak and frail—our enemy strong, powerful, and ferocious—as you know, O merciful Father." The writing closes: "Father, into your hands we commend our bodies, lives, honor, goods, souls, and spirits. Everything we have received from you we wish to offer back unto you as a sacrifice. You give and you take away; may your name be praised. Amen, and may it be ever so."

Grebel, Mantz, Blaurock, and other Anabaptists of the area had been incarcerated since the third disputation on baptism early in November. They lay in the feared New Tower, popularly called the *Ketzerturm* or Heretics Tower. During the winter more and more of their fellow believers joined them. On March 7 the frustrated authorities, with Zwingli's approval, issued a mandate setting death by drowning as the penalty for anyone who rebaptized another person. Grebel, Mantz, Blaurock, and others were at the same time condemned to life imprisonment. Later in the same month, however, the entire group escaped from the Ketzerturm.

Hubmaier must have spent much time in his austere and unhealthy Wellenberg cell—whenever he was free from torture and interrogation—thinking of his changed situation following the death mandate of March 7. Was his situation now much different from what it would be anywhere else, even inside Austrian territory? True, he had not had opportunity to baptize anyone since the death mandate, but this brought little assurance. The Zurich council was giving priority to imprisoned Anabaptists who were their own citizens, but by now it must have placed Hubmaier in a similar category. He surely considered himself to be one with the Swiss Brethren and, despite their differences on one or two points of doctrine, most of them probably thought of him in the same way.

Zwingli and the councilors must have begun to realize that Hubmaier's recantations were insincere and only for self-preservation. He would never become their dependable convert, as Hofmeister had; so they wished to be rid of him.

They asked for a further recantation statement, and upon receiving it, took him from the Wellenberg on April 6. A week later, again upon request, he began the process of reading the recantation in three churches. These included one church in the Gruningen district where Anabaptism was strongest. Knowing that the recantation was insincere, the authorities still desired to use it to the fullest in their battle against the Swiss Brethren. Some officials do seem to have been helpful—and Zwingli later claimed a part in this— keeping him in secrecy and safety until he was able to slip quietly out of Zurich and across the border some time about the end of April.

Hubmaier and his wife made the perilous, weary way to Constance. Some of his faithful parishioners in Waldshut had fled there when their town was becoming Catholic again, and the Hubmaiers evidently went first to these friends. They must have encouraged him to resume his role as an Anabaptist activist. Reports indicate that he was soon meeting in Constance with reform pastors who supported Zwingli, defending believer's baptism and complaining of the harsh treatment he had received in Zurich.

The Hubmaiers proceeded after a few days to Augsburg and must have arrived there early in May 1526. It was his native area, the town of Friedberg being only a few miles away. Eight years earlier, Balthasar Hubmaier the priest had reported there to the imperial diet in the presence of the emperor on the question of the Regensburg Jews. This time the Hubmaiers stayed about two months in Augsburg. Luther and Zwingli both had strong followings in the city and there was a small conventicle of believers who called themselves True Christians, established by Ludwig Haetzer, who had cooperated for a while with Grebel and his party in Zurich. Expelled from Augsburg as he had been from Zurich, Haetzer was followed by Hans Denck as leader of the conventicle.

Petrus Gynoraeus, a representative of Zwinglian reform in Augsburg, wrote to Zwingli on August 22 that Hubmaier had succeeded in gaining many adherents for the Anabaptist cause in the city. It is likely that Hans Denck was among

those baptized by Hubmaier. Others in the old Haetzer group were baptized at this time, and it became, under the lead of Hans Denck, an important congregation of the Brethren. There Denck baptized the radical itinerant evangelist and eschatological preacher Hans Hut.

Hubmaier also had some contact with Lutheran pastors in Augsburg. He complained to them, as well as to Zwinglian sympathizers there, about the harsh treatment meted out to him in Zurich. This criticism was not favorably received by the clergy, some of whom must have informed the local authorities. Hubmaier began to experience insecurity even in the free city of Augsburg.

It must have been in early July 1526 that he left for Moravia, a land about three hundred miles to the east which offered considerable freedom of faith and had not come under the rule of Hapsburgs.

Beginnings in Nikolsburg

For a year, beginning in July 1526, Balthasar Hubmaier was able to work without major hindrance in Nikolsburg, Moravia—which is now Mikulov, Czechoslovakia. It was then a frontier town, forty-five miles northeast of Vienna on the important post road between that imperial city and Brünn (Brno), the chief city of Moravia, which was even closer to Nikolsburg than was Vienna. The population was predominantly German. Moravia, smaller in area than the state of Vermont, was traditionally united with Bohemia (Czech lands) as a margravate held by the younger sons of the kings of Bohemia. But royal power was almost nonexistent in Moravia. Local nobility—since 1249, the Liechtenstein family—ruled the land. In the 1520s Leonhard and his nephew Hans von Liechtenstein governed. They were inclined to grant considerable freedom to their people, including freedom in religious matters.

Roman Catholicism still maintained its presence, but since the work of Jan Hus in Prague (the Bohemian capital) before and after the turn of the century in 1400, the spirit of reform dominated church life in Bohemia and Moravia. The followers of Hus fought bitterly, dividing into the conserva-

tive Utraquists, and those more radical who developed into the *Unitas Fratrum*, or Bohemian Brethren, then the Moravian Brethren. Lutheran ideas took hold in the 1520s, apparently under the lead of Hans Spittelmaier, chaplain to the Liechtenstein family.

Other pastors in Nikolsburg who came shortly before the arrival of Hubmaier were Oswald Glaidt, who had been a monk or priest earlier in life, and Martin Göschl, the former coadjutor bishop in another part of the land. These now supported the Reformation also, as did the lords of Liechtenstein, Leonhard and Hans. Another nobleman, high in rank and in office, was Johann of Pernstein, who remained a Utraquist but accepted and promoted Reformation ideas. Still another was Jan Dubcansky, a disciple of Zwingli's, who had arranged for a disputation in Austerlitz in March 1526 with the purpose of winning the Utraquists—the largest religious group in Moravia—to Zwinglian reform. The conference was not successful. The Utraquists began to diverge even further from those seeking fundamental reform.

Simprecht Sorg, called Froschauer, was Hubmaier's printer in Nikolsburg. He came from a family of Augsburg, well known in the trade. He seems to have moved to Zurich in 1524 to work with his uncle Christoph Froschauer, who was Zwingli's printer. Simprecht must have become a disciple of Hubmaier's while the latter was imprisoned in Zurich. He followed the Anabaptist leader to Nikolsburg, where he printed sixteen of the reformer's works. Several of these were obviously brought there in a completed or almost-completed form.

The Judgment of Ancient and of Very Recent Teachers came out first. It seeks to list statements about baptism and against infant baptism from primitive Christian writers in the first part and from Hubmaier's contemporaries in the second part. It came out in two editions at about the same time; in each the preface is dated July 21, 1526. Internal evidence indicates that this work was started in Waldshut early in 1525, continued perhaps later in Zurich and in the libraries of Augsburg. There are many mistakes and other

weaknesses, especially in the second edition. Hubmaier was not at his best in historical work, even for most recent times. His strength lay, rather, in expositing Scripture and delineating Christian teachings. The first edition, about 4,500 words, and the second, more than a quarter longer, were both dedicated to Goschl.

In the first part Hubmaier presents material from Origen, Athanasius, Augustine, Tertullian, Eusebius, and others, including councils and popes; the quotations are not direct and are often used out of context. In the second part—with reference to the teachings of Erasmus, Luther, Oecolampadius, Zwingli, Jud, Hofmeister, Haetzer, and others—some valid points are made, but nothing new. The entire section on Martin Luther reads: "Luther six years ago had a sermon on the mass. The seventeenth article in it declared that the signs such as baptism and the Lord's Supper should not be given unless there is preceding faith. These signs would otherwise be as a sheath without a knife in it, a box without its jewels, a barrel-hoop before the wine-house but no wine." Hubmaier concludes the work with a few pages of comment on his own. "Whoever does not believe," he writes, "will be condemned.... First must be the preaching; next, faith; third, being baptized; fourth, salvation."

The Moravian political situation took an ominous turn not long after Hubmaier's arrival in Nikolsburg. King Ludwig II of Hungary and Bohemia died in battle with the Turks, August 1526, at the age of sixteen. Two months later the Bohemian diet elected Archduke Ferdinand of Austria as king of Bohemia; a month later he became margrave of Moravia. He began at once trying to strengthen royal power and Roman Catholicism in his newly acquired territories. He seemed to have his eye particularly on Balthasar Hubmaier, who had caused him so much trouble elsewhere and whom his officials had never been able to apprehend. Even now, however, his task was not easy. Leonhard and Hans von Liechtenstein managed to hold on to power in Moravia, as their successors would for decades, but their position was not as secure as before. One will wonder whether the final disposition they would make in regard to Hubmaier might be a part of the price they had to pay to retain their position and authority in Moravia.

By the fall of 1526 Hubmaier seems to have made great progress in winning over the leaders of church and state in Nikolsburg to moderate Anabaptist principles. Hans Spittelmaier, Oswald Glaidt, and Martin Goschl seem to have joined Hubmaier wholeheartedly in making the Nikolsburg church into one or more Brethren congregations of baptized believers. Hubmaier himself evidently baptized Leonhard von Liechtenstein. His nephew Hans supported the reform movements but less prominently than his uncle did, and there is no evidence he received believer's baptism. During the coming winter Hans was absent, spending several months in Prague in connection with the coronation of King Ferdinand. Hubmaier and his colleagues built up Anabaptist congregations in and around Nikolsburg totaling perhaps as many as six thousand members. Many of them were refugees from persecution elsewhere. Hubmaier and his colleagues allowed some ancient practices to continue or be revived such as the ringing of church bells for the hours of prayer—morning, noon, and evening.

Hubmaier Undertakes His Literary Defense

Libelous reports and continuing accusations of enemies followed Hubmaier to faraway Moravia. New friends there suggested that he publish a booklet in his own defense, explaining his views and some past events in print as he had presented these orally in Nikolsburg. Reluctantly, for fear it might seem like self-praise, he took up the task. *A Short Apology*, about 4,800 words in length, appeared probably in the early fall of 1526. It was dedicated to Leonhard and Hans von Liechtenstein.

Among the charges of "new teachings" Hubmaier says had been leveled against him, some he might well have admitted straightaway, e.g., that he practiced "rebaptism," rejected transubstantiation, confession to a priest, extreme unction, church-regulated fasting, many festivals, intercession of saints for worshipers, papal authority, convents, priestly vows, payment of tithe taxes, and usury.

Others, he felt, were patently untrue: "That I am a preacher of new teachings ... do away with prayer ... am a rioter and misled the people ... preach that one should not be obedient to the authorities ... am the worst Lutheran arch-heretic one could find ... apostate from the faith." Still others he considered ridiculous: "that I am possessed of seven devils that speak through me ... a cross is burned under my heels, and I have goat's feet."

Hubmaier begins his defense: "I know nothing of any new teaching; I preach Christ and him crucified.... I recognize the pure virgin Mary ... truly mother of God.... The dear saints in God I honor as his instruments.... That they are mediators for us and helpers in our troubles before God, I deny. We have an intercessor and helper in our need, even Christ Jesus (Matthew 11; 1 John 2; 1 Timothy 2; John 14). Prayer? I teach it ceaselessly ... but to mumble much with the lips and the heart nowhere near, I hate that (Luke 18; 1 Thessalonians 5; Matthew 6; Luke 11). One should fast daily by avoiding excess in food and drink.... Extreme unction.... I hold to be not only a mockery but even idolatry, for people attribute forgiveness of sins to it." The writer explains the basis of his judgments: "The holy Fathers, councils, and men's teachings I test on the touchstone of holy Scripture (1 John 4)."

Hubmaier continues, "I recognize three baptisms: that of the Spirit, which takes place inwardly, in faith ... water baptism, which takes place outwardly with oral affirmation of faith before the church ... [and] that of the blood of the martyrs or the dying, of which Christ speaks in Luke 12.... No one should be frightened by persecution or suffering, for Christ himself had to suffer and so to enter into his glory (Luke 24). Paul writes, 'All who wish to live godly lives in Christ Jesus will suffer persecution' (1 Timothy 3). That is the third and last baptism."

"I have never taught rebaptism," Hubmaier protests. "The true baptism of Christ, preceded by teaching and oral testimony of faith, I do teach; I also declare that infant baptism is robbery of the true baptism of Christ and a misuse of the holy name of God the Father, Son, and Holy Spirit, entirely contrary to the way it was instituted by Christ and practiced by the apostles (Matthew 28; Mark 16; Acts 2, 8, 9, 10, 11, 16, 18, 19, 22; 1 Peter 3; Hebrews 10). Still, it is properly and correctly called infant baptism. For what on this earth can be more infantile than to take a baby two hours old and ask the child in Latin if it renounces the devil? The child is supposed to answer in German that it renounces him—as if the infant had studied two languages in its mother's womb. O what childishness, what blindness!

"The altar? Yes, I would destroy that—on which Christ Jesus ... is [presumably] crucified and killed anew.... I don't find the word 'mass' anywhere in Scripture.... I regard the priestly mass [*mess*] just about as highly as I do the Frankfurt fair [*mess*]—nothing but buying and selling day after day. The only difference is that the priestly mass [supposedly] takes place spiritually."

The writer relates how he had been mistreated in Zurich and hunted down by Ferdinand's officers, who put pressure on Zurich and the confederation to hand him over to them. He maintains his innocence of crime and heresy. Instead of responding to his plea for instruction from the Word of God, the so-called great ones sought to teach, he says, "with arrest, imprisonment, killing, and the executioner's work. But faith is a work of God and not of the Heretics' Tower, from which a prisoner sees neither sun nor moon and lives on bread and water alone." Asking for nothing but a fair hearing and justice, he testifies, "All [can be endured] except injury to God's Word and the troubling of believers."

Hubmaier warns, "Beware, beware, O authorities, that your hands are not polluted, and then washed in the blood of the innocent.... Keep well in mind that you also have a Judge who is over you in heaven.... You cannot escape his judgment. Also it will not help you to say, 'I had to do it. My gracious lord [ruler] commanded me to do it. He wants to have it so.' No, not so. One must obey God rather than men.... You should be no respecter of persons in court, but give a hearing to the small person just as you do to the great one, and fear no one, for the judgment is God's.... The judge sits in the place of God.... Rage and fury and the shedding of innocent blood will not help.... The Lord in heaven laughs at you. You make a grave and will fall into it yourselves.... Turn to God, dear masters and friends, and he will graciously remove the iron scourge from us. Truth is immortal."

Christian Doctrines and the Ordinances

Another booklet, *A Simple Instruction,* about 7,600 words in length, concerned primarily Jesus' words "This is my body," in observance of the Lord's Supper. It was a contribution to the heated discussion which had been going on among reform-minded churchmen already before Hubmaier arrived in Nikolsburg. Some favored Luther's interpretation that Christ was somehow present in the elements and others Zwingli's, that the Supper, like baptism, was a symbol and sign. Hubmaier held to the latter view. Although he objected to Zwingli saying, "this is my body" means "this signifies my body," the two men come out essentially at the same place in this dispute. Hubmaier dedicated the work to Leonhard von Liechtenstein, whom he praises in extravagant language. The booklet, apparently well received, came out in a second edition not long after the first.

It begins with a repudiation of various views of transubstantiation and related doctrines concerning the real presence of Christ in the elements. In the process the writer further explains his method of biblical interpretation: "Wherever certain statements of Scripture are obscure or the matter is presented very briefly from which discord could come, one should set, alongside the short or obscure passage, other passages—as many as possible on the subject—which are somewhat clearer and more specific; these should be used—as one might use many lighted candles bound together for brighter illumination—in order to clarify the scriptural passage."

Hubmaier quotes, along with other passages, the classic Scripture on the subject from 1 Corinthians 11: "This is my body, which is given for you.... This do in remembrance of me." He comments, "The previous statement should be understood according to the latter.... The bread is not in itself the body, for bread is not crucified and has not died; so the bread must be the body of Christ—in remembrance." Christ is here physically present at a farewell meal with his disciples, the writer relates; so it is impossible that his body should be in the bread. Likewise, in present observances, "The breaking, distribution, and eating of the bread is not a breaking, distribution, and eating of the body of Christ, who sits at God's right hand in heaven. All of this is a remembrance of the breaking and dissemination of the body in his suffering."

Hubmaier gives illustrations: "I see a portrait of the emperor Nero and say, 'That is the emperor Nero.' Taken literally the statement is false. So rather I say, 'That is a remembrance of the emperor Nero,' and the statement is true." Similarly with the wine in the ordinance: "This is my blood . . . held in remembrance. . . . For the wine of the Supper was not shed for the remission of our sins, but the rose-colored blood of Good Friday's cross was. It became the blood of the new testament through his death. . . . The Lord's Supper is a remembrance, a memorial, an admonition from the sufferings of Christ—and not a sacrifice—until he comes."

With so many people from so many lands and so many levels of society coming into the Anabaptist church in Nikolsburg, there was a burning need for a sort of catechism or handbook of doctrine. At the urgent request of Martin Goschl, Hubmaier prepared such a handbook, of about 8,000 words, and dedicated it to Goschl, whom he addresses as "gracious sir [or lord] and brother." Entitled *A Manual of Christian Teaching Which Each Person Should Know Before He Is Baptized*, it is presented in the form of a dialogue between Leonhard and Hans von Liechtenstein. In the preface Hubmaier introduces them as "great lovers of the holy gospel, our gracious lords."

Explaining the general need for instruction the author writes, also in the preface, of his former positions as professor in Ingolstadt and cathedral preacher in Regensburg when he and others "made many priests and monks, none of whom knew how to translate into German or even to read properly the epistles of Paul. . . . I myself was made a doctor in the holy Scriptures . . . and still did not understand the Christian principles presented in this little book. At that time I had read none of the Gospels, nor the epistles of Paul, from beginning to end. How could I therefore teach any sacred Word or preach to others?. . . People picked out some parts and patches of the gospel for us but so much of the straw and hulls of human elaboration and addition was mixed in with it that we did not find the sweetness of the kernel and the real wheat."

This catechism booklet treats various doctrines of the faith, using the Apostles' Creed as part of the instructional material; Leonhard speaks as the teacher asking the questions (he was forty-four years of age at the time), Hans (twenty-six) answering somewhat as a disciple. In this interchange the gospel is outlined—the death of Christ for man's sins, the preaching of the Word, the work of the Holy Spirit, confession of sin, faith, the church, new birth, baptism, the Lord's Supper, prayer, church discipline, eternal life, hell, and the second coming of Christ. Asked why he was not baptized in infancy, Hans answers: "Because I had not yet believed, nor did I know what faith or Christ or baptism was." Infant baptism, he says, "robs the child of the true baptism of Christ. . . . If we desire to have water baptism, even if one is a hundred years old, it is not rebaptism, because infant baptism is no baptism at all—it is quite unworthy even of the name baptism."

There are questions then about "brotherly discipline" in the church and the ordinance of the Supper. Confession of sins, it comes out, is "to God, but to no monk or priest." Images are rejected as aids to worship. Fasting is "daily— using food and drink in moderation." As for prayer to the saints, Hans exclaims, "Whoever runs to the saints and cries out for them to pray to Christ to be merciful toward him, blasphemes [Christ], who is the most gracious and most merciful one in all of heaven, our only advocate and gracious mediator before the Father." Extensive models are given for prayer before meals. The necessity of good works, empowered by the Spirit of God, is emphasized.

In this connection an interesting detail of customary home life, as well as school life, is revealed. Leonhard asks Hans why God would condemn a person "since no one, in and of himself, can do anything good." God "does not condemn him for what he does but for what he does not do," Hans answers, "just as a schoolmaster beats his pupils not for what they learned but for not learning. Similarly, a man beats his wife not for what she does but for what she doesn't do. God in like manner condemns people not for works they do but for those they do not do according to God's will and his good pleasure."

Opposing what he regarded as Lutheran doctrine, the writer says, "There is still something in us of the image of God, in which we were originally created (Genesis 1). This is, however, obscured, taken captive and fettered, by the disobedience of Adam. There we are stuck, until Christ makes us free."

Cause and Reason Why Every Person Who Was Baptized Early in His Childhood Should Be Baptized According to the Ordinance of Christ Even if He Were a Hundred Years Old, a tract of approximately 3,400 words, appeared about the same time as the one just discussed—at the turn of the year 1526-27. It is in the main a reprinting of the latter part of Hubmaier's book on baptism published about a year and a half earlier. Some new points appear in the closing part of the later publication which suggest that they were written amid church conditions known to prevail at the time in Moravia. *Cause and Reason* is dedicated to Johann von Pernstein.

Tracts on Practical Issues

A series of four tracts by Hubmaier on practical matters of church life in Nikolsburg—baptism, the Lord's Supper, discipline, and the ban—were written near the end of the year 1526 and printed early the next year. The shortest of these, *A Form for Baptizing*, runs to only about 1,550 words. It was dedicated to the nobleman Jan Dubcansky in an effort evidently to win him for the Anabaptist cause, or at least to gain his support as mediator and protector. In the brief writing, Hubmaier outlines the baptismal services as conducted by him and his associates. He refers to the minister as "bishop," using the word in its New Testament sense of "overseer" of the congregation. He emphasizes the need for adequate instruction of the candidate preceding baptism, his or her confession of faith, and vows taken before the church.

The bishop dips up a bit of water and pours this over the head of the candidate saying "I baptize you in the name of the Father, the Son, and the Holy Spirit for the forgiveness of your sins. Amen. May it be so." The administrator then calls upon the church to pray for the new convert "that God and all Christian people should cause his faith to increase and give to all of us the power and endurance that we persevere in the Christian faith and be found in it to the end." After a congregational prayer, the bishop lays his hand on the head of the new member and says, "I give you the testimony and the authority that from this time on you be counted a part of the Christian fellowship, to participate in the use of its keys, to break bread and pray with Christian sisters and brothers. May God be with you and with your spirit. Amen."

Likewise, *A Form for Observance of the Supper*, about 4,300 words, describes the practice in Nikolsburg and seeks to meet the current need for instruction of new members. Here again administrators are called "bishops," also "priests." Both terms as used mean simply congregational leaders. The tract is dedicated to Burian Sobek of Kornice, one of the lesser nobility, doctor of laws and member of the *Unitas Fratrum;* he had translated Luther's writings into Czech (Bohemian) and favored radical reform. He might be, Hubmaier must have reasoned, a good Anabaptist prospect.

As brothers and sisters "modestly dressed" are gathered for observance of the Supper, sitting quietly—not babbling or boisterous—"each participant should call himself to account before God, acknowledging his sins and his guilt," Hubmaier writes. "It is not improper, to start with, that the priest, along with the congregation, falls to his knees and prays from his heart the following: 'Father, we have sinned.... Be merciful to us, sinners ... through Jesus

Christ our Lord and Savior. Amen.' " The congregation takes the "pledge of love." Everyone sits again and the priest teaches of Christ, his suffering and death; passages are suggested for exposition.

Members who do not understand something may ask questions—but only male members! "Women are to be quiet and remain silent in church. If they want to learn about something, they should ask their husbands when they get home, so that all things may proceed in an orderly fashion (1 Corinthians 11 and 14).... Remembrance involves the following—that the person surely and fully believes that Christ gave up his body and poured out his rose-colored blood on the cross for us. Let the person also test himself in regard to thankfulness ... shown in word and deed ... the true fellowship of the saints ... of all the host of heaven and the universal Christian church, outside which there is no salvation. In this light the bread and the wine of the table of God are so important."

The booklet on general church discipline, *Concerning Brotherly Discipline,* runs to about 3,300 words. The remainder of the title states the thesis: "Where it is not practiced, there is certainly no church, even if water baptism and the Lord's Supper are observed." The text states, "After people have heard the Word of God, received it, and believed it, they make a promise to God, committing themselves in baptism before the church to live thereafter according to the Word.... Water baptism and the breaking of bread is in vain, useless and fruitless, where brotherly discipline and the Christian ban [excommunication] is not practiced along with them—discipline bearing a relationship to baptism, and the ban, to communion and fellowship."

Referring to 1 Timothy 5:20, the writer declares, "Those who sin openly should be disciplined before the whole group in order that others may fear. Christ disciplined Peter in this way. Peter had suggested to him in just a few kind and well-intentioned words that he watch out for himself and not go to Jerusalem, so that nothing bad should happen to him" (Matthew 16:23). Hubmaier gives another example in the "disciplining" of Simon of Samaria (Acts 8:18-24). The writer says secret sins should be dealt with secretly, and here gives the example of Nathan going privately to King David (2 Kings 12) and Christ speaking privately to Judas, although in the presence of the other disciples (Matthew 26:25). In cases where the offending member is obstinate in his sin, the matter must be brought before the church; and if he or she will not acknowledge guilt and repent, the congregation must decide on the penalty. The ultimate penalty, which would be dealt with in another writing, was the ban or exclusion from the church.

"Observe, devout Christians, how helpful and beneficial brotherly discipline is," Hubmaier writes, "especially if one recognizes its redemptive quality and dutifully accepts it." It is no valid excuse for a member of the congregation to protest that he is himself a sinner and therefore unworthy of judging. There is in fact a benefit to those making the judgment, as well as to the offending member, for it is a challenge to them to examine their own lives, first of all, and get themselves more perfectly attuned to the will of God, then, to fulfill their Christian responsibility toward the offending member. This all belongs to the believer's original commitment of everything to Christ, and to the sign of loyalty given in baptism.

"Where there is no baptism according to the ordinance of Christ," Hubmaier writes in the concluding paragraph, "it is impossible for one to receive helpful brotherly discipline from the others. Nobody really knows, then, who is in the church and who is outside of it; none has any authority over the other, but all are scattered as sheep without a shepherd, without pasture, without ordinances.... May God help us all, that we may enter by the right door into the sheepfold of Christ Jesus and not by another way—against the express ordering of Christ. Amen. Truth is immortal."

The companion tract on discipline, *Concerning the Christian Ban*, about 4,900 words, also brings out its thesis in the rest of the title: "Where it is not instituted and practiced, according to the serious and orderly command of Christ, there sin, shame, and vice rule." Those who could not be reclaimed for consistent Christian living by other measures of discipline such as serious exhortation or excluding the offender from the Lord's Supper, were to be excommunicated, but only after every brotherly effort had been made to help them. The tract begins: "After the sinner has been seriously admonished by his brother, correction thus being attempted secretly, then [if needed], before two or three witnesses, and then [again, if needed] before the entire congregation (Matthew 18) . . . and he will not improve or forsake his sin, then he is to be excluded from the church and excommunicated according to the command of Christ."

As for the relationship of church people toward the excommunicated one, "With the banned person you are not to fraternize in eating, drinking, greetings, or any other way . . . otherwise we become party to his evil activity. We should regard him as a heathen and a publican. . . . All this occurs in honor to God, with benefit to the church and for the good of the disciplined one himself, to the end that he becomes ashamed, forsakes the sins, and changes his life. We should still not regard him as an enemy; we are not to beat him, strike him, or put him to death—simply avoid him, flee from him, have nothing to do with him. That is, in short, the will of God." There follows a discussion of Scriptures on the subject such as 1 Corinthians 5. "Discipline and the ban do not take place out of hate," the author emphasizes, "nor to anyone's detriment, but rather out of Christian love." Other churches should be notified about the excluded member, the writer states, "that they may know also to beware of him."

Then Hubmaier presents the more positive side of excommunication: "If the excluded person acknowledges his error and his miserable state, forsakes the sins in deed, turns back, repents, asks God for mercy, and straightens out his life, then the church should receive him again with great rejoicing, opening again the kingdom of Christ in the power of the keys granted to it according to the command of Christ: 'Whatever you loose on earth shall be loosed in heaven.' This may happen not seven times only but seventy times seven, 490 times. . . . This is to be understood as: so often as the sinner repents and feels sorrow for his sin, it will be remitted through the sufferings of Christ. That means, however, real sorrow and repentance for the sin."

Can Everyone Respond to God's Grace and Guidance?

Hubmaier entered the controversy about the doctrine of free will with two booklets on the subject; even here, his primary interest was practical, as always, and not literary. *Concerning Freedom of the Will,* approximately 7,500 words, is summarized as others in the remainder of the title: ". . . which God through his Word vouchsafes to all people and in free will gives the power to become his children, also the choice to will and to do the good, or to remain children of wrath which they are by nature." The booklet bears the date of April 1, 1527, and it is dedicated to the godly George of Brandenburg-Ansbach, a promoter of Lutheranism and protector of various reformers throughout a wide area, including Moravia. *The Second Booklet on Man's Freedom of Will,* dated May 20 and almost half again as long as the former, is dedicated to Count Friedrich II von Liegnitz. The territories he ruled bordered on Moravia. He was early won for the Reformation and promoted it, often in its more radical and spiritualist aspects. He would later give refuge to the printer Simprecht Sorg, Oswald Glaidt, and others from Nikolsburg when Hubmaier was no longer there and reform came under new pressures. The rest of the title reads: ". . . in which it is shown from Scripture that God through his Word gives power to become his children, leaving freely to them the choice to will and do the good."

Although Reformation preaching had been going on in many areas for years, Hubmaier writes, "Still I find very many people who unfortunately have learned and understand no more than two points from all the preaching: They say, (1) 'We believe, and this faith saves us,' and (2) 'We are incapable of doing anything good. God works in us both the willing and the doing. We have no free will.' Such talk is only half-truth, from which one can draw no more than half a judgment. Whoever draws a full judgment from it and does not lay counter-Scriptures on the scales with it, makes the half-truth much more harmful than a total lie. From this sort of thing come all kinds of sects, quarreling and heresies. . . . The world is worse than it has been in a thousand years . . . everything taking place, sad to state, under the pretense of the gospel. . . . People say, 'All things happen because of God's ordinance, and must happen.' They therefore believe their sinning is allowed . . . justify all license of the flesh and hang all the sins and guilt on God, as Adam blamed his sin on Eve, and Eve, hers on the serpent."

The individual soul has the power, granted by the Father through Christ, to respond to God's grace, the writer emphasizes, and this is his or her free will. That soul has the free will also to reject it, for "God wants to have uncoerced, willing, and joyful disciples and followers; these he loves to have. For God forces no one, except through the sending out of his Word with its appeal. . . . For the gospel is the power of God to save all believers."

In the conclusion Hubmaier repeats his argument: "Through the denial of free will, many excuses are given for evildoers, that they may lay the responsibility for their sins and iniquity on God. They say, 'It is the will of God that I commit whoremongering and adultery. Whatever God wills, that must take place. Who can resist his will? If it were not his will, I could not sin. Whenever it is his will, I shall stop sinning.' I refrain from comment [on this blasphemy]. Through such false thinking many people are led astray into slothfulness and wickedness, thinking, 'Since I can neither will nor do anything good, and all things happen of necessity, I shall remain as I am. If God wants me, he will surely draw me to himself. If he does not want me, my own will is exercised fruitlessly and in vain.' Such people wait for some special, unusual, and miraculous drawing which God may use with them, as if the sending of his holy Word, to draw them and help them forward, were not enough."

In his second book on free will Hubmaier complains that some of his "dear friends" deny the doctrine "in a very heated way." These "come to me daily," he writes, "quoting many Scriptures by which they hope to dispose of free will entirely." He hoped in this second booklet on the subject "to clear out of the way such offensive stones of opposition and deal these stones such a blow with the sword of God's Word that no one may stumble over them or be injured by them."

This writing is influenced in its form and scriptural selection by a book of Erasmus on the subject; it is obviously influenced also by Hans Denck's *The Assertion that Scripture Says God Practices and Produces Good and Evil,* published in 1526. *The Second Book on Man's Free Will* is divided into three sections. The first discusses many passages of the Old Testament and the New, taken to support free will. The second section lists many epigrammatic statements on the subject, which made it useful in disputations. The third answers fifteen different "arguments" against free will. Scripture references and quotations abound.

"Whoever understands what is involved in the rebirth experience will not deny man's free will," Hubmaier writes. "It would be a deceptive God who would invite all the people to a supper and offer, in all seriousness, his lovingkindness to everyone, if it were not indeed his desire that they come. It would be a false God who should say with his mouth, 'Come hither,' while thinking secretly in his heart, 'Stay there.' It would be a faithless God who would openly give his grace to a person, clothing that person in a new robe, while secretly taking it away and preparing hell for him." The writer refers several times to the positive and negative aspects of God's will—God's "turning-toward" will and his "turning-from" will. "God's positive will is that of his love. His negative will is that of his wrath or punishment." Hubmaier makes the application: "That all persons are not saved God is not to blame; he gave his most beloved Son unto death for us all. We ourselves are to blame."

An "argument" raised against free will is that "God has mercy on whom he will and whom he will he hardens (Romans 9). Here my dear friend cries out against me, 'Look here, everything depends on God and nothing is in our own power. What God wills, that shall and must come to pass.' Answer: These are words about the almighty and secret will of God, which no man is responsible for. God can without any injustice have mercy on whom he will, or harden the same one—save him or condemn him. . . . He can make us what he will, a vessel of honor or of dishonor, as the potter has such power over his clay—and we cannot rightly say, 'Why do you do it so?' "

In contrast to this secret will of God, however, "There is also a revealed will of God according to which he desires all people to be saved and come to the knowledge of the truth"; John 3:16 is quoted as documentation. "He suffered for our sins," Hubmaier continues, "and not for our sins only but for the sins of the whole world. He gave himself for the redemption of all people. He is also the true light that lightens all persons who come into this world. To all those who receive him he gives the power to become sons of God. And after that he commands them to preach the gospel to every creature so that everyone who receives and believes it and is baptized will be saved."

Questions of Eschatology and the Sword

While Hubmaier was preparing the second of his booklets on free will, Hans Hut, the fiery Anabaptist preacher from South Germany, entered Nikolsburg. He agreed essentially with most other Anabaptists on basic doctrines—baptism, the Lord's Supper, the church, and renunciation of "the sword" (nonparticipation in government and military service). He seems to have opposed as well the payment of taxes when these might be used for military purposes. His pacifism did not apply to the time of Christ's reign on earth, however, when worldly powers would be toppled and the ungodly destroyed. He seems to have set exact dates, some two years hence, for the second coming of Christ. His favorite subject for preaching was the exciting developments at the end of the age.

Hut attended several services where Hubmaier preached, but he was not satisfied with what he saw and heard. He was more attracted to an opposition group which advocated community of goods for Christians. He had apparently never taught this himself, but he liked the radical approach of these people. Oswald Glaidt and many others joined Hut. Hubmaier, realizing that the unity of his work as a whole was being threatened, went on the offensive. He got together a collection of Hut's teachings and alleged teachings and reduced them to seven "Theses Against Hut." He planned to have these printed but did not get it arranged. The writing was used, however, for discussions near the middle of May between Hubmaier and Hut, later in a small circle of pastors and laymen, then for a larger gathering in the church, and finally, in the castle on the hill, at the insistence of Leonhard von Liechtenstein, in the presence of Leonhard, other nobles, and some councilmen.

Even at the last of these meetings Hubmaier was quite harsh with Hut in the discussions, and some of the nobles spoke up asking him to give Hut more freedom to speak his mind; this was done. Still, the radical Hut seems to have shown no restraint. The Liechtenstein lords were convinced that he was teaching insurrection for the present time, and universal violence at the time of the imminent return of Christ. They forcibly detained him in the castle that Monday evening, after the discussions ended. The incarceration was not very tight, it seems, and Hut escaped during the night. It is possible his treatment was arranged in this way to get him to leave the country. Fleeing to Augsburg, then to Vienna, he apparently worked for awhile with Oswald Glaidt.

Hut's teaching on baptism was basically that of Hubmaier, but Hut gave more emphasis to what he called the real spiritual baptism, which should follow water baptism as a special gift of God's grace, and to the "baptism of suffering," which would inevitably follow conversion for the true Christian. He also compared baptism with the seal worn on the foreheads of the 144,000 servants of God in Revelation 7:4. This documents again Hut's teachings about last things. He was obsessed with the theme, preaching on it repeatedly from passages in Daniel and Revelation. He seems to have set the duration of the antichrist's reign at three and a half years. Hubmaier worked out figures in the same passages Hut had used for the antichrist's reign and arrived at a period of 1,277 years instead of three and a half. This was probably done to show that Scripture should not be used in such a way.

The two differed greatly on the question of "the sword," and Hubmaier wrote a booklet on the subject. *Concerning the Sword,* dated June 24, 1527, and comprising about 9,700 words, was the last of the books printed by Simprecht Sorg for Hubmaier. It was dedicated to Arkleb von Boskovic, who belonged to a noble family of Moravia, held the highest administrative offices in the land, and supported the Lutheran cause. Arkleb would die in the same city and on the same day as would Hubmaier, but—in contrast to the latter—from natural causes. The subtitle: "A Christian exposition of Scriptures so earnestly quoted by certain brethren against the magistracy, holding that Christians should not sit in judgment nor bear the sword."

The writer quotes Jesus as he speaks to Pilate, " 'My kingdom is not of this world; if it were of this world my servants would surely fight for me, that I should not be delivered to the Jews' (John 18). From this Scripture some brothers say that a Christian may not bear the sword, since the kingdom of Christ is not of this world." In answer Hubmaier says, "Our kingdom *should* not be of this world, but unfortunately we must confess before God that it is ... a kingdom of sin, death, and hell.... Christ alone can say with truth, 'My kingdom is not of this world.' ... The most devout and godly Christians must acknowledge themselves unholy even until death."

Another quoted passage relates the effort of Peter to attack those who came to arrest Christ in the Garden of Gethsemane. "Put up your sword into its place.... This thing must happen in this way" (Matthew 26). Hubmaier notes that Peter is not reproached for carrying a sword, nor is he told to throw it away, but to put it back in its scabbard. Jesus' time has come; he knows it and desires no interference in the Father's plan. Moreover, if some force were to be applied, it should not be by Peter but by the authorities, those who are chosen as magistrates to protect the good and punish the evil. He is saying to Peter, 'You are not in authority.... You have not been called or elected to such a position.' He who takes up the sword shall perish by the sword. These who 'take up the sword' are those who use it without election, in a disorderly way, and on their own authority."

Hubmaier elaborates further: "One of the people spoke to the Lord, 'Master, say to my brother that he divide the inheritance with me.' But he said to him, 'Man, who has appointed me judge or the divider of inheritances over you?' (Luke 12)." The writer explains that Jesus is saying, " 'I am not chosen or set up as a judge. It is not my office. It belongs to others.' Notice, Christ does not condemn the judge's office.... Rather, he shows that no one should undertake to be a judge who is not appointed, or chosen for the position. So there are elections for burgomasters, mayors, and judges."

It is better, Hubmaier writes, for Christians to suffer wrong rather than bring disputes to court; yet "if Christians wish to go to law and not be at peace with one another, they would sin still more—doubly so—if they would take their case before an unbelieving judge and not before a Christian.... A Christian may, according to the good ordinance of God, bear the sword in the place of God and against the evildoer to punish him. He is also ordained of God for the protection and defense of godly people from evil ones."

Hubmaier distinguishes between this external, coercive authority of government and the pacifist discipline in church according to Matthew 18:15-17: "See now, dear brethren, that these two offices and commandments—concerning the ban and the secular sword—are not set in opposition to each other, since both are from God. The Christian ban has its frequent place and propriety—as, for example, in [dealing with] the many private sins in which the sword may by no means be used.... In this manner the church with its ban, and the authorities with their sword, must exist side by side, with neither grasping after the office of the other."

A True and a False Magistracy

In regard to the injunction of Jesus, "Love your enemies" (Matthew 6:44), Hubmaier says, "An enemy is he whom one hates and envies. A Christian should not hate or envy any-

body but love everyone; a Christian magistrate has no
enemy, for he hates and envies no one. What he does with
the sword he does not do out of envy or hate but according to
the command of God, . . . on the basis of justice . . . yet not
only on the basis of justice but also out of the great love that
he bears toward the evildoer—not his evil deed—that the
magistrate can and should punish him."

The opposing brethren are made to quote Matthew 5:21,
"You shall not kill." Hubmaier then contrasts this to Old
Testament passages recording God's orders to kill, as well as
New Testament passages such as the command to rulers to
wield the sword in Romans 13. Pious opponents ask, "How
then can this 'Kill!' and 'Do not kill' stand one with another?"
Hubmaier answers, "Quite well!" Then he lists thirty-three
paradoxical statements from various parts of the Bible,
which Hubmaier believes can stand together: "having
nothing yet possessing everything, 2 Corinthians 6 . . . loving father and mother and hating them, Exodus 20, Luke 14
. . . swearing by the name of God and not swearing,
Deuteronomy 6, Matthew 5 . . . being told we should not do
good works before men and still should do them that men
see our good works, Matthew 5, 23 . . . finding out that Abraham was justified by faith and yet by works, Romans 4,
James 2, Hebrews 11 . . . being asked to please our neighbor
and yet not to please men, Romans 15, Galatians 1 . . . and
reading that God does not tempt, yet that he tempted Abraham; James 1; Genesis 22."

Hubmaier refers again to the command not to kill (Matthew 5:21), which was followed by Jesus' condemning
anyone for being angry with his brother or saying "Raca" or
"Fool" to him. "Reading that, dear brothers, you see clearly
the kind of killing Christ forbade, namely, killing which
takes place out of anger, ridicule, or abuse. The magistrate,
however—I speak of the just magistrate—does not kill in
anger. He is not motivated by words of ridicule and abuse
but by the orders of God, who has earnestly commanded him
to do away with the wicked and maintain the devout in
peace. . . . Those who do not wish evildoers to be killed but
want them to live, actually sin against the commandment

'Do not kill'; for whoever does not protect the righteous person, kills him, and is guilty of his death just as much as he who does not feed the hungry."

The author pleads with his opponents, "So, dear brothers, do not make patchwork of Scripture, but put the preceding words and the following words together for a total judgment, then you will come to a complete understanding of the Scripture; and you will see how it does not forbid the magistracy of Christians as you do but teaches us not to quarrel, war, and fight, or to conquer land and people with force and the sword. That is against God. Also we should not long to be exalted lords and nobles, worldly kings, princes, and rulers. For the magistracy is not lordly and aristocratic but serves according to the ordinance of God."

The writer warns further, "Worldly authorities have power over temporal goods and the flesh or the physical body alone, but not over the soul. The sword is entrusted to them by God's ordinance not that they should noisily fight, war, quarrel, castigate, strive, and tyrannize—but to defend orphans, protect widows, take care of the devout, provide for all who are troubled and repressed. This is the duty of the one in an office of authority, as God himself shows manifold times in Scripture. This cannot take place without the shedding of blood and killing; for this reason, therefore, God has hung a sword at the magistrates' side, not a fox's tail."

Taking Romans 13 as the strongest argument for submitting to valid government authority, which is authorized by God, Hubmaier says, "This Scripture alone is enough, dear brothers, to affirm the magistracy, against all the gates of hell." Going further he says, "The magistrate will punish the wicked, as he is duty-bound to do for his own soul's salvation, and if he has not reached the point where he can do this alone, and calls on his subjects—by bell or alarm signals, by letter or other summons—they are duty-bound, also for their souls' salvation, to stand by their ruler and help him, so that the wicked may be exterminated and rooted out."

In keeping with the medieval tradition that people had the right to replace a totally unworthy prince or magistrate,

Hubmaier explains: "Subjects should carefully test the spirit of their ruler, whether he is motivated and stimulated more by haughtiness, pride, intoxication, envy, hatred, or his own interests than by love for the common good and the peace of the land. When the latter is the case he does not bear the sword according to the ordinance of God. . . . If a ruler should be childish or foolish, even entirely unfit to rule, one can then quite justifiably take leave of him and submit to another. . . . For because of a wicked ruler God has often punished an entire land. But if it cannot be done in an orderly way and peaceably, without great destruction and general uprising, one should rather endure the ruler as one whom God has given us in his wrath for the purpose of chastising us for our sins, we who are unworthy of anything better."

Hubmaier then caps his argument: "To sum up: No one can deny that to protect the devout and punish the wicked is the earnest command of God, which stands until the judgment day." Eight Scriptures are listed in support of this. Therefore, Hubmaier concludes, "the magistrate is a servant of God. . . . Now, where is it written that a Christian may not be such a servant of God, fulfilling the command of God to bring good to all the people? Or that he may not carry out such godly work (as Paul himself calls it) according to the ordinance of God? . . . The peace of God be with us all. Amen. Truth is immortal."

The Prosecution Prepares, as Does the Defense

Amid great pomp and ceremony Archduke Ferdinand had been crowned king of Bohemia in February 1527. One of the first issues to which he turned his attention in his realms was the elimination of heresy, especially that of the hated Anabaptists. He was drawing up a general mandate against heretics which stated that those who submitted to the blasphemous practice of rebaptism would be outlawed, punished in body and life. The mandate was published later that same year. Working closely with the king in this program was the king's counselor, Johann Faber, former friend of Hubmaier, yet zealous persecutor of heretics. Faber probably took the initiative and administered the king's program against Anabaptists, to begin with Hubmaier.

Plans were laid, patiently and carefully. Since leading nobles in Moravia were involved in reform and Anabaptist movements, the Catholic king was without doubt advised to bring pressure on them, especially Leonhard von Liechtenstein. Leonhard was surely brought to see that, when the program against heretics achieved full momentum, he would be extremely vulnerable. Perhaps he was promised immunity and the right to remain without question in his high position—even permitted to continue with a considerable amount of religious freedom in Moravia—if he would bring Hubmaier to Vienna for the Austrians to question him.

Heresy was not the open charge against the Anabaptist at this time, but rather sedition and insurrection in his Waldshut days. Leonhard von Liechtenstein and his nephew Hans could hardly refuse the king's order to subject Hubmaier to questioning on such a serious charge, without jeopardizing their own position and freedom. In any case, they obeyed. Perhaps the new faith was not strong enough, even for Leonhard, to enable them to risk everything for it. So they had Hubmaier delivered to the authorities in Vienna, probably in the early part of July. There he was imprisoned, along with his wife, and questioned for long hours.

Ferdinand wrote on July 22 to the Austrian officials in Freiburg to gather all possible materials about Hubmaier's part in the earlier uprising of the peasants and of Waldshut. The king said his order should also be sent to the regional government in Ensisheim so that materials could be gathered there too. Similar instructions went to the Austrian authorities in Innsbruck.

After a few days the Hubmaiers were taken from Vienna to the Kreuzenstein, an old, dank and dingy castle north of Vienna, where they were incarcerated separately. There the questioning continued, under torture. The charges now included heresy as well as insurrection.

Hubmaier, realizing his weakness when faced with physical torture and hardship, spent long uncomfortable hours reflecting on his desperate situation. Could anything be saved from the debacle? Knowing that his old friend Faber was a key person, and a very close counselor to the king, the prisoner determined as a first step to request talks with Faber. Surely his old university fellow would moderate his and the king's position toward a friend of former days. The Anabaptist, in view of his otherwise hopeless situation, was prepared to meet his opponents halfway and give in a bit here and there, particularly in respect to doctrinal and practical distinctives of rigid Catholicism, which he regarded as of little importance one way or the other. He would try to hold firm on vital points but play down the controversial elements as much as possible. He sent the king a request to speak with Faber. The request was granted and conversations between Hubmaier and Faber, lasting several days, took place in the Kreuzenstein Castle at the end of 1527.

In addition to these two principals, two others were present—Ambrosius Salzer, rector of the University of Vienna, and Markus Beckh von Leopoldsdorf, governor of Lower Austria—but they apparently took no part in the discussions. Beckh attended because Ferdinand had ordered the government of Lower Austria, in whose jurisdiction Kreuzenstein was located, to conduct the case against the Anabaptist leader.

Hubmaier composed an extensive Statement of Faith— about 12,500 words—addressed to Ferdinand; it was, of course, not printed at the time. In a preface he expresses his appreciation to the king that the latter had, "out of his particular graciousness and generosity, sent to me the worthy Dr. Johann Faber who ... conducted himself in a kind and praiseworthy fashion in all his actions toward me." The imprisoned writer then takes up the question of "salvation by faith alone," for that gives him the opportunity to castigate Lutherans and place himself, as it were, on the Catholic side. Quoting Galatians 5:6, "faith working through love," he insists that "faith alone is like a green fig tree without fruit, a cistern without water, clouds without rain." He refers to many passages, including Philippians 2:12,

"Work out your own salvation," and James 1:22, "Be doers of the Word and not hearers only," concluding, "Those people who say they can do nothing which is good deceive themselves and there is no true faith in them."

Teaching the Ten Commandments frequently is encouraged, as is prayer. At the close of the section on the latter theme Hubmaier gives a moving tribute to his wife, Elsbeth: "O most gracious king, how I would long to be with my wife, as I am indeed with her in spirit. I do not speak to praise her, yet I have never seen or heard of a person, in all my life, more earnest and more fervent in prayer than she."

On the subject of the Christian congregation, the writer says, "The church is an external gathering and a communion of believers in one Lord, one faith, and one baptism." As for the ordinances, Hubmaier tries to avoid controversial aspects and instead exhausts his argument by attacking Hans Hut. "I can say in good conscience and on the basis of the divine Word that he misused both rites [baptism and the Lord's Supper], contrary to the ordinance of Christ.... I have taught nothing concerning baptism except that it is a public and oral confession of the Christian faith and a renunciation one must make of the devil and all his works, so that a person calmly submits himself in the power of God the Father, Son, and Holy Spirit, is willing to suffer, die, and be buried, in faith, that he may also be raised with Christ into eternal life (Romans 6). One testifies to this in water baptism.

"In the Supper of Christ, as I have taught, we find a testimony of brotherly love; and as we have loved Christ, even unto death, so we should love one another and fulfill works of mercy to one another.... So the baptism I have taught and the baptism brought forward by Hut are as far apart from one another as are heaven and hell, as the east is from the west, as Christ is from Belial—and so also with the Supper." As noted earlier, Hubmaier and Hut actually did agree on the meaning of the Lord's Supper. As for baptism the tendency of Hut to connect it to his eschatological teachings, as indicated above, is about the only point with which Hubmaier could fairly find fault.

The church should practice discipline and the ban, Hubmaier underscores in his present statement; this is "necessary medicine among Christians."

Differences between Hut and Hubmaier on the Christian's relationship to earthly governments were quite real, and Hubmaier made the most of this situation—to separate himself not only from Hut and his followers, but perhaps from other persecuted Anabaptists as well. He referred to his published writings, especially *Concerning the Sword,* to prove he had taught that respect, honor, and obedience—as well as taxes—should be paid to the authorities. Repeating his arguments for Christians taking part in government, with appropriate scriptural quotations as usual, Hubmaier boasts: "Such have I said to Hut and others to their faces; I rejected completely their seductive insurrectionist teachings, as may be found in the articles against him which I defended publicly."

Eschatological differences between Hubmaier and Hut are also highlighted: "Although Christ has given us many signs to know that the day of his coming again is near, no one knows that day except God alone.... I have therefore been very firm against Johann Hut and his followers because they set a specific time for the last day, namely next Whitsunday. They have presented this in an imaginative manner before simple people and caused them to sell their property, leave their wives and children, give up their daily work, leading simple people to run after them—a seductive error growing out of a great misunderstanding of the Scripture."

Hubmaier then lists three kinds of confessions: before God, before the person wronged, and before the church through acknowledgment of sins. He approves of fasting, so that more time and dedication may be given to prayer. Sunday is affirmed as the Christian Sabbath, and a few other holidays may well be observed. As for the intercession of the saints on the worshiper's behalf, Hubmaier states: "Since our Head, Christ Jesus, prays to his heavenly Father for us, I hold that the dear saints who are in heaven and at one in will with their Head, Christ, as members of his body, also pray with Christ ... but I know of absolutely no Scripture indicating that we should call upon them for help and blessings in our time of trouble; for all Scripture points us to Christ as our advocate and intercessor (Matthew 11; 1 Timothy 2; 1 John 2; Romans 8)." As for Mary, the mother of Jesus, "Holy Scripture shows plainly and clearly her virginity ... ever a chaste virgin, before, during and after the birth of Jesus.... Mary alone is mother of Christ, mother of God.... The Lord Jesus is truly God, so it must follow that she is also mother of the true God." Regarding purgatory, the writer says: "That there is, in addition to heaven and hell, a special purgatory, I know of no basis in Scripture."

Martyrdom of the Hubmaiers

Hubmaier must have realized that such negative statements as that on purgatory and the intercession of saints for the faithful, with the omission of any reference to other Catholic tenets of faith, such as transubstantiation, would make his writing useless for the purpose of saving his life. Since this must have indeed been its purpose, it is surprising not that he made concessions, but that he made so few. He gave up nothing in his teachings on biblical authority, baptism, the church, and the Supper, although everything was indeed expressed in as conciliatory a way as conscience allowed. He also went on to say, near the end of the statement, that he would be willing to leave the controversial questions to the decision of a general council of the Catholic Church, which many expected to be called soon. Meanwhile, Hubmaier offered to stop the practice and teaching of baptism and the Supper as he had understood them. "If, however, his majesty does not desire to wait for a council," the eager suppliant continued, "I beg his majesty that I may be permitted to defend these articles with the holy Scriptures before your majesty's honorable council and university representatives. Your majesty may then himself be the judge, according to the answers he has heard."

It is doubtful that Ferdinand ever saw this confession or statement which was addressed to him. He wrote angrily to the government of Lower Austria on February 26, 1528, ordering it to hurry the case against Hubmaier and the other Anabaptist prisoners. In their reply of March 4 the authorities excused themselves on the ground that Hubmaier had promised, in the meetings with Faber, to renounce his teachings; he had then sent to the governor only a "half opinion" (the statement, discussed above, which Hubmaier intended for Ferdinand). The Lower Austrian government, therefore, had ordered Hubmaier to prepare another statement, its reply to Ferdinand continues, dealing especially with the questions of baptism and the Supper. The poor, battered prisoner had prepared it, before the end of February, according to the official letter, and it had been sent through the usual channels—to the bishop, then to the Lower Austrian government, and finally to the king. Nothing more is known of this particular writing.

In any case Ferdinand had gathered enough material to bring the matter to a close. Hubmaier was brought back to Vienna, as was his wife. Subjected to further hearings and torture, he was made to write out another confession—"of guilt." He states boldly in this document, however, that he does not hold to the sacrament on the altar or to infant baptism. He admits that he had rendered some assistance and counsel to the peasants in Waldshut. This confession was read in a public gathering of several thousand Viennese, it seems, and Faber later published it. On the basis of the confession Hubmaier was burned at the stake on March 10, 1528, for heresy and insurrection. He went without complaint, courageous at the end.

Dean Stephanus Sprügel of the University of Vienna claimed to be an eyewitness. He wrote that as Hubmaier was being taken to the place of execution, he repeated for his own consolation verses of Scripture and remained to the last "fixed like an immovable rock in his heresy." Accompanied by armed guards and a large crowd of people, the "heretic" came to the stake which had brush and faggots around it for his burning. He cried out, "O gracious God, in this my great torment, forgive my sins. O Father, I give you thanks that you will today take me out of this vale of tears. I desire to die with rejoicing, and come to you. O Lamb, O Lamb, take away the sins of the world. O God, into your hands I commit my spirit." To the people he cried out, "O dear brothers and sisters, if I have injured anyone, in word or deed, may they forgive me for the sake of my merciful God. I forgive all those who have harmed me."

Later he spoke in Latin, "O Lord, into your hands I commit my spirit." As sulphur and gunpowder were rubbed into his beard, which he wore rather long, he said, "O salt me well, salt me well." Raising his head he called out to the people, "O dear brothers, pray God that he will grant me patience in my suffering." When the fire began to lap up about him, he said in a loud voice, "O my heavenly Father, O my gracious God," and as his hair and beard began to burn he cried out, "O Jesus, Jesus!" And so, overcome with smoke, he breathed his last.

Three days later his noble wife, Elsbeth—of whom their persecutors said, "She was hardened in the same heresy, more constant than her husband"—was thrown into the Danube, a large stone tied to her neck, and drowned.

Anabaptists of Hubmaier's persuasion, evidently under the lead of Hans Spittelmaier, and including Leonhard von Liechtenstein, continued in Moravia; but the party of those opposing the holding of private property by Christians gained the upper hand. They were viewed as being quite contentious, however. Leonhard and Hans von Liechtenstein urged them to moderate their views, or leave. They chose the latter course and established a commune in Austerlitz, Moravia; others grouped in Auspitz—which came under the leadership of Jacob Huter from Tyrol—and other places. They came to be known as Hutterites, whose traditions reflect great respect for the works of Hubmaier (especially those on baptism, the Lord's Supper, discipline, and free will), and his life and death—although they themselves held to Christian communism, nonviolence, nonparticipation in government and nonpayment of military taxes.

A hymn of eighteen stanzas generally attributed to Hubmaier, "A Song in Praise of God's Word," has survived the centuries. It tells the story of numerous biblical heroes such as Adam, Noah, Abraham, David, the writer of each

Gospel, Peter, Paul, and especially of Jesus Christ. Here are the first and last stanzas:

*Frewt euch, frewt euch in
    diser zeyt,
jr werden Christen alle!
Wann yetz in allen landen
    weyt
Gots wort her dringt mit
    schalle.
Est ist kein man, ders weren
    kan,
das habt ir wol vernummen,
Dann Gottes wort bleybt
    ewig stan
den bösen als den frummen.*

Rejoice, rejoice in this our
    time,
All you who are true
    Christians,
That now in all lands far and
    wide
God's Word comes through
    as joyful sound.
No man can prevail against
    it,
As you have all observed,
The Word of God stands sure
    forever,
For evil men as for the good.

*Lobt Gott, lobt Gott in
    eynigkeyt,
jr Christen all gemeyne!
Das er seyn wort hatt
    ausgepreyt,
das ist seyn werck alleyne.
Keins menschen wan nicht
    helffen kan,
wie hoch er sey mit namen,
Dan Gottes wort bleybt ewig
    stan,
Nun singen wir fröhlich,
    Amen!*

Praise God, praise God in
    unity,
You Christian people
    everywhere!
He's caused his Word to
    break forth,
That is his work, his alone.
And human notions cannot
    help,
No matter how exalted,
For God's own Word stands
    forever,
And so, joyfully, we sing—
    Amen!

• NOTES •

Numerical references in Bible quotations give chapters only; the use of verse divisions came later.

See Selected Bibliography, below, for bibliographical data.

Books and articles are here generally referred to by the name of author or editor; occasionally—e.g., when an author has more than one work listed in the bibliography—a part of the title is given.

Augsburger = Michael Sattler (unpublished dissertation)
von Beck = *Die Geschichtsbücher* . . .
Bender = *Conrad Grebel*
Blanke = *Brothers in Christ* (English edition)
Bullinger = *Reformationsgeschichte*
Estep = English translation of Bergsten's Hubmaier biography
Goertz = *Profiles of Radical Reformers*
Krajewski = *Leben . . . Felix Mantz*
ME = *The Mennonite Encyclopedia*
ML = *Mennonitisches Lexikon*
Moore = *Der starke Jörg*
MQR = *Mennonite Quarterly Review*
Q I, Q II = *Quellen zur Geschichte der Täufer in der Schweiz*, Volumes I and II
Schriften = Denck, *Schriften* (in the chapter on Denck); Hubmaier, *Schriften* (in the chapter on Hubmaier)
Snyder = *The Life and Thought of Michael Sattler*
Yoder = *The Legacy of Michael Sattler*

1. CONRAD GREBEL:
Founder of the Swiss Brethren

Life: Bender, *Conrad Grebel;* Goertz, pp. 118-131; ME II, pp. 566-574; ML II, pp. 163-169.

Lively Student Days
Bender, pp. 9-29.
Zurich: ME IV, pp. 1042-1047; ML IV, pp. 625-640.

Decline and Fall of Serious Studies
In Paris: Bender, pp. 27-52.
Vadian: ME IV, p. 796; ML IV, p. 401.

Struggle for a Foothold in Life
Settling in Zurich, briefly in Basel: Bender, pp. 53-64.
Zurich: ME IV, pp. 1042-1047; ML IV, pp. 625-640.
Basel: ME I, pp. 241-246; ML I, pp. 129-134.
With Zwingli et al.: Bender, pp. 56-59, 72-75.
Zwingli: ME IV, pp. 1052-1054; ML IV, pp. 648-653.
Grebel's poem: Bender, p. 281.

Problems Also in Romance
Love affair and marriage: Bender, pp. 59-64.

Fellow Worker in Zwinglian Reform
Zwingli's supporter: Bender, pp. 76-88.
January 1523 disputation: Bender, pp. 92-96.

Breach in the Groundwork of Unity
October 1523 disputation: Bender, pp. 96-99.
Beginnings of estrangement: Bender, pp. 95-102

Search for the Truth
Proposals of Grebel et al.: Bender, pp. 103-107.
December 1523 letter to Vadian: Q I, p. 8.
September 1524 letter to Vadian: Q I, pp. 11-13.

Additional Issues Raised
Contacts with various reformers: Bender, pp. 108-110, 120-123, 196-202, 256.
Brötli: ME I, pp. 439, ML I, p. 275; Moore, "Johannes Brötli," *The Baptist
    Quarterly*, January 1953, pp. 29-34.
Reublin: ME IV, pp. 304-307; ML III, pp. 477-481.
Zollikon: ME III, pp. 785-789; ML III, pp. 187f.
Müntzer: ME III, pp. 785-789; ML III, pp. 187f.

The Undelivered Letter
Letter to Müntzer: Q I, pp. 13-21; Williams and Mergal, pp. 71-85; Bender,
    pp. 110f., 198f.

First Baptism Disputation
Council's announcement: Q I, p. 33; Bender, pp. 133f.
The disputation: Bullinger II, p. 238.
Mandates, banishments: Q I, pp. 34-36.

Birthday of the Movement
Forbidden meeting, baptisms: Zieglschmied, p. 47; von Beck, pp. 15-20;
    Bender, pp. 136f., 217-219.
First week, Zollikon: Blanke, *passim.*

Missionary Labors Near and Far
Schaffhausen: ME IV, pp. 439-441; ML IV, pp. 41-44; Bender, pp. 139-142
Ulimann: ME IV, pp. 787f.; ML IV, pp. 393f.; Q II, pp. 604f., 636.
St. Gall: ME IV, pp. 401f.

Disputations and mass baptism: Bender, p. 143; Estep, *The Anabaptist...*, pp. 28, 177; Q II, pp. 605, 610; cf. Q II, p. 382.
Further on Vadian: Bender, pp. 127, 142, 145, *passim*.

Finding a Field of Work
Letter to Castelberger: Bender, pp. 146, 265f.; cf. ME, pp. 523f.; ML I, p. 71.
In Waldshut: Bender, pp. 147f.; Q I, p. 194; cf. ML IV, pp. 457f.
Grüningen: Bender, pp. 148-156; ME II, pp. 604-606; ML II, pp. 193-195; Q I, pp. 91f., 183-188.
Grebel and Bosshart: Q I, pp. 86, 89, 96.

The Authorities Tighten the Noose
Anabaptists from Waldshut: Bender, p. 152; Q I, pp. 108f.
Arrest and imprisonment: Bender, pp. 152-154; Q I, pp. 109-111.
November 1525 disputation: Bender, p. 155; Q I, pp. 115-141f., 389; Bullinger I, pp. 294-298.
Trials and sentencing: Bender, p. 156; Q I, pp. 120-125, 136.
March 1526 sentencing, capital punishment threatened: Q I, p. 178.

Grebel's Final Labors
Escape from prison: Bender, p. 160; Q I, pp. 191-193.
Grebel's tract on baptism: Bender, pp. 161, 186-191.
Death: Bender, pp. 161f.; Q II, p. 631.

2. FELIX MANTZ: Anabaptist Martyr

Life: Ekkehard Krajewski, *Leben und Sterben des Zürcher Täuferführers Felix Mantz*, the only complete biography; ME III, pp. 472-474; ML III, pp. 22-24.
Parentage and youth: Krajewski, pp. 15-21.
Study with Zwingli: Krajewski, pp. 22-28; Q I, pp. 127, 260; Zieglschmied, p. 45.

Formation of Parties
Discussions with Zwingli: Krajewski, pp. 29-33; Blanke, p. 12.
Plans for school of prophecy: Krajewski, pp. 33-36.
Letter to Müntzer: Q I, pp. 13-21; Krajewski, pp. 48-59.
Carlstadt's tracts: Krajewski, pp. 43-47.
Carlstadt: ME I, pp. 519-521; ML II, pp. 463-465.
Tuesday discussions: Krajewski, pp. 60-63; Blanke, p. 17.

Mantz's Letter of Defense
Krajewski, pp. 63-67; Q I, pp. 23-28; Blanke, p. 18.
Zwingli's *Those Who Incite ...: Wer Ursache gebe zu Aufruhr.*
Requests to be heard in writing: Krajewski, p. 65; Q I, pp. 51, 73, 93, 174.
Meetings at Mantz house: Krajewski, p. 38; Q I, p. 127.

Brethren Beginnings and Early Development
January 1525 disputation: Krajewski, pp. 67-71; Q I, p. 33.
Council mandates: Q I, pp. 35f.
First Anabaptist baptisms: Krajewski, pp. 74-79; von Beck, pp. 15-20; Zieglschmied, p. 47.
Baptism of Jörg Schad, Hans Bruggbach et al.: Q I, pp. 41-43; Blanke, pp.

21-23, 25-28; cf. ME IV, p. 438, ML IV, p. 40.

Standing Firm While Many Weaken

First arrests and trials: Krajewski, pp. 86-92; Blanke, pp. 43-48; Q I, pp. 38-47.
Letter to Zurich council: Q I, pp. 49f.
February 18 sentence: Q I, pp. 50f.
Brötli's letter: Q I, pp. 44-46; Moore, "Johannes Brötli," pp. 32f.; cf. ME I, p. 439, ML I, p. 275.

Continuing Persecution—and Mission Work

Baptisms by Schad et al.: Krajewski, p. 92; Blanke, p. 53; Q I, p. 63.
March disputation: Krajewski, pp. 93-97; Q I, p. 70.
March 25 hearings: Q I, pp. 73-75; Blanke, p. 59.
Escape from prison: Krajewski, pp. 99-101; Q I, pp. 93f.
In Schaffhausen: Krajewski, pp. 104-107; Q I, pp. 123, 214, 216.
In Graubünden: Q II, p. 501; cf. ME II, pp. 584-586, ML II, pp. 157-159.
Arrest, return to Zurich: Krajewski, pp. 107-109; Q I, p. 92f.

Out of Prison and Back in Again

Mantz's hearing: Krajewski, pp. 109-111; Q I, pp. 93f.
Release from second imprisonment: Krajewski, p. 111; Q I, p. 216.
In Grüningen: Krajewski, pp. 112-116; Q I, pp. 109f., 115f.
Third arrest and imprisonment: Krajewski, pp. 116f., 121; cf. Q I, p. 191.

More Disputation, Less Tolerance

Third disputation on baptism: Krajewski, pp. 117-121; Q I, pp. 118, 132, 389; Bullinger I, pp. 295-297.
Berger's December 8 letter to council: Q I, p. 145.
Hubmaier in Zurich: Krajewski, p. 123; Q I, pp. 158-162, 175, 193-197, 390-393.
March 1526 hearings, trials: Krajewski, pp. 123-127; Q I, pp. 174-181.
Death penalty decreed: Krajewski, pp. 125f.; Q I, p. 181.
Sentencing for Mantz et al.: Krajewski, pp. 124f.; Q I, p. 178.
Escape: Krajewski, pp. 127f.; Q I, pp. 191-193.

Widespread Evangelism and Church Growth

In Embrach: Krajewski, p. 129; Q I, p. 216.
In Grüningen: Krajewski, p. 130; Q I, pp. 203f.
In Basel area: Krajewski, pp. 130-132.
In St. Gall area: Krajewski, pp. 133-135; Q I, pp. 117, 133-135; Q II, pp. 423-426, 631.

Last Labors and Trial

Hearings, trials, and the end: Krajewski, pp. 138-141; Q I, pp. 214-218; von Beck, p. 21.
Letter and hymn: Krajewski, pp. 141f.; Q I, pp. 218-221; Wackernagel, Vol. III, pp. 451f.; *Ausbund,* pp. 41-46.

Martyred for the Cause

Death sentence: Krajewski, pp. 142-144; Q I, pp. 222-224.
Drowning: Krajewski, pp. 146f.; Bullinger I, p. 382; van Bracht, p. 415.

3. BLAUROCK: He Was Called Strong George

Life: Moore, *Der starke Jörg*, a brief biography; "George Blaurock," *Baptist History and Heritage*, July 1967, pp. 104-113, and January 1969, pp. 55-65. ME I, pp. 354-359; ML I, pp. 227-234.

Choosing Sides for Reform
Arrival in Zurich: von Beck, p. 34; Zieglschmied, p. 46; Moore, pp. 7-10; Blanke, p. 36, Q I, pp. 109f. (Blaurock's appearance).
Els Blaurock: Q II, pp. 199, 248, 424.
January 17 disputation and council mandates: Q I, pp. 33-36; Bullinger I, pp. 11-13; Blanke, pp. 19f.; Moore, pp. 11-13.

Starting the New Movement
The first baptisms: von Beck, p. 35; Zieglschmied, p. 47; Williams and Mergal, pp. 39-46; Blanke, pp. 21f.; Moore, pp. 13f.

Effective Witness in a Zollikon Home
Zollikon: ME IV, pp. 1036f.; ML IV, pp. 619-621.
At Rüdi Thomann's, Hans Mürer's et al., Q I, pp. 37-43; Blanke, pp. 24-29; Moore, pp. 15-17.

The Putsch That Failed
Numerical achievements in first week: Blanke, p. 41.
Blaurock in Zollikon church: Q I, p. 39; Blanke, pp. 29-31, Moore, pp. 17f.

Hopes Are Dashed Once Again
Arrest, imprisonment, hearings for Zollikon group: Q I, pp. 39-42; Blanke, pp. 43-45.
For Blaurock: Q I, pp. 42f.; Blanke, p. 51.
Sentencing of the larger group: Q I, p. 47; Blanke, p. 47; Moore, p. 19.

Tireless Evangelism in Zurich and Zollikon
February 18 hearing: Q I, p. 50.
Blaurock's release: Q I, p. 51; Blanke, p. 49.
Heinrich Aberli: ME I, pp. 7f.; ML I, p. 11.
At Aberli's, Rogenacher's, Murer's et al.: Q I, pp. 58-62; Blanke, pp. 49-51.
Baptism of Aberli: Q I, p. 62; Blanke, p. 51.
Schad baptizes forty: Q I, pp. 63, 105, 107; Blanke, p. 53.

Struggle of the Brethren for Survival
Decree of council: Q I, pp. 60f.
R. Hottinger's testimony: Q I, p. 62; Blanke, p. 56.
Arrest, imprisonment, and hearings: Q I, pp. 61-74; Blanke, pp. 56-59.
March "disputation": Q I, p. 70; Bullinger I, p. 239; von Beck, pp. 7-9.

Blaurock's Labors Far and Wide
Exiled to Chur: Q I, pp. 74f.; cf. Q II, p. 501, note 1.
Commander: ME I, p. 356; Q II, pp. 502f.

Another Putsch Fails
Hinwil: ME II, pp. 745f.; ML II, pp. 317f.
In the Hinwil church: Q I, pp. 109-111, 388-389; Moore, pp. 24-26.

Authorities Talk, Then Threaten the Worst
November disputation: Q I, pp. 115f., 389; Bullinger I, pp. 295f.; Moore, pp. 26f.

Report to Zollikon that Anabaptists fairly heard: Q I, pp. 138-140; cf. Q I, pp. 114f.
Sentence for Blaurock et al.: Q I, p. 136.
Blaurock's letter and testimony: Q I, pp. 125f.
March 1526 hearings: Q I, pp. 174f.
Testimony and sentencing: Q I, pp. 174-178.
Death penalty for rebaptizing: Q I, p. 178.

Escape, Manifold Labors, and Recapture
Escape: Q I, pp. 191-193; cf. pp. 215, 217; Bullinger I, p. 261; Moore, p. 29.
In Grüningen: Q I, pp. 212-217, 284, 287.
Blaurock on church discipline: Q I, p. 217; Moore, p. 30.
Willingness to continue baptizing: Q I, p. 223.

Final Work in Switzerland
Sentences for Mantz, Blaurock: Q I, pp. 222-228; Bullinger I, pp. 381f., cf. II, p. 382; Moore, pp. 30-35.
In Bern canton: Grätz, pp. 15f., 20; cf. ME I, pp. 287-298; ML I, pp. 168-196; ME II, p. 71; ML I, p. 282.
Appenzell: Q I, p. 301; cf. Q II, p. 204; ME I, p. 143; ML I, p. 80.
In Wil: Q I, pp. 215, 217.

The New Field in Tyrol; The Voice of Strong George Silenced at Last; Blaurock's Hymns
Tyrol: ME IV, pp. 724-728; ML IV, pp. 332-340; von Beck, pp. 27-29, 79-81, 90.
Kirschner: ME III, pp. 261f.; ML II, p. 602.
Blaurock's work, arrest, trial, execution: van Braght, pp. 430-432; Zieglschmid, p. 56; von Beck, p. 29; Moore, pp. 34-38.
Blaurock's hymns: *Ausbund*, pp. 35-41, 186-190; Wackernagel III, pp. 447-450.

4. MICHAEL SATTLER:
Holiness in Church, in Life, and in Death

Life: Snyder, pp. 23-107; Goertz, pp. 132-143; Augsburger, Michael Sattler, pp. 1-20; Wiswedel, *Bilder* III, pp. 9-23; Yoder, *Legacy*, pp. 10f.; ME IV, pp. 427-434; ML IV, pp. 29-38; Estep, *The Anabaptist Story*, pp. 40-47.
Sattler in Switzerland: Snyder, pp. 76-88; Q I, p. 136.

Seeking His Way and His Work
Strasbourg: ME IV, pp. 639-642; ML IV, pp. 252-254; Snyder, pp. 89-97.
Bucer and Capito: ME I, pp. 455-460, 512-516; ML I, pp. 307-313, 326-333
Twenty-point letter to Strasbourg: Augsburger, pp. 261-266; Yoder, pp. 22f.
Reublin: ME IV, pp. 304-307; ML III, pp. 477-481.

Tracts on Doctrine and Christian Living
English translations here basically those of John C. Wenger, MQR, October 1946 and January, April, October 1947 and in Augsburger, pp. 277-318.

The Gathering in Schleitheim
Quotation from Yoder: Statement to college classes, according to Augsburger, p. xiii.
The "false brethren": Yoder, pp. 27-34; Meihuizen, "Who ..." MQR, July 1967, pp. 200-222.
Schleitheim: ME IV, pp. 460f.; ML IV, pp. 68-70.

The Schleitheim Confession
Text etc.: Jenny, pp. 9-18; Yoder, pp. 34-43; ME I, pp. 447f.: ML IV, pp. 70f.; Snyder, pp. 114-123.

Relationships with Government
Use of force and the sword: Snyder, pp. 140-150; Yoder, pp. 39-41; cf. *Stayer, Anabaptists and the Sword*, also 2nd ed., *Passim.*
The oath: Yoder, pp. 41f.
Conclusion: Yoder, pp. 42f.
"Congregational Order": Yoder, pp. 44f.

Ever the Pastor, Even in Prison; Saints in the Dock; A Verdict of Infamy
Letter to Horb congregation: Yoder, pp. 58-65; Snyder, pp. 123-128; Augsburger, p. 30 and *passim.*
Trial and death: Williams and Mergal, pp. 136-144; Yoder, pp. 66-85; Estep, "Michael Sattler's ... " MQR, July 1951, pp. 205-van Braght, pp. 416-420; Q I, pp. 250-253 (Reublin's account).

Death Not the Last Word
Capito's letter: Yoder, p. 87.
Hymn, "When Christ... ," *Ausbund*, pp. 46-48; Augsburger, pp. 267-272 (English translation).
Hymn, "If there now... ," *Ausbund*, pp. 791-793; Augsburger, pp. 273-276 (English translation).

5. HANS DENCK: God Speaks His Word in Everyman's Heart

Life: Coutts, *Hans Denck...* ; Keller, *Ein Apostel...* ;
Denck, *Schriften*, 2. Teil, pp. 8-19; Kiwiet, "The Life ... "; Goertz, pp. 62-72; Wiswedel I, pp. 137-152; MQR, October 1957, pp. 227-259; ME II, pp. 32-35; ML I, pp. 401-414.

The Wandering Humanist Scholar
Veit Bild correspondence: *Schriften*, 1. Teil, pp. 67f.; 3. Teil, pp. 129-131.
T. Gaza Greek grammar: *Schriften*, 1. Teil, pp. 65f., 3. Teil, p. 128.

An Independent Thinker Is Born
Nurnberg: ME III, pp. 926-928, ML III, pp. 279-282.
Osiander: ME IV, pp. 89f.; ML III, pp. 312f.
Hearings and banishment: *Schriften*, 1. Teil, pp. 10f.

The Theologian Emerges; The Mystic Tries to Be Practical; Driven Hither and Yon
Statement for council: *Schriften*, 2. Teil, pp. 20-26; *Selected Writings* (English translation), pp. 12-23.
Evaluation by the pastors: *Schriften*, 3. Teil, pp. 136-142; *Selected Writings*, pp. 24-35.

A Committed Christian but Ever the Seeker
St. Gall: Q II, pp. 274, 614f.; ME IV, pp. 401f.
Kessler's *Sabbata*, Q II, pp. 596-638.

Ministry of Writing Discovered
Augsburg: ME I, pp. 182-185.

U. Rhegius: ME IV, p. 314; ML III, pp. 486f.
Written statement to council: *Schriften*, 3. Teil, pp. 132f.; Selected Writings, pp. 36-39.

God's Purpose and Human Response

The Assertion . . . = Was geredt sei, das die schrift sagt, Gott thue und Mache guts and böses: Schriften, 2. Teil, pp. 27-47; Williams and Mergal, pp. 86-111.
Denck's mysticism: Packull, *Mysticism . . .* pp. 35-61.

Anabaptism Espoused, Writing Continued

Augsburg: ME I, pp. 182-185.
Denck's baptism: Packull, "Denck's Alleged Baptism . . ." MQR, 1973, pp. 327-336; but compare standard sources on Denck's life, e.g., Bergsten, p. 396, Estep, p. 310.
H. Hut: ME II, pp. 846-850; ML II, pp. 370-375.

Law and Gospel

The Law . . . = Vom Gesatz Gottes, Schriften, 2. Teil, pp. 48-66; *Selected Writings*, pp. 40-72.

Use and Misuse of Scripture

He Who Truly Loves . . . = Wer die wahrhait warlich lieb hat: Schriften, 2. Teil, pp. 67-74; *Selected Writings*, pp. 132-143.

Persona non Grata in Augsburg and Strasbourg

Strasbourg: ME IV, pp. 639-642; ML IV, pp. 252-254.
Bucer: ME I, pp. 455-460; ML I, pp. 307-313.
Capito: ME I, pp. 512-516; ML I, pp. 326-333.

Evangelist, Translator, and Author

Bergzabern: ME I, p. 283; ML I, p. 166.
Landau: ME III, p. 279; ML II, p. 608.
Bader: ME I, pp. 210f.; ML I, p. 109.
Translation of the prophets = Alle Propheten nach hebräischer Sprache verdeutscht: Schriften, 1. Teil, pp. 32ff.; ME IV, pp. 983f.; ML IV, pp. 565f.

God's Good Plan and Man's Fateful Choice

God's Order . . . = Ordnung Gottes und der creaturen werck, Schriften, 2. Teil, pp. 87-103; *Selected Writings*, pp. 73-98.

Needs Never Greater Than Divine Love

Worms: ME IV, p. 983; ML IV, p. 565.
Hätzer: ME II, pp. 621-626; ML II, pp. 225-231.
Kautz: ME, pp. 159f.; ML II, pp. 476-478.

Difficulties in Active Mission

Martyr's Synod: ME III, pp. 529-531; ML III, pp. 53-56; Kiwiet, "The Life . . . ," MQR, October 1957, pp. 256f.
Oecolampadius: ME IV, pp. 18-20.
Denck's letter: Kiwiet, *ibid.*, p. 257.
Recantation . . . = Hans Dencken Widerruf; Protest . . . = Protestation und bekantnuss: Schriften, 2. Teil, pp. 104-110; *Selected Writings*, pp. 120-131.

Hans Denck's Last Words

Fundamental Articles = *Etliche hauptreden.*

Micah commentary: *Schriften,* 3. Teil, pp. 7-98.

Denck's continuing influence: Kiwiet, "The Theology ...," MQR, January 1959, pp. 23-27.

6. BALTHASAR HUBMAIER: Truth Is Immortal

Life: Bergsten, *Balthasar Hubmaier* and English translation.

Estep, ed., *Balthasar Hubmaier;* Vedder, *Balthasar Hübmaier;* Goertz, pp. 144-157.

Gunnar Westin and Torsten Bergsten, eds., *Balthasar Hubmaier Schriften,* pp. 9-43; ME II, pp. 826-834; ML II, pp. 353-363.

Spelling of Hubmaier's name: Vedder, pp. 66-68.

Prominent Priest, Preacher, and Leader

Oppression of Jews in Regensburg: Bergsten, pp. 74-86; Estep, pp. 52-60; Vedder, pp. 37-44.

At Beauteous Mary Chapel: Bergsten, pp. 86-93; Estep, pp. 60-66; Vedder, pp. 44-50.

Seeking, Far and Wide, for Right Ways

In Waldshut: Bergsten, pp. 94-103; Estep, pp. 68-75; Vedder, pp. 51-55; ML IV, pp. 457f.

Back to Regensburg: Bergsten, pp. 103-105; Estep, pp. 75-77; Vedder, pp. 55f.

Identifying with Swiss Reform

Beginnings of reform in Waldshut: Bergsten, pp. 106-108; Estep, pp. 77f.

Relationships with Swiss reformers: Bergsten, pp. 108-112; Estep, pp. 78-82.

Third baptism disputation in Zurich: Bergsten, pp. 113-116; Estep, pp. 82-84; Vedder, pp. 57-66.

Threats from High Places Fail to Intimidate

Waldshut's controversy with Austria: Bergsten, pp. 120-127; Estep, pp. 90-96.

Called Back to Regensburg: Bergsten, pp. 139-141; Estep, p. 104; Vedder, pp. 55f.

Reform in Waldshut Given a Manifesto

The Eighteen Articles = *Achtzehen schlussrede so betreffende eyn gantz Christlich leben, Schriften,* pp. 69-74.

Changes at Whitsuntide: Bergsten, pp. 132f.; Estep, pp. 99-101.

Another call from Regensburg: Bergsten, pp. 141-143; Estep, pp. 105f.; Vedder, pp. 77-79.

Waldshut Seeks Allies and Hubmaier a Refuge

Waldshut and the Stühlingen Peasants: Bergsten, pp. 146-151; Estep, pp. 107-112.

Hubmaier in Schaffhausen: Bergsten, pp. 166-186; Estep, pp. 124-141.

Petitions to Schaffhausen and a Polemic to Eck

An Earnest Christian Petition = *Ein ernstliche Christenlich erbietung an einen Ersamen Rate ze Schaffhusen: Schriften,* pp. 75-84.

Theses Against Eck = Axiomata quae Baldazar Pacimontanus, Musca, Huldrychi Zuinglij in Christo frater, Ioanni Eckio and the German edition: *Schlussreden die Baldasar Friedberger, Pfarrer zu Waldshut, ein Bruder Huldrychs Zwinglis, dem Joanni Eckio zu Ingolstatt, die meysterlich zu examinieren fürbotten hat: Schriften,* pp. 85-94; Vedder, pp. 89-91.

Striking a Blow for Toleration
Concerning Heretics and Those Who Burn Them = Von ketzern und iren verbrennern. Vergleichung der geschrifften, zesamenzogen durch doctor Balthazerem Friedbergern, pastor in Waldshut: Schriften, pp. 95-100; Vedder, pp. 84-88.

Volunteers from Zurich: Bergsten, pp. 157-165; Estep, pp. 115-121.

Struggle of Waldshut for Freedom of the Word
Hubmaier's return and further reform: Bergsten, pp. 192-195; Estep, pp. 144-146.

Rheinfelden conference: Bergsten, pp. 195-198; Estep, pp. 146-149.

Constance conference: Bergsten, pp. 221-233; Estep, pp. 165-172.

Reform Marches on, Despite Increasing Peril
Ulm conference: Bergsten, pp. 241-244; Estep, pp. 176-179.

Hubmaier's marriage: Bergsten, p. 275; Estep, pp. 205f.

Writing to Oecolampadius et al, about baptism: Bergsten, pp. 261-271; Estep, pp. 195-202; Vedder, pp. 108f.

Some Articles on the Teaching of the Mass = Ettlich beschlussreden von Doktor Paltus Fridberger zu Waldshut allen christen von underricht der mess: Schriften, pp. 101-104.

Anabaptism Comes to Waldshut; Believer's Baptism Is Defended
A Public Invitation ... = Balthazar Friedbergers zu Waldshut Offentliche erbietung an all Christgläubig menschen ...: Schriften, pp. 105-107.

Reublin and Hubmaier baptize: Bergsten, pp. 304-311; Estep, pp. 230-236; Vedder, pp. 108-112.

On the form of baptism among Anabaptists: Vedder, pp. 142-145.

Summary ... = Ain Summ ains gantzen Christlichen lebens ...; The Christian Baptism of Believers = Von dem Christenlichen Tauff der glaubigen. Durch Balthasarn Hüebmör von Fridberg, yetz zu Waldshut, ausgangen. Die warheit ist untödlich: Schriften, pp. 108-163; Bergsten, pp. 326-334; Estep, pp. 249-255; Vedder, pp. 114-117.

No Letup in the Baptism Debate
A Discussion ... = Ein gesprech Balthasar Hubmörs von Fridberg, Doctors, auf Mayster Ulrichs Zwinglens zu Zürch, Tauffbuchlen von dem Kindertauff. Die Warhayt ist untödlich: Schriften, pp. 164-214.

Concerning Infant Baptism = Von dem khindertauff: Ecolampadius, Thomas Augustinianer Leesmaister, M. Jacob Immelen, M. Vuolffg. Weissenburger; Schriften, pp. 256-269.

The Capitulation of Waldshut
Hubmaier tries to attend third baptism disputation in Zurich: Bergsten, pp. 344f., Estep, pp. 264f.

The fall of Waldshut, departure of Hubmaier: Bergsten, pp. 346-354; Estep, pp. 265-271.

Drama in the Fraumünster
Arrest, imprisonment, discussions: Bergsten, pp. 383-389; Estep, pp. 300-304.
The Fraumünster episode: Bergsten, pp. 389f.; Estep, pp. 304f.; Q II, p. 613.
Twelve Articles ... = Die zwelf Artickel Christenlichs glaubens, zu Zürch im Wasserthurn, in Bettweis gestelt: Schriften, pp. 215-220, Bergsten, p. 394; Estep, p. 308.

From Zurich to Augsburg
The Lord's Prayer, in Brief = Ein kurtzes Vaterunser ...: Schriften, pp. 221-223.
In Constance and Augsburg: Bergsten, pp. 395-397; Estep, pp. 309-311; Zeman, pp. 127-130; Packull, "Denck's Alleged Baptism by Hubmaier," MQR, Oct. 1973, pp. 327-337.

Beginnings in Nikolsburg
Nikolsburg: ME III, pp. 883-886; ML III, pp. 256-260.
Leonhard von Liechtenstein: ME III, p. 338; Zeman, pp. 84-89.
Spittelmayer: ME IV, p. 599.
Glaidt: ME II, pp. 522f.; ML II, pp. 117-119.
Göschl: ME II, p. 546; Zeman, pp. 179-189.
The Judgment ... Teachers = Der Uralten unnd gar neuen Leerern Urteil, das man die jungen khindlen nit tauffen solle, biss sy im glauben unnderricht sind: Schriften, pp. 224-255.

Hubmaier Undertakes His Literary Defense
A Short Apology ... = Ein kurtze entschuldigung D. Balthasar Huebmors von Fridberg an alle Christglaubige menschen, das sy sich an den erdichtenn unwarhayten, so imm sein missgönner zu legen, nit ergern: Schriften, pp. 270-283.

Christian Doctrines and the Ordinances
A Simple Instruction ... = Ein ain feltige underricht auff die wort: Das ist der Leib mein, in dem Nachtmal Christi: Schriften, pp. 284-304.
A Manual ... = Ein Christennliche Leertafel, die ein yedlicher mensch, ee und er im Wasser getaufft wirt, vor wissenn solle: Schriften, pp. 305-326.
Cause and Reason ... = Grund und Ursach, das einn yedlicher mensch der gleich in seiner Khindthait getaufft ist, schuldig sei sich recht nach der Ordnung Christi ze tauffen lassen, ob er schon hundert jar allt were: Schriften, pp. 327-336.

Tracts on Practical Issues
A Form for Baptizing = Ein Form ze Tauffen im wasser die unnderrichten im glauben: Schriften, pp. 347-352.
A Form for Observance of the Supper = Ein Form des Nachtmals Christi: Schriften, pp. 351-365.
Concerning Brotherly Discipline ... = Von der Briederlichen straff. Wo die nit ist, da ist gewisslich auch khain Kirch, ob schon der Wassertauff und das Nachtmal Christj daselbs gehaltenn werdent: Schriften, pp. 337-346.
Concerning the Christian Ban ... = Von dem Christenlichen Bann. Wo der selb nit auffgericht und gebraucht wirdt nach dem ordenlichen und ernstlichen bevelh Christi, da selbs regiert nichts denn sünd, schand und laster: Schriften, pp. 366-378.

Can Everyone Respond to God's Grace and Guidance?

Concerning Freedom of the Will ... = *Von der Freyhait des Willens, die Gott durch sein gesendet wort anbeüt allen menschen, und inen dar in gwalt gibt seine Khinder ze werden, auch die waal gütes ze wollen und zethon. Oder sy aber Khinder des Zorns, wie sy denn von natur seind, ze bleiben lassen: Schriften,* pp. 398-431; Williams and Mergal, pp. 112-135 (English); cf. Bergsten, pp. 436-451; Estep, pp. 348-360.

Questions of Eschatology and the Sword; A True and a False Magistracy

H. Hut: Goertz, pp. 54-61; Wiswedel I, pp. 125-136. ME II, pp. 846-850; ML II, pp. 370-375.

Hubmaier-Hut controversy: Bergsten, pp. 451-475; Estep, pp. 361-377.

Concerning the Sword = *Von dem Schwert. Ein Christennliche erklerung der Schrifften, so wider die Oberkait (das ist, das die Christen nit sollent im Gwalt sitzen, noch das schwert fiern) von etlichen Bruedern gar ernstlich angezogen werdent): Schriften,* pp. 432-457; Vedder, pp. 273-310.

The Prosecution Prepares, as Does the Defense; Martyrdom of the Hubmaiers

Imprisonment, Trial, and Death: Bergsten, pp. 476-481; Estep, pp. 377-380; Vedder, pp. 219-244; van Bracht, p. 465.

J. Faber: ME II, pp. 285f.

Statement of Faith = *An den ... herrn Ferdinannd ... Ein Rechenschafft des Glaubens ...: Schriften,* pp. 458-491.

Anabaptism later in Moravia and Hubmaier's wider influence: Bergsten, pp. 482-502; Estep, pp. 382-398; Vedder, pp. 245-271.

Hubmaier's hymn: Wackernagel III, pp. 126-128.

• SELECTED •
BIBLIOGRAPHY

Augsburger, Myron S., Michael Sattler, d. 1527, Theologian of the Swiss Brethren Movement. Unpublished dissertation, Union Theological Seminary, Richmond, Virginia, May 1964.

_____, *Pilgrim Aflame*. (Fictionized biography of Sattler.) Scottdale, Pennsylvania: Herald Press, 1967.

Ausbund ... Etliche schöne Christliche Lieder ..., 13.Auflage. Lancaster County, Pennsylvania: Verlag von den Amischen Gemeinden, 1955.

Beck, Joseph R. von (with material from Joseph Loserth), *Georg Blaurock und die Anfänge des Anabaptismus in Graubünden und Tirol*. Berlin, 1899.

_____, ed., *Die Geschichtsbücher der Wiedertäufer in Oester-reich-Ungarn*. Nieuwkoop, the Netherlands: B. de Graaf, 1967.

Bender, Harold S., *Conrad Grebel, c. 1498-1526: the Founder of the Swiss Brethren, Sometimes Called Anabaptists*. Goshen, Indiana: The Mennonite Historical Society, 1950.

Bergsten, Torsten, *Balthasar Hubmaier: Seine Stellung zu Reformation und Täufertum, 1521-1528*. Kassel, Germany: J. G. Oncken Verlag, 1961.

_____, William R. Estep, ed., *Balthasar Hubmaier: Anabaptist Theologian and Martyr*. Valley Forge, Pennsylvania: Judson Press, 1978.

Blanke, Fritz, *Brüder in Christo: Die Geschichte der ältesten Täufergemeinde* (Zollikon). Zurich: Zwingli Verlag, 1955.

_____, Joseph Nordenhaug, translator: *Brothers in Christ: the History of the Oldest Anabaptist Congregation, Zollikon near Zurich, Switzerland*. Scottdale, Pennsylvania: Herald Press, 1961.

Bossert, Gustav, Jr., "Michael Sattler's Trial and Martyrdom in

1527," *Mennonite Quarterly Review*, July 1951, pp. 201-218.

Braght, Thieleman J. van, ed., *The Bloody Theatre or Martyrs Mirror of the Defenseless Christians*. Scottdale, Pennsylvania: Mennonite Publishing House, 1950.

Bullinger, Heinrich, *Reformationsgeschichte nach dem Autographen*, three volumes. Frauenfeld, Switzerland, 1838-1840.

──────, *Der Widertäufferen Ursprung*. Zurich, 1560.

Coutts, Alfred, *Hans Denck, Humanist and Heretic*. Edinburgh: Macniven and Wallace, 1927.

Denck, Hans, *Schriften, 1. Teil, Bibliographie*, Georg Baring, ed., Gütersloh, Germany: C. Bertelsmann Verlag, 1955; *2. Teil, Religiöse Schriften* (and "Das Leben Dencks"), Walter Fellmann, ed., 1956; *3. Teil, Exegetische Schriften, Gedichte und Briefe*, Walter Fellmann, ed., Gerd Mohn: Gutersloher Verlagshaus, 1960.

──────, *Selected Writings of Hans Denck*, translated, edited by Edward J. Furcha, Ford Lewis Battles. Pittsburgh, Pennsylvania: The Pickwick Press, 1975.

──────, *Anabaptist Beginnings, a Source Book* (1523-1533). Nieuwkoop, The Netherlands: B. de Graaf, 1976.

Estep, William R., *The Anabaptist Story*. Grand Rapids, Michigan: William B. Eerdmans Publishing Company, revised edition, 1975.

──────, "Von Ketzern und iren Verbrennern: A Sixteenth-Century Tract on Religious Liberty," *Mennonite Quarterly Review*, October 1969, pp. 271-282.

──────, "Martyr Without Honor," *Baptist History and Heritage*, April 1978, pp. 5-10.

──────, "Michael Sattler's Trial and Martyrdom in 1527," *Mennonite Quarterly Review*, July 1951, pp. 205-218.

Goertz, Hans-Jürgen, ed. (Walter Klassen, English edition editor. Translated from the original German edition), *Profiles of Radical Reformers: Biographical Sketches from Thomas Müntzer to Paracelsus*. Kitchener, Ontario, and Scottdale, Pennsylvania: Herald Press 1982.

Gratz, Delbert L., *Bernese Anabaptists and Their American Descendants*. Scottdale, Pennsylvania: Herald Press, 1953.

Hubmaier, Balthasar, *Schriften*, edited by Gunnar Westin and Torsten Bergsten. Gerd Mohn, Germany: Gütersloher Verlagshaus, 1962.

──────, The Writings of Balthasar Hubmaier, translated by George D. Davidson, William Jewell College, Liberty, Missouri; collected and photographed by W. O. Lewis, 1939. Microfilm copies of typescript available in numerous libraries.

Hopper, John David, Balthasar Hubmaier's Doctrine of the Church, unpublished Th.M. thesis, Southwestern Baptist

Theological Seminary, Fort Worth, Texas, 1966.

Jenny, Beatrice, ed., *Das Schleitheimer Täuferbekenntnis* 1927. Thayngen, Germany: Karl Augustin Verlag, 1951.

Keller, Ludwig, *Ein Apostel der Wiedertäufer* (Hans Denck). Leipzig, Germany, 1882.

Kiwiet, Jan J., "The Life of Hans Denck," *Mennonite Quarterly Review*, October 1957, pp. 227-259.

_____, "The Theology of Hans Denck," *Mennonite Quarterly Review*, January 1958, pp. 3-27.

Krajewski, Ekkehard, *Leben und Sterben des Zürcher Täuferführers Felix Mantz*. Kassel, Germany: J. G. Oncken Verlag, 1957.

_____, "The Theology of Felix Mantz," *Mennonite Quarterly Review*, January 1962, pp. 76-87.

Littell, Franklin H., *The Anabaptist View of the Church, A Study in the Origins of Sectarian Protestantism*, second edition, Boston: Starr King Press, 1958.

Loserth, Joseph, *Doctor Balthasar Hubmaier und die Anfänge der Wiedertäufer in Mähren*. Brünn, Moravia, 1893.

Meihuizen, H. W., "Who Were the False Brethren Mentioned in the Schleitheim Articles?" *Mennonite Quarterly Review*, July 1967, pp. 200-222.

The Mennonite Encyclopedia, four volumes. Scottdale, Pennsylvania: Mennonite Publishing House; Newton, Kansas: Mennonite Publication Office; Hillsboro, Kansas: Mennonite Brethren Publishing House, 1955-1959.

Mennonitisches Lexikon, four volumes. Frankfurt a.M., Weierhof, Karlsruhe, Germany, 1913-1959.

Moore, John Allen, *Der Starke Jörg, Die Geschichte Jörg Blaurocks, des Täuferführers und Missionars*. Kassel, Germany: J. G. Oncken Verlag, 1955.

_____, "Felix Manz, Anabaptist Martyr," *The Fraternal* (London), July 1952, pp. 21-24.

_____, "George Blaurock, Pioneer Anabaptist Evangelist," *Baptist History and Heritage* (Nashville), July 1967, pp. 104-113.

_____, "George Blaurock, Later Work and Martyrdom," *Baptist History and Heritage*, July 1969, pp. 55-65.

_____, "Johannes Brötli," *The Baptist Quarterly* (London), January 1953, pp. 29-34.

Newman, Albert H., "Balthazar Hubmaier and the Moravian Anabaptists," *The Goshen College Record Review Supplement*, September 1926, pp. 4-22.

_____, *History of Anti-Pedobaptism, From the Rise of Pedobaptism to A.D. 1609*. Philadelphia: American Baptist Publication Society, 1896.

Packull, Werner O. "Denck's Alleged Baptism by Hubmaier," *Mennonite Quarterly Review*, October 1973, pp. 327-337.

_____, *Mysticism and the Early South German-Austrian Anabaptist Movement, 1525-1531*. Scottdale, Pennsylvania: Herald Press, 1977.

Quellen zur Geschichte der Täufer in der Schweiz, Erster Band, Zürich, edited by Leonhard von Muralt and Walter Schmid. Zurich: S. Hirzel Verlag, 1952.

Quellen zur Geschichte der Täufer in der Schweiz, Zweiter Band, Ostschweiz, edited by Heinhold Fast. Zurich: Theologischer Verlag, Zurich, 1973.

Ruth, John L., *Conrad Grebel, Son of Zurich*. Scottdale, Pennsylvania: Herald Press, 1975 (fictionized).

Sachsee, D. *Balthasar Hubmaier als Theologe*. Berlin, 1914.

Smithson, R. J., *The Anabaptists, Their Contribution to Our Protestant Heritage*. London: James Clark and Co., 1935.

Snyder, C. Arnold, *The Life and Thought of Michael Sattler*, Scottdale, Pennsylvania, and Kitchener, Ontario: Herald Press, 1984.

Stayer, James A., *Anabaptists and the Sword*. Lawrence, Kansas: Colorado Press, 1972. Also 2nd revised edition, 1976.

Vedder, Henry C., *Balthasar Hübmaier, the Leader of the Anabaptists*. New York: G. P. Putnam's Sons, 1905.

Wackernagel, Philipp, ed., *Das deutsche Kirchenlied von der ältesten Zeit bis zu Anfang des XVII. Jahrhunderts*, five volumes. Leipzig, Germany, 1864-1877.

Williams, George H., *The Radical Reformation*. Philadelphia: The Westminster Press, 1962.

_____ and Angel M. Mergal, eds., *Spiritual and Anabaptist Writers: Documents Illustrative of the Radical Reformation* (The Library of Christian Classics, Vol. XXV). Philadelphia: The Westminster Press, 1957.

Weiss, F. L., *The Life, Teachings and Works of Johannes Denck*. Strasbourg, 1924.

Wiswedel, Wilhelm, *Balthasar Hubmaier: Der Vorkämpfer für Glaubens- und Gewissensfreiheit*. Kassel, Germany: J. G. Oncken Verlag, 1939.

_____, *Bilder und Führergestalten aus dem täufertum*, three volumes. Kassel, Germany: J. G. Oncken Verlag, 1928-1952.

Yoder, John H., "Balthasar Hubmaier and the Beginnings of Swiss Anabaptism," *Mennonite Quarterly Review*, January 1959, pp. 5-17.

_____, ed., *The Legacy of Michael Sattler*. Scottdale, Pennsylvania: Herald Press, 1978.

_____, *Täufertum und Reformation in der Schweiz, I, Die Gespräche zwischen Täufern und Reformatoren, 1523-1538*. Karlsruhe, Germany, 1962.

Zeman, Jarold K., *The Anabaptists and the Czech Brethren in Moravia, 1526-1628*. The Hague, the Netherlands: Mouton, 1969.

Zieglschmid, A.J.F., ed., *Die älteste Chronik der Hutterischen Brüder*. Ithaca, New York: The Cayuga Press, 1943.

• THE AUTHOR •

John Allen Moore taught church history and other subjects for many years at the international Baptist Theological Seminary in Ruschlikon, just outside Zurich, Switzerland—the birthplace of Anabaptism. He walked in the footsteps of Brethren pioneers in Switzerland, Austria, Czechoslovakia, and Germany, seeking to visualize and understand their ministry.

A native of Mississippi, Moore grew up in the town of Tupelo. He took his BA at Mississippi College in Clinton, majoring in English and Christianity. He earned the ThM and PhD degrees at Southern Baptist Theological Seminary in Louisville, Kentucky, and did additional work at the University of Zurich and Union Theological Seminary in New York City.

The Foreign Mission Board of the Southern Baptist Convention appointed him missionary in 1938, and he served in Europe for forty years. He was sent first to Yugoslavia, where he established a small seminary. His fiancée, Pauline Willingham of Macon, Georgia, soon joined him; they were married in Rome and proceeded then to Belgrade.

Forced out of Europe by the second world war, the Moores were loaned by the Foreign Mission Board to the United Nations Relief and Rehabilitation Administration, and they worked as welfare officers in Yugoslav refugee camps in Egypt, 1944-45.

Moore taught in the English department of Howard College (now Samford University) in Birmingham, Alabama, 1945-47, then a year in the Bible department of Baylor University of Waco, Texas, but retained affiliation with the Foreign Mission Board.

In the spring of 1948 the board assigned the Moores to help establish a seminary in Switzerland, and they went to Zurich in August of that year; the new institution opened in the fall of 1949.

Professor Moore taught there for twenty years, working each year with students from about twenty countries, of several continents; he served one year as acting president.

At the request of the Baptists of Europe he began in 1961 the European Baptist Press Service, and wrote many hundreds of news stories and feature articles.

Moore also served as the Southern Baptists' fraternal representative to the Baptists of Eastern Europe. He visited regularly among churches and seminaries in that part of Europe, counseling, lecturing, preaching, and administering financial assistance wherever possible.

In 1969 Moore became the board's field representative for Europe, giving up his seminary teaching in Rüschlikon but retaining Eastern Europe responsibilities. As field representative he worked with about 115 Southern Baptist missionaries and with nationals in nine or ten countries of Western Europe.

The Moores returned to the U.S. for final furlough in October 1976 and settled in Brownwood, Texas. After a brief assignment in Germany, they retired, early in 1978.

They have two children, both born, although of different parents, on the same day in Germany in 1950—and adopted in the following year. Daughter Marilyn is married and lives in Louisville, Kentucky; she and her husband have an adopted daughter. The son, Edward, is back in his native Germany; he and his wife have an infant son.

John and Pauline Moore are active in local church work in Brownwood. They travel widely, making visits and attending conferences at home and abroad.